PSYCHOLOGICAL THERAPIES FOR THE ELDERLY

Psychological Therapies for the Elderly

Edited by IAN HANLEY and MARY GILHOOLY

CROOM HELM
London & Sydney

Croom Helm Ltd, Provident House, Burrell Row,
Beckenham, Kent BR3 1AT
Croom Helm Australia Pty Ltd, Suite 4, 6th Floor,
64–76 Kippax Street, NSW 2010, Australia

British Library Cataloguing in Publication Data

Psychological therapies for the elderly.
1. Geriatric psychiatry 2. Psychotherapy
I. Hanley, Ian II. Gilhooly, Mary
618.97′68914 RC451.4.A5

ISBN 0-7099-3762-8

Filmset by Mayhew Typesetting, Bristol, England
Printed and bound in Great Britain by
Biddles Ltd, Guildford and King's Lynn

CONTENTS

List of Contributors

Preface

1. Issues in Psychological Therapy with Elderly People *Mike Church* 1
2. Dynamic Psychotherapy with the Elderly *Peter Hildebrand* 22
3. Issues in the Therapeutic Use of Reminiscence with Elderly People *Peter Coleman* 41
4. Reality Orientation in the Care of the Elderly Patient with Dementia — Three Case Studies *Ian Hanley* 65
5. Psychological Considerations in the Day Care of Elderly People *Victor G. Cicirelli and Ellen Browne* 80
6. Self Help and Family Support Groups *Rachel Filinson* 101
7. The Systems Approach to Changing Practice in Residential Care *David P. Jeffery* 124
8. 'Over the Hill and Far Away': The Production of a Video-Assisted Training Package *Gerry Murphy* 151
9. Group Care and Natural Living in a Residential Home for the Elderly *Edith McCallum and Ian Hanley* 163
10. Ethical and Legal Issues in Therapy with the Elderly *Mary L.M. Gilhooly* 173

Index 198

CONTRIBUTORS

Dr Ellen Browne, Parkside Human Services Corporation, USA.

Dr Victor Cicirelli, Professor of Developmental and Ageing Psychology, Purdue University, West Lafayette, Indiana, USA.

Mr Mike Church, Principal Clinical Psychologist, Middlewood Hospital, Sheffield, England.

Dr Peter Coleman, Senior Lecturer in Social Gerontology, University of Southampton, England.

Dr Rachel Filinson, Department of Behavioural Sciences, Purdue University, Calumet, Hammond, Indiana, USA.

Dr Mary Gilhooly, Lecturer, Behavioural Sciences Group, University of Glasgow, Scotland.

Dr Ian Hanley, District Clinical Psychologist, East Cumbria Health Authority, England.

Dr Peter Hildebrand, The Tavistock Clinic, 120 Belsize Lane, London, England.

Mr David Jeffery, Senior Clinical Psychologist, Torbay Health Authority, Torquay, England.

Edith McCallum, Residential Social Worker, Aberdeenshire, Scotland.

Mr Gerry Murphy, Training Consultant, East Sussex Consultancy and Training Agency, Brighton, England.

PREFACE

This book can be seen as a follow-on to an earlier book, *Psychological Approaches to the Care of the Elderly*, edited by Hanley and Hodge (Croom Helm, London/Methuen, New York, 1984). It shares with this text the overall purpose of attempting to provide an up-to-the-minute reflection on the usefulness of applied psychology in dealing with some of the problems experienced by elderly people. Whereas the first volume devoted almost equal attention to the themes of assessment and therapy and concluded with a review of issues in effective service provision, the current collection of papers focuses on a selection of psychological treatments and then examines issues relevant to systems or contexts of care.

Hopefully, both technique and context are given equal weight, as the complexity of the considerations involved in providing a truly therapeutic service cannot be encompassed by consideration of therapeutic techniques alone. It is a truism that elderly people become more dependent on their environment. What they can achieve and how far they can become instrumental in their own psychological welfare will depend fundamentally on the functioning of the system that cares for them.

Textbooks and research papers rarely manage to convey a sense of 'what actually happens' when any form of psychological treatment approach is put into practice. This is especially true of work with the elderly, as any clinician will attest from working experience. This book has not aimed for neat, succinct reviews, but hopes to convey the views of those speaking, in part at least, from their working experience.

We sincerely hope that the material presented in this book will not become rapidly redundant. The wayside of the psychology of ageing is littered with the abandoned remains of bandwagons of past decades. The reader, if old enough, may wish to recall the days, not that long ago, when psychologists pronounced at length on the intellectual deficits of ageing, held to the view that well adjusted elderly people were 'disengaged' and spent considerable amounts of time differentially diagnosing dementia from depression. Even reality orientation, one of the newer psychological offerings adopted with relish by so many only a few years ago, has fallen from favour. Lest the conclusion be drawn that at best psychologists are a fickle lot, the reader should contemplate the relationship between theory and practice. Only in recent years have psychologists had the opportunity to play a significant role in the provision of health services to the elderly. As a result we are 'maturing' rapidly, have the opportunity to test in practice what was often conceived of through research and theory formation, and can measure the effectiveness of our ideas and activities through their real impact on the perceptions of other professionals and elderly people themselves.

This notion of experience is central to the format adopted here. All the contributors have worked with elderly people and those that care for them. By happy accident, however, not all the contributors are clinical psychologists. Clearly, psychologists are not the sole agency through which sound psychological practices are exercised. Certainly, we may have a leading role to play in raising the psychological awareness of other professionals, but often too we can benefit from the psychological skills of non-psychologists. Indeed, it is essential to harness and develop this other expertise if we are to become effective agents of change in the way organisations function. We need 'allies within' who have the authority to introduce change — a simple point, but one too often forgotten.

Fundamentally then, this book does not present itself as a textbook. It does not assume the reader to be either a newcomer to working with elderly people or in search of a 'cookbook' of psychological techniques. It is intended that each chapter reflects issues currently relevant to practice and that the book will appeal both to psychologists working with the elderly, those working in other fields who may wish to catch the flavour of what is happening in this specialist area and to a variety of others who either work directly with elderly people or are engaged in the training of those that do.

Before introducing the contents some comment is apposite on what has been omitted from the book. Perhaps we are all guilty of neglecting the potential contribution of therapeutic approaches developed for one specific problem area or grouping of clients. Often we assume that these are not applicable to the elderly. It is not our purpose to dwell at length on what may be obvious to many — that family therapy, behavioural approaches to anxiety management, group and individual psychotherapy of various shades, counselling and many other types of intervention too numerous to mention, all have a worthwhile place in our therapeutic armorarium. Neither is it our aim to give space to issues that deserve considerably more attention than we can offer here. We have particularly in mind the areas of bereavement and death and dying, both of which have been well covered in other books.

We had hoped originally to cover behavioural treatments as we have increasing reservations about the relevance and indeed the ethics of behaviour therapy with elderly people. A chapter was offered by a leading authority on this subject, but this never materialised. Is the epitaph of operant work with the elderly perhaps sounded in the explanation offered namely 'I find myself having some doubts about the directions behavioural work seems to be taking with the elderly'? We would certainly echo this view for mainline operant work while acknowledging the contributions of Lindsley and Powell Lawton among others to the potential of discriminant control of behaviour through the environment. Developments in this area are not really seen to be linked with behaviour therapy, however, and will be referred to at different points in this book.

The layout of the book is as follows. Three of the first four chapters deal with particular types of psychological therapy. The next five chapters address the therapeutic value of different contexts or systems for providing good psychological care and look at two possible mechanisms for bringing about change in systems. The final chapter examines the ethics of psychological therapy with the elderly. We have tried to be deliberately selective in presenting a variety of issues of living concern.

Emerging fields such as reminiscence work deserve careful consideration if they are to find appropriate application from the outset and avoid being rejected at a later date simply because too much was expected to begin with. Likewise, we need to re-examine the value of approaches such as reality orientation, which are currently being viewed with a measure of disaffection and are in danger of being lost prematurely. We need also to examine the relative contributions of systems theory and staff training to the problem of changing the way care is provided to elderly people. These are some of the issues addressed in this book.

Chapter 1 opens with the assertion from Mike Church that elderly people have suffered more than their fair share of ill-considered (therapeutic) interventions. He goes on to explore some issues in psychological therapy by developing the theme of their special needs as reflected by the processes of normal and abnormal ageing. Specific issues at both the level of direct client intervention and the context of the interventions are raised. As Church points out, there may be many instances 'where changing a specific organisational factor can be more effective than any number of individual psychological interventions'.

In Chapter 2 Peter Hildebrand highlights the recent emergence of interest in dynamic psychotherapy with the elderly. Tracing the evolution of the focus of psychoanalytic and psychotherapeutic thought in part to the emergence of lifespan developmental psychology, he illustrates how different views are today from those of Freud who claimed that 'psychotherapy is not possible near or above the age of 50'. Illustrated by examples from his own casework, Hildebrand argues that the converse is true. Through a greater understanding of the developmental problems of later life has come a dynamic psychotherapeutic approach with older people which 'has the potentiality for them to explore, come to grips with and hopefully resolve the difficulties which we must all encounter in later life'.

Reminiscence is becoming a household word wherever elderly people are cared for. In the United Kingdom at least 'reminiscence therapy' is widely employed. Peter Coleman has researched the functions of reminiscence since the late 1960s: part of his extensive research was longitudinal and extended throughout the 1970s. In Chapter 3 he examines in detail the link between reminiscence and psychological adjustment. What emerges is a clearly differential analysis with considerable variation noted in elderly people's orientation to this activity. Coleman illustrates graphically the link between attitude to reminiscing and subsequent adjustment and shatters the simplistic perspective that reminiscence suits everyone equally.

In Chapter 4 Ian Hanley describes a number of case studies where the pragmatic application of reality orientation principles in case management resolved a range of behavioural problems in elderly patients with dementia. The careful, individually tailored treatment plans described serve to highlight the selective potential of an approach which, partly through extravagant early claims for its effectiveness and partly through the failure of inappropriately designed evaluative trials, is in danger of being abandoned by many.

Victor Cicirelli and Ellen Browne provide an overview of day care in Chapter 5. This is an increasingly popular context for providing psychological care to elderly people and has a crucial role in the long-term care system. Cicirelli and Browne examine current issues in the use of day care, present some findings from existing evaluations of day care and draw some conclusions about the strength of day care and how it might be improved.

In the final chapter of the earlier book, *Psychological Approaches to the Care of the Elderly*, Jeffrey and Saxby argued that 'our first priority must be to influence systems so that effective psychological care may be provided for the elderly as a population'. This, they argued, could never be achieved through work with individual elderly clients alone. In Chapter 6 of the current book, Rachel Filinson reviews the role of self-help groups for the elderly and their families as 'a cost-effective vehicle for social action, personal change and mutual aid'. Four main directions of the self-help approach are discussed, namely self-help groups formed of the elderly themselves, self-help groups for caregivers, peer counselling and informal mutual help networks. Although most of the developments described are from the United States, this model of intervention is pertinent to the provision of psychological services to the elderly in Great Britain and elsewhere, where shortage of psychologist manpower is always likely to be a major influence on the type and extent of services that can be provided realistically.

David Jeffrey continues this theme of cost-effective provision of psychological services in Chapter 7. He argues that 'giving away' psychological therapy skills to a wide range of other people working with the elderly is a necessary but by no means sufficient answer to the problem of ensuring that the elderly receive appropriate psychological treatment. It is remarkably difficult to ensure that the staff who are to implement the therapy do so; if they do implement the therapy it is as difficult to ensure that the programme is maintained over time. After examining the effect of the behaviour of care staff on residents and the relationship between care staff behaviour and organisational variables, Jeffrey goes on to outline the human systems approach to change, to describe his system for changing practice in residential care and to draw together principles for successful interventions in care systems.

Staff training and in-service education provisions traditionally have been regarded as of key importance in ensuring appropriate care of the elderly, psychological and otherwise. It can be deduced from the chapter by Jeffrey that such efforts will not be wholly successful without first considering the many other factors involved in organisational change. However, improving the quality of training packages is likely to enhance their effect. Too often the tendency has been to provide in-service education programmes that dwell at length on aspects of physical care while providing only cursory coverage of the psychological side of caring. Where psychological factors are considered, programmes are often piecemeal, lack a practice base or are pitched at an inappropriate level relative to the background of those at either the presenting or receiving end. In Chapter 8 Gerry Murphy describes 'Over the Hill and Far Away', a five-day video-assisted course offering a comprehensive introduction to work with elderly mentally infirm people that is specifically designed to be used with direct care workers.

The preceding two chapters deal specifically with issues relating to the systematic improvement of practices in residential care of the elderly. Therefore, both are concerned at least indirectly, with the quality of life available to the elderly being 'looked after' in institutions. Debate still goes on as to what constitutes 'quality of life'. Many of the elderly being cared for are unable to tell us coherently what their view is. Often we feel forced to make decisions for them with the only direction provided by loose conceptual systems such as normalisation. Yet some of us have had the experience of visiting or working in settings caring for the elderly where somehow the care 'feels' right, where one gets the sense the psychological principles are actually being applied in practice.

Often this seems like a special experience given the sort of practices we get used to seeing in institutional care. What we might assume is that such 'good' practice must have been systematically devised from first (psychological) principles. Quite often it is not. What we are seeing cannot be so readily accounted for. In this sense, Chapter 9 is a little different from the others. It is essentially an account of what care is like in one residential home for the elderly in the North of Scotland. No apology is made for the fact that it is essentially a personal account. Some of the general principles behind the approach are outlined briefly but the intention is that the reader gets a 'feel' for what life might be like there, rather than a more academic, contrived analysis. Those readers who would prefer a more systematic approach to the presentation of the issues in residential care of the elderly might wish to miss out this chapter.

The book concludes with a review of the ethical and legal issues in therapy with the elderly. The reason for including this chapter by Mary Gilhooly is twofold. First, the elderly are a group vulnerable to ethical abuses, and second, little in the way of ethics is taught during the training of psychologists. The issues involved are of fundamental importance, especially in relationship to the areas of diagnosis, consent, confidentiality and the role of the psychologist.

This book, albeit unintentionally, reflects an all too common tendency, namely, that it is most often the young who venture forth with views concerning the welfare of the elderly. No contributor here, for example, is over the age of 50. No doubt this reflects the relative youth of the psychology profession and is no major detraction in itself from the value of the exercise. However, we all need to consciously make the effort to listen to what the elderly have to tell us. We should seek to understand the issues involved in psychological wellbeing at least in part through the eyes of our clients. We should not give any unnecessary prominence to the notion of the elderly as dependent.

An anecdote may illustrate this last point. When one of us (IH) went fishing a couple of days before this preface was written, he met an angler by the river who was in his late 70s. This man said he always fished in the same pool near the car park. The assumption was made that this was because he was now too frail to make the journey up the riverside path to other pools. As the conversation proceeded, this turned out to be far from the truth: the man quite simply had no good reason to go further afield — he caught quite sufficient salmon where he was (in contrast to the writer!). He referred in his own words to an 'old chap' who also fished the same pool. Even in their 70s some people do not view themselves as elderly.

Ian Hanley and Mary Gilhooly

1 ISSUES IN PSYCHOLOGICAL THERAPY WITH ELDERLY PEOPLE

Mike Church

When therapeutic interventions begin to be made with new client groups, it is to be expected that they will be characterised by ill-considered as well as cogent planning. Unfortunately, the literature on psychological therapy indicates that elderly people have suffered more than their fair share of ill-considered interventions. Perhaps we should not be surprised at this when many professionals who have caring contacts with elderly people continue to use language which stereotypes and dehumanises them. The psychologists who report their studies of 'dements', the neurologist who describes a cognitively unimpaired 70-year-old woman suffering from hallucinations because of an impending blindness as having 'delusions from a senile brain', are but two of an endless number of examples of how elderly people are categorised as somehow less than human. Since language reflects and creates our perception of reality, how can a psychologist who uses such expressions make psychological interventions which are based on the needs of the individual?

It is ironic that much of the literature on psychological therapy with elderly people has focused on the difficulties that this client group present for therapists and therapies of different persuasions. This more subtle discrimination says more about the therapists and therapies than about elderly people. It may not be too cynical to comment that a summary of the present literature indicates there is increasing evidence that clinicians and researchers do show some ability to learn under the right conditions! Within this last statement I have indicated what I wish to present as the central theme of this chapter: that we must begin to fully accept our own responsibilities as to whether or not we intervene effectively with elderly people.

To achieve such a goal, we must have a foundation based on the recognition of every elderly person as being a unique individual, yet undergoing a common process — that of ageing — and have as our keystone pragmatism rather than an allegiance to any monolithic psychological theory. In common with other groups of people with special needs who have come under the psychiatric umbrella, the elderly have suffered as a matter of course the violation of many basic rights. In mental handicap the subtlety and variety of these violations have been explored through the concept of normalisation. With elderly people this situation has been compounded by a failure to consider adequately their special needs as reflected by the process of normal and abnormal ageing.

The common effect of all ageing is to reduce the body's spare capacity for dealing with change. This can can be illustrated simply by considering a young person who may have 95 per cent of his capacity in reserve as compared to an elderly person who may have 5 per cent or less in reserve. If both undergo an experience which calls upon the use of 10 per cent of the spare capacity, this will be barely noticed by the young individual but will mean acute distress for the elderly person. The direct consequence of such a reduction in spare capacity as a result of ageing is to increase dependence on the environment in its broader sense. The potential significance of the environment to the psychological and physical well being of the elderly person still goes largely unrecognised.

A recent study by Finlay, Bayles, Rosen, *et al.* (1983) looked at residents of three old peoples homes in Britain who were unable to rise unaided out of the seats provided for them (N = 39). When Department of Health and Social Security recommended chairs were provided, they found that 77 per cent (N = 30) could then get up themselves. Finlay *et al.* (1983) concluded 'at today's prices, £1,830 was spent on what was found to be unsuitable chairs for this group. Had current guidelines been used in the selection of chairs for the homes, staff would also be saved a minimum of 300 lifts a day for meals and toileting . . .'

Whether in terms of enforced dependency or cost implication, this result, if repeated around the country (and there is no reason to suppose it would not be), almost defies comprehension. It would be missing the point to blame the staff of old people's homes, who often receive little support and training for their work with elderly people. In response to an enquiry, the present author made about the availability of suitable chairs for elderly people, a researcher at the Institute of Consumer Ergonomics, University of Loughborough, recently wrote 'as yet we do not know of any manufacturer who has produced a range which fits our design criteria'.

Designing appropriate physical environments for elderly people is not easy. Continuing with the previous example of chair design, there are a minimum of 21 design features which should be considered when designing this common, everyday piece of furniture (Table 1.1). It is also clear that some design features, for example, having cloth chair covering rather than plastic, though highly desirable for comfort and the possible prevention of skin infections, may also raise difficulties if,

Table 1.1: Factors in Chair Design for Elderly People

1.	Seat height (approximately 18")
2.	Arm rests
3.	Correct arm rest height (approximately 10")
4.	Rounded arm rest ends (for gripping)
5.	Arm rest length
6.	Seat length
7.	Seat declination reduced
8.	Seat width
9.	Adequate seat padding (over frame)
10.	Back height
11.	Lumber support
12.	Rake of seat back
13.	Sharp edges padded
14.	No bar between chair legs
15.	Room under chair legs (to put legs for rising)
16.	No head wings (reduce interaction)
17.	Cloth v. plastic covering
18.	Fire resistance
19.	Fixed chair v. castors (furniture used to aid mobility)
20.	Stability of chair
21.	Avoid grossly splayed chair legs (reduces trips)

for instance, the elderly person is frequently incontinent. It is not possible in this chapter to even begin to do justice to this important and complex subject. Interested readers are referred to a short manual discussing psychological factors, which remains the most comprehensive account, by Henneman (1982).

In the next two sections, on elderly people with dementia and elderly people with functional problems, some issues in psychological therapy will be explored by developing the theme of their special needs as reflected by normal and abnormal ageing. In doing this, specific issues at the level of direct client intervention and the context of the interventions, for instance, service organisation, will both be addressed. The development of a service which delivers effective psychological interventions is dependent both on sound psychological theory in practice with the client group and upon organisational factors such as the kind of service offered and the way it is delivered.

It is a rather spurious argument that clinical psychologists should concentrate their work on one of these aspects to the detriment of the other, as these areas are inter-related. It is clear that there may be many instances where changing a specific organisational factor can be more effective than any number of individual psychological interventions. In the previous example regarding mobility and chair design, improving elderly clients' mobility in a number of residential old people's homes would be best served by initial intervention at the level of chair supply rather than implementing individual behavioural programmes. Likewise, the specific research finding that memory for facial recognition is relatively well preserved in dementia has specific implications for one-to-one client contact, which leads to certain conclusions about how best any support service for elderly people with dementia might be organised and delivered, as will be seen in the next section.

Elderly People with Dementia

The area of therapeutic intervention with elderly people suffering from dementia provides one of the clearest examples of how psychologists have failed to think through the implications of 'abnormal' ageing. The notion of the prosthetic environment suggested by Lindsley (1964) and its effect in facilitating attempts at behavioural intervention has been clearly acknowledged (Baltes and Barton, 1977; Patterson and Jackson, 1980). However, in adopting this view, those using behavioural interventions have almost completely missed what should be the central consideration — that any environmental change made should be closely dependent on the nature of the deficits being compensated for. In particular when considering abnormal ageing, the pattern of neuropsychological deficits and those abilities remaining to the elderly person will be important determinants of behaviour in any environment. This has been illustrated previously by the present author (Church, 1985a, 1985b) in relation to language difficulty, a relatively common problem in dementia. Several strategies which might be used with a person who suffers from a language difficulty have been suggested by research in the neuropsychological literature; it should be noted that for a number of years all these strategies have been regarded as important components of reality orientation.

Myers-Pease and Goodglass (1978) have shown that the use of first sound cueing, for example, 'Ma' for 'Margaret' for aphasics with word-finding difficulties, was considerably more effective in aiding word retrieval than cues which mobilised semantic knowledge such as function cueing (for example, 'You cut better with a . . .'). Albert and Bear (1957) looked at receptive language function when they presented a single case study of a man with a 'word deafness . . . suggestive of a resolving Wernickes aphasia'. This man's comprehension was markedly improved when the examiner reduced his speed of speech to a third or less of normal rate, and this finding was later confirmed experimentally. Goodglass, Blumstein, Gleason *et al.* (1979) showed that the expansion of subject-embedded sentences into two similar propositions (for example, 'The man making love to his wife was standing on his head' — 'The man was making love to his wife and standing on his head') facilitated understanding, particularly in Brocas aphasics.

A further but more subtle aspect of such strategies is the manner in which these are used, that is, the social skills of the staff. Both the verbal and nonverbal skill with which cueing and sentence simplification are used may be important determinants of the elderly person's behaviour. The timing with which the cue is provided to someone who is searching for a word is crucial. Repeatedly presenting the cue too soon will reduce the recipient's experience of success and may precipitate or magnify depressed mood; presenting the cue too late may lead to anger and frustration.

Indeed, the optimum timing is likely to vary considerably from individual to individual and situation to situation. If an elderly person has an expressive aphasia and talks mainly in jargon, then saying verbally to them, 'I know you are trying to tell me something, I'll keep trying to understand you' is likely to have a different effect than saying 'Oh, try to make sense; I can't understand a word you say'. In this case where receptive function may well be impaired, it is likely that the accompanying nonverbal behaviour indicating attentiveness, eye contact and empathy may be more important than the reply itself. It is all to easy to express nonverbally disinterest and lack of time.

Although language is only one of a number of possible areas of neuropsychological dysfunction occurring in organic brain states, the brief examples given clearly illustrate the necessity of carrying out a full analysis of the elderly person's neuropsychological assets and deficits prior to any possible behavioural intervention. It is not hard to imagine what would be the likely outcome of a behavioural programme which relied on the use of verbal instructions if the recipients had an impairment of receptive language. Hodge's (1984) detailed analysis of this issue remains an island in a sea of neglect by those carrying out research with this client group. In his paper, he argued that group designs with a greater matching of subjects, or the use of single case studies, would improve the quality of research in this area. The present author would go further and say that the use of group experimental design as a research method is totally inappropriate with people suffering from organic brain damage. It is surprising that psychologists should have been seduced by the group design model so influential in psychiatric research because of its compatibility with the psychiatric diagnostic model. The limitations of psychiatric diagnosis are well known, while there are numerous psychiatric diagnostic categories (see World Health Organization, 1978) there are probably only four main psychiatric physical treatments of proven usefulness.

The use of single case experimental methodology is also further necessitated by the fact that two individuals with the same psychiatric diagnosis will have different patterns of neuropsychological dysfunction. Furthermore, these neuropsychological deficits will have an interactive effect in producing any particular behaviour problem. The case of an elderly man with an occipital stroke presented by Church and Wattis (1984a) illustrates this point. One management problem that this man presented to hospital staff, but not his wife, was occasional physical aggression on being approached. It was discovered that this behaviour was more likely to occur when he was approached from the left-hand side, in the region of his left visual field defect. The effects of this deficit were compounded by the presence of a poor short-term memory and visual agnosia. His experience must have been somewhat similar to being suddenly physically accosted in the street by a stranger. The behavioural consequences of these neuropsychological deficits were greatly reduced by getting staff to approach him within the range of his intact visual field and to use politeness and a reality-orientated set of skills.

Hodge (1984) also emphasised the importance of taking into account previous social and personal experiences. In the above case, the man had held an important position in a local council department for much of his life: it was clear from observations that he resented being approached in an over-familiar fashion by young nursing staff.

Preserved Abilities in Dementia

Some of the most interesting research regarding the preservation of abilities in dementia has come from the experimental rather than the clinical literature. One consequence of this has been the failure of psychologists carrying out clinical research to be influenced by relatively important experimental findings. An example of this is given in a review by Squire (1982). He presented evidence indicating that certain types of learning were well-preserved even in the presence of a considerable degree of brain damage, findings which had been available since 1962. He suggested that there was a difference between declarative learning, that is, the learning of facts, information and rules (for example, learning some local street names) and procedural learning, or learning by action (for example, as one does when learning tennis). It seems that learning by action can remain unimpaired even when the ability to learn information is grossly impaired, as in Korsikoff's psychosis or post-encephalitis.

The implication for patient care is that skills can be retained or retrained by the use of behavioural practice, even when someone has a considerable degree of dementia. This research finding may explain the effectiveness of ward-orientation (Hanley, 1981). The training procedure in ward-orientation allows the elderly person with dementia to learn through action and it is interesting that for those who do benefit from this approach, there is little relationship to the degree of dementia. It can be suggested that the appropriate use of behaviour modification involving the techniques of shaping, physical prompting, behavioural rehearsal and reinforcement because they utilise an area of intact functioning, will allow the elderly person, even with severe dementia, to maintain higher levels of independence in self-care for much longer.

Ferris, Crook, Clarke, *et al.* (1980) give a more recent example of preserved ability in senile dementia. They found that although facial recognition was lower for two elderly groups than for young normals, they found no different in ability between a normal elderly group and an elderly group with mild to moderate senile dementia. This indicated that facial recognition memory, although declining due to normal ageing, apparently showed no further decline as a result of mild or moderate senile dementia. It suggests that the first few contacts made by, for example, a home help, with an elderly person suffering from dementia will be crucial in determining whether or not that person can perform a useful role as a supporter. Although the elderly person with dementia may not be able to learn the home help's name, he will soon come to recognise them as someone who is potentially helpful and friendly, or as someone who is associated with unpleasant experiences.

Any training for home helps should emphasise the importance of developing a good relationship with the client first of all, rather than being activity-orientated. Training in the use of strategies for dealing with confused talk from an elderly client (Holden and Woods, 1982) would be an important part of this. The service would be organised most effectively if it were able to provide input by the same one or two home helps who knew the person well, rather than by providing a different home help every two or three months, as often happens. It could be further argued that, for example, if a home help, for whatever reasons, developed a poor relationship with the client then rather than persisting, the service should be flexible enough to provide a new home help who could effectively start from scratch in developing a good relationship.

In summary, an understanding of the special needs of an elderly person with dementia arises from the consideration of the behavioural consequences of the neuropsychological assets and deficits. This will have implications from the level of one-to-one contact, through to the level of service delivery and organisation. If psychologists are to guide developments at either of these levels, then there is an urgent need for clinicians both to employ the appropriate research designs and to utilise the experimental research findings that already exist.

Elderly People with Functional Problems

Individual Therapy

Elderly people, in common with other groups, suffer from a wide range of functional problems. These may have a recent origin or be problems which have developed prior to or during early adulthood. In terms of this range of chronicity of presenting problem alone, it seems unlikely that any one therapeutic approach would be suitable for all elderly people. Unfortunately, as in other areas of endeavour with elderly people, therapeutic rigidity has prevented a realistic appraisal of their special needs in relation to psychological therapy.

Psychoanalytic psychotherapy has had particular difficulties in this respect. While it was realised that psychoanalytic therapy would have to be modified for use with this client group, the modifications suggested have been conceptualised within the analytic framework. Thus, for example, Karpf (1980) in a brief review article, wrote '. . . that unconscious resistance to remembering is lessened and free association comes more readily . . .' and warned that '. . . id derivatives may be uncovered at too rapid pace for effective analysis'.

Not only are such descriptions unhelpful in facilitating communication between therapists of different persuasions, the phenomena they refer to may be more parsimoniously explained. Thus the present author reviewed some of the evidence relating to changes in language, memory, and abstract ability that occurred in normal ageing (Church, 1983). This evidence, although tentative, suggested that as therapy becomes more verbal and interpretive in its nature, the elderly client will have increasing difficulty. The value of such experimental findings is that they indicate specific modifications to the way in which a therapist might carry out therapy regardless of therapeutic persuasion. Such findings taken in the light of other reviews, for instance, Sparacino (1979), must put in doubt the applicability of traditional analysis to any elderly person.

In considering the effects of ageing, a number of authors have made the cogent suggestion that not only do elderly people have special needs as compared with younger people, but that the over-60 or over-65 population is not necessarily homogeneous of itself (Mintz, Sener and Jarvick, 1981). In terms of cognitive ability, this is most dramatically illustrated by Walker (1982) who found that failure rate on a test of ability to shift set rose from 10 per cent in those aged 60 to 64 years, to 92 per cent in those aged over 80. In considering one therapeutic model, Sparacino (1978) has speculated as to how attributions may differ between the younger and older elderly. He reported one study in which 50 per cent of those aged between 64 to 75 years expected to live at least another 10 years, while only 10 per cent of those aged 85 to 95 had this expectation. It was suggested that such a reduction in time perspective led to a change in perception of the causal locus of a person's actions, towards residing within a person rather than externally in the environment. It is interesting that the main effect of ageing is in fact the reverse of this, making environmental factors more rather than less important. Although the role of attributions and therapeutic change is still the subject of much controversy, it undoubtedly is the case that an accurate understanding of a person's attributions enhances the development of the therapeutic relationship.

A further area of interest with the elderly relates to the phenomonology of problems presented. While some work has been done using the traditional psychiatric diagnostic system, for example, on hypochondriasis and depression (De Alarcon, 1964), there is little relating to problems such as the presentation of anxiety in the elderly. It is the author's clinical impression that hyperventilation is both a much commoner presentation of anxiety among the elderly and also in some individuals much more resistant to therapeutic intervention.

Lum (1977) has reported impressive success rates in correcting dysfunctional breathing patterns in younger populations. It remains to be seen whether this success can be emulated with elderly people who have a lifelong poor breathing pattern or have greater physical infirmity. This may be an instance where the emphasis should be on the early identification of difficulties and preventative work. However, at present, there is not enough phenomenological evidence to act as a springboard from which to set such priorities.

It is encouraging that some more recent reviews have addressed themselves in detail to the modifications which need to be made to increase the effectiveness of work with elderly clients (Mintz *et al.*, 1981; Sholomskas, Chevron, Prusoff *et al.*, 1983). It is not possible here to

Table 1.2: Factors Enhancing Therapeutic Contact with Elderly People

1. Less abstract, interpretive approach
2. Compensate for reduction in memory for meaning
3. Flexible session length (client comfort)
4. Flexibility of session location (client's home versus office)
5. Time-limited contract
6. Explicit, concrete, realistic goals
7. Awareness of real social and physical limitations
8. Provision of formal social resources and support
9. Interpersonal context of problem ('family' or 'institutional')
10. Active rather than passive therapist
11. Awareness of age contrast in goal-setting and empathy
12. Absence of ageism in therapist
13. Awareness of drug effects in the elderly
14. Assessment of physical factors which may exacerbate 'psychological' problems

review this area in depth, but Table 1.2 presents a summary of a number of factors which might be considered by any therapist. Again, the unifying theme is the tendency of ageing to increase dependency on the environment in its broadest sense. In clinical practice, the weight with which the therapist assigns to each of these factors should depend on their assessment of each elderly individual.

One particular issue of importance which has often been neglected is the possibility, especially with the very old, of, the development of organic states, such as senile dementia of the Alzheimer's type. These may be evidenced by subtle changes in orientation and naming ability (nominal aphasia), probably the most sensitive indicators of organic damage (Gilleard, 1984; Skelton-Robinson and Jones, 1984), or there may be a dramatic change such as in a stroke. If this happens there will need to be a revision of therapeutic strategies and goals in the light of the neuropsychological impairments presented. There are very few instances of such work being reported in the literature (Church, 1984). Counselling individuals with progressive organic pathology is an area fraught with difficulties, as evidenced by Spy (1984).

For a variety of reasons, psychologists have often had a more limited involvement in the management of people with severe psychological and psychiatric disturbance, who suffer repeated admissions in distress and present the greatest burden upon health service resources. While the difficulties faced in carrying out appropriate psychological interventions within inpatient settings can be immense, a considerable proportion of people who are most in need of help will not receive it if psychologists ignore this problem. One substantial group of elderly people who might benefit from a greater psychological contribution are those with depressive illness. Their poor response to traditional psychiatric treatment is well documented (Murphy, 1983). To make a contribution in this area, psychologists will have to fully understand and employ the multi-level model of depression (Akiskal and McKinney, 1975).

Thus the levels of intervention, whether biochemical, psychological or social, are seen as different and co-existing rather than competitive alternatives. Despite the acceptance of such a model within the literature, psychiatric practice still rests heavily on physical treatments, and is often poorly acquainted even with the how of implementing psychological interventions, let alone what kind of intervention might best be used. This fact has often been crucial in determining psychologists' willingness to engage in inpatient work. Conversely, it might be said that psychologists' understanding and acceptance of the appropriate use of physical treatments must influence their acceptance by their psychiatric colleagues.

Church and Wattis (1984b) presented a brief case study of a depressed 69-year-old married woman who was admitted at a greater than yearly frequency with depressive illness (including four suicide attempts) in a 13-year period up to her admission in 1981. According to her notes, before 1981 there was no attempt at a psychological understanding of her difficulties, only at diagnoses. This case illustrated the need for true multidisciplinary teamwork, because of the variety of factors which emerged during the course of her treatment.

Table 1.3 shows the main interventions employed and their timing. It is not possible to discuss this case in detail, but it should be noted that these interventions were carefully planned and timed responses to the changes in problems presented by the patient. It can be seen that psychological aspects were tackled in different ways throughout the stages of her recovery. Thus when she was suffering from depressive delusions (for example, 'There is no blood in my body'; 'I'm dead'; 'I'm no good, I can't do that') it was possible to develop a cognitive behavioural strategy with the staff to cope constructively with these statements and her lack of co-operation.

The behavioural aspects of this strategy involved structuring an increase in staff-initiated contact with her, but a reduction in the time spent with her when she was being negative or unco-operative. The cognitive part of the programme was based on the idea that the meaning she was taking from what staff were saying to her may not have been what was intended. For example, nursing staff would sometimes argue with her during their well-meaning attempts to persuade her that her fixed ideas

Table 1.3: Treatments Interventions with a Severely Depressed Woman

Intervention	Time span
1. Section for admission and treatment	1st week–4th week
2. Antidepressant therapy (amitryptyline)	1st week–54th week
3. Behavioural/cognitive strategy for delusions	3rd week–9th week
4. Counselling and advice for daughters	3rd week–onwards
5. Martial cotherapy (problem solving/ cognitive)	9th week–onwards
6. Discharge and follow-up: (a) Compliance; (b) Problem-solving (c) Gradual reduction in reliance of hospital staff	18th week–onwards
7. Identification and treatment of new medical state (arthritis)	25th week
8. Social change (house move to live near daughter and grandchildren)	32nd week onwards

were not particular realistic. It seemed that these arguments, rather than being seen as helpful or believable by her, were taken to be a further confirmation of her worthlessness.

In practice then, a typical nursing interaction might involve the nurse going up to her and saying 'Let's get your hair done this afternoon and make it look really nice'. The woman's response: 'I'm no good; I'm ugly'. Nurse's response: 'I know you believe that, but you are not ugly and I am not going to stay here and listen to you being hurtful to yourself like that'; and then walking away for a ten-minute period.

Nursing staff also learnt to initiate interaction with the woman when she spontaneously did something constructive. This involved taking a helpful interest in other patients on the ward. The importance of giving nursing staff constructive ways to interact with patients whose intransigent behaviour is brought about by the fixed ideas characteristic of severe depression cannot be underestimated. The alternative is often the patient acquiring a meaningless and destructive label such as 'manipulative'. It is interesting to note in this case that when this woman recovered, she was able to joke about her delusions and it was clear that she remembered many of her experiences while severely depressed.

At a later stage, marital work was begun because her improvement had plateaued after some weeks on a therapeutic dose of antidepressants, and the observation that despite her spouse's daily attendance there was almost no interaction between them. While the initial sessions were fraught, it was possible to improve their immediate relationship by, for example, examining the validity of the woman's belief that her husband did not care for her because he had put her into hospital.

Whatever the profession of the key worker involved in such a case, that person must have a wide range of skills, including the knowledge of other professional areas of expertise. In this case, on two occasions during follow-up a premature attempt was made to discontinue the woman's antidepressant medication, these attempts being circumvented by the key worker. The issue of compliance of elderly people with antidepressant medication has received scant attention in literature and a recent computer research by the present author unearthed no references to research in this area.

While no single intervention produced a dramatic change, neglecting any one might well have led to a treatment failure or a partial response. Indeed, it seems likely that a social change has been responsible for her continued wellbeing. Some three months after her discharge it was possible to re-house the women near her daughter and grandchildren, by means of a letter giving medical priority. This move, which was wanted by her whole family, allowed her to regain the constructive life she had lost when her children had started to leave home, and which resulted in the onset of her episodes of depressive illness. At the time of writing, she has been well for two years (without antidepressants for one year).

Family Therapy

Any therapeutic work with elderly people must consider their context within the social network of family, friends or care staff. For a variety of reasons, such as physical health, retirement or loss of roles, the common effect of ageing is to make the elderly more dependent on their social network. Thus the elderly person's quality and nature of these interpersonal contacts may be an important factor in the maintenance of their problem. A few more detailed accounts emphasising this interactional view have usually adopted a realistic and pragmatic approach. Some of the skills encouraged, for instance, a detailed review of the family members' attempts at solutions (failed or otherwise) and the results of these problem-solving efforts, are potentially useful in any therapeutic endeavour (Herr and Weakland, 1979).

At a more general level, family therapy has been imbued with a mystic unparalleled in most other therapeutic models, this arising in part from the charisma of the main proponents of different family models (Selvini-Palazzoli, Cechin, Prata, *et al.*, 1979). More recently, some of the central concepts within these different models of family therapy, such as homeostasis, have been subject to major revisions (Dell, 1982). One overriding view which emerges from literature in this area is the importance of holding therapy sessions with all the 'family' members present. However, as Watzlawick and Coyne (1980) point out, because there is an interactional system, '. . . appropriate change in a subsystem (e.g. one family member) can bring about major changes in the entire system'. Although it is generally desirable to assess the family initially, it is possible to take Watzlawick's and Coyne's view further and suggest that some work may be more effectively carried out *without* family presence, that is, on an individual basis. In practice, there seems to be three broad ways of working with families.

The first group, where it is desirable to see the family together, is often more closely knit, perhaps because of cultural or religious reasons. There is often considerable pressure on outside agencies to do something, despite the often very different picture of needs and abilities presented by the elderly person himself. Direct advice and information about the elderly relative's needs and abilities as given to other family members is often poorly tolerated. The family often takes the view that 'we've tried everything, and nothing works'.

In the second group of families, particular those who care for an elderly relative with a life-long functional problem such as depression or a recently developed chronic problem such as dementia, it may be best to see the main care giver alone. These kind of carers are often eager for specific practical advice which they have often been unable to obtain elsewhere and are not threatened by receiving such direct advice. For example, they may want to know the best course of action if mother telephones about twice a week at three o'clock in the morning saying she is having a heart attack, but appears quite all right when the daughter arrives on the doorstep. Obviously, it is not easy to give specific advice if the mother is present during a session. Similarly, when counselling a relative whose spouse or partner has dementia, separate sessions will always be necessary. In this group, then, it is not possible to work effectively on some issues with all family members present, but there is no reason why other family sessions cannot be held; these may be an important adjunct to the individual intervention.

The third group consists of those in which it is impractical or even impossible to gather family members for therapeutic sessions. Church and Wattis (1984a) presented an example of an elderly woman with a lifelong history of hypochrondriachial complaints, who showed the psychiatrist the door on his assessment interview. Because of this and the desire of the caring, competent daughter for help, only the daughter was seen. The intervention involved the daughter redistributing her precious time (she also cared for her divorced father who had dementia) in a way that improved the quality of their interactions. A marked improvement occurred within six weeks and this was maintained over a year.

As discussed earlier in the section on dementia, the interactional system is particularly important within institutions. It is often impossible to get the relevant caregivers together for a family interview in institutions because of the shift system. This problem may be heightened in a private old people's home because of the emphasis on running a profitable business. In such situations, making an effective intervention within the system to help a client may require luck as well as acumen. One case which illustrates this involved a very pleasant but unhappy lady, who had lost her husband, became depressed and had been put into a private old person's home by her relatives within the space of four months. This was a devastating experience for her and individual intervention involved bereavement work and treatment with antidepressants. However, one of her main complaints was the way in which she was treated by Mrs P, who was in charge of her part of the old people's home. The home consisted of two separate buildings, one of which was overseen by the owner, the matron, and the other by Mrs P, who was the matron's sister. Through meeting Mrs P, conversations with other care staff and using the client's comments, a picture emerged of Mrs P as a rather unhappy woman who found it difficult to manage effectively, treated the elderly people in her care as children and who was under pressure from the matron to do her job better.

Mrs P appeared to actively ignore the initial advice given her to help the author's client and eventually took to standing outside the door during my individual sessions with the client, apparently eavesdropping. In this situation, my over-riding concern was to make an intervention which would result in an improved state of affairs for my client rather than deal with my own angry feelings. The intervention was based on the idea that Mrs P, despite being quite destructive, was well-meaning in her behaviour and that she felt considerable pressure from the matron. It involved sending a letter to the matron under the guise of keeping her informed, which positively connotated, that is, praised, Mrs P's actions with regard to my client. This letter was sent knowing (or perhaps hoping) that the contents would be passed on by the matron to Mrs P. The change in Mrs P's co-operation on my next visit was dramatic, and this was later confirmed by other staff. At the end of my individual work and at six months' follow-up, the situation remained much more positive. It can easily be imagined what might have happened if I had informed the matron of difficulties with her sister, Mrs P, rather than making this kind of strategic intervention.

This example indicates that the interactional context of the psychologist's work is much broader than just involving direct interventions with elderly people and their families, but can and should be utilised during indirect work for elderly people, for example, on committees or planning teams, in order to influence policy.

Conclusion

Although many issues remain to be explained and developed, enough is known about the implications of ageing to considerably improve the quality of care that elderly people receive. The understanding of ageing leads directly to an understanding of the special needs of the elderly person. However, a gulf still separates the care elderly people actually receive and the care that they could or should receive.

This is not just because of misunderstanding about ageing, but rather because most services which exist today are not organised with the psychological wellbeing of the elderly and their families in mind. Psychiatric and geriatric services are often organised without rhyme or reason, and remain almost totally lacking in accountability for the quality of service given. Within such services, it may be impossible to institute effective psychological care without altering their organisation. Indeed, altering any procedure or practice which has become routine in such a setting becomes a major task. For example, it was still possible in a teaching hospital in 1984 to find elderly people suffering urinary incontinence being routinely cathetorised on admission to an acute geriatric ward rather than the staff attempting retraining (Chung, 1984). As in this case, it can take months of persistent effort to get a change in such a procedure considered.

The importance of the environment in determining behaviour has been repeatedly emphasised in this paper. In a similar way, the staff who work in such services (usually with little support and inadequate funding) should not be blamed. Rather, one should look at their environment and the organisational structure they work in. Changing this can produce much more effective and permanent change in care practice than any individual psychological intervention. Table 1.4 lists some of the possible organisational factors which influence the efficiency of a psychogeriatric service. This is by no means comprehensive and, indeed, some of these factors may be very hard to implement in practice. For example, the issue of

Table 1.4: Organisational Factors Influencing Efficiency of a Psychogeriatric Service

1. Size of permanent facility (for example, ward, day centre)	As small as possible (suggested maximum of 15 beds/facility)
2. Physical design of facility	Accommodate needs of client and staff, and their interaction. Reduce effects of normal and abnormal ageing
3. Single team per facility	Allows development of coherent team and policies. Allows the assessment of the team service effectiveness as compared to other psychogeriatric teams (that is, accountability increased)
4. Decision-making models	Shared decision-making versus authoritarianism promotes responsibility, acceptance of other special skills, common service aims and increased service efficiency
5. Consultative planning	Multidisciplinary planning teams promote effective, whole-person planning
6. Hospital-based versus community-based services	Majority of services should be community-based. They should reflect client need not staff convenience
7. Multi-level versus medical model of care	A multi-level, whole-person approach increases probability of successful client management. Requires different set of skills to traditional medical diagnostic interviewing
8. Assessment procedures should be predictive and problem-oriented	Use of common and valid assessment procedures such as CAPE (Pattie and Gilleard, 1976) promotes communication within teams and between health services and community services
9. Team worker control of resource allocation	Key workers should have access for allocating money available for client support. Promotes meeting of client need rather than matching client to existing support service

shared versus authoritarian decision-making is a difficult one, not least because the consultant, in law, has the medical responsibility. However, in practice, it is possible to run a team with a key worker system who takes on the central role of decision-making regarding their clients, in close consultation with other members of the team. The more supportive the team, the more likely that areas of disagreement will be solved constructively for the client's benefit.

Because most health authorities in Britain and agencies in other countries are now committed to a move towards community care for elderly people, the next few years will be crucial for many workers in determining the kind of service their client group receives. They will have an opportunity either to develop services which are organised to serve and support their clients or to recapitulate the organisational disasters which already exist. If the latter occurs, there is no doubt that the community-based service will be every bit as bad as the institutional service it replaces.

At present, there is contradictory evidence about which aspects of a community service can provide significant help to elderly people and their relatives. Gilleard, Belford, Gilleard, *et al.* (1984) found that levels of formal and informal community support were not related to supporters' mental health as measured by the General Household Questionnaire. However, Levin, Sinclair and Gorbach (1984) found, for example, that the build-up of strain among those whose relatives were still at home about a year after their initial interview was less if they had been receiving the services of home helps, community nurses, day care, relief care or attendance allowance on their first interview than if they were not.

It is worth noting that Levin *et al.* specifically picked their study areas on the basis of being community-orientated, and having a reputation for sound, interesting practice, whereas Gilleard *et al.* picked the existing service in Edinburgh. Levin *et al.* (1984) also looked at the supporters' perception of the services received. Prompt interviews, sensitivity in dealing with the elderly person, clear explanations and an agreed clear and promptly implemented plan of action were some of the things commented on by the supporters. Any reorganised service must look to meeting these client wishes. The range of need which elderly people have implies a range and flexibility of psychological approach which is probably unparalleled in any other client group. Similarly, a range and flexibility of services will be needed to provide effective community care.

Traditional community services have often not evolved in a way to allow this. Thus, the client, whatever his needs, is fitted into the existing service provision, however inappropriate, because there is nothing else available. As it is only too well known, services organised in this way respond at an almost imperceptible pace to even major changes in the degree and nature of the needs of the client group. One way to get round this problem would be to carry out detailed surveys of the elderly population and their supporters, particularly those not known to existing services, and to provide some method of using this information to quickly develop new client-based services.

The Kent Community Project, reported by Challis and Davis (1980), shows how an organisational change can lead to an effective flexible support service for some elderly clients. They looked at elderly people who were on the edge of institutional care, but who wanted to remain in their own homes. Specialist social workers with reduced case loads were allowed to use up to two-thirds of the money which would have been used for institutional care in *any* way they wished to provide support at home for each elderly person. In the event, the commonest use of the money was to pay helpers, neighbours and friends for particular 'tasks'. In this controlled study, the results showed that, as compared to traditionally organised services, they were able to dramatically reduce admission to residential care. It should be noted that the Kent Community Project also incorporated other good organisational practices such as the use of a problem-orientated approach.

Finally, it should be said that however good the skills or however well-organised the community support services, there will always be some elderly people, particularly those with severe dementia, who need 24-hour care. Anyone who has been in a typical long-stay ward with 35 people with severe dementia and four nurses, cannot doubt there is a more humane alternative. It will cost more, but then surely how we care for those in society who are least able to speak for themselves is the measure of our civilisation.

References

Akiskal, H.S. and McKinney, W.T. (1975) 'Overview of Recent Research in Depression', *Archives of General Psychiatry, 32*, pp. 285–304

Albert, M.C. and Bear, D. (1957) 'Time to Understand. A Case Study of Word Deafness with Reference to the Role of Time in Auditory Comprehension', *Brain, 97*, pp. 373–84

Baltes, M.M. and Barton, C.M. (1977) 'New Approaches Towards Ageing: A Case for the Operant Model', *Educational Gerontology, 2*, pp. 383–405.

Challis, D. and Davies, B. (1980) 'A New Approach to Community Care for the Elderly', *British Journal of Social Work, 10*

Chung, E. (1984) personal communication

Church, M.A. (1983) 'Psychological Therapy with Elderly People', *Bulletin of the British Psychological Society, 36*, pp. 110–12.

——— (1984) 'Some Aspects of Bereavement Counselling with Elderly People', *Psychologists Special Interest Group in the Elderly Newsletter, 12*, pp. 6–9
——— (1985a) 'Forgotten Something', *Nursing Times*, 24 July, pp. 23–4
——— (1985b) 'Cues to Clarity', *Nursing Times*, 31 July, pp. 35–7
——— and Wattis, J.P. (1984a) 'Psychological Approaches: Neuropsychological Assessment', *Geriatric Medicine*, November, pp. 833–8
——— and Wattis, J.P. (1984b) 'Multidisciplinary Treatment of Depression in the Elderly, a Case Study', paper presented at the Royal College of Psychiatry Conference: *Psychiatry and Psychologists — Co-operation or Confrontation?*, November 15
De Alarcon, R. (1964) 'Hypochondriasis and Depression in the Aged', *Geront. Clin. 6*, pp. 266–77
Dell, P.F. (1982) 'Beyond Homeostasis: Towards a Concept of Coherence', *Family Process, Inc., 21*, pp. 21–41
Ferris, S.H., Crook, T., Clarke, E., *et al.* (1980) 'Facial Recognition Memory Deficits in Normal Ageing and Senile Dementia', *J. of Geront, 35*, pp. 707–14
Finlay, O.E., Bayles, T.B., Rosen, C., *et al.* (1983) 'Effects of Chair Design. Age and Cognitive Status on Mobility', *Age and Ageing, 12*, pp. 328–31
Gilleard, C. (1984) 'Assessment of Cognitive Impairment in the Elderly: A Review' in I. Hanley and J. Hodge (eds), *Psychological Approaches to the Care of the Elderly*, Croom Helm, London
——— Belford, H., Gilleard, E. *et al.* (1984) 'Emotional Distress Amongst the Supporters of the Elderly Mentally Infirm', *British Journal of Psychiatry, 145*, pp. 172–7
Goodglass, H., Blumstein, S.E., Gleason, J.B. *et al.* (1979) 'The Effect of Syntactic/Encoding on Sentence Comprehension in Aphasia', *Brain and Language, 7*, pp. 201–9
Hanley, I.G. (1981) 'The Use of Sign Posts and Active Training to Modify Ward Disorientation in Elderly Patients', *Journal of Behaviour and Experimental Psychiatry, 12 (3)*, pp. 241–7
Henneman, L. (1982) *Short Manual Discussing Psychological Factors in the Design of Environments for the Elderly Sick* (contact Lynda Henneman, Principal Psychologist, Elderly Development Team, Exminster Hospital, Exeter, EX6 8AB)
Herr, J.J. and Weakland, J.H. (1979) *Counselling Elders and their Families. Practical Techniques for Applied Gerontology*, Springer, New York
Hodge, J. (1984) 'Towards a Behavioural Analysis of Dementia' in I. Hanley and J. Hodge (eds), *Psychological Approaches to the Care of the Elderly*, Croom Helm, London
Holden, U.P. and Woods, R.T. (1982) 'Reality Orientation', *Psychological Approaches to the 'Confused' Elderly*, Churchill Livingstone, London
Karpf, R.J. (1980) 'Modalities of Psychotherapy with the Elderly', *Journal of the American Geriatrics Society, 28* (8), pp. 367–71
Levin, E., Sinclair, I. and Gorbach, P. (1984) *The Supporters of Confused Elderly Persons at Home*, unpublished research study, extract from the main report, National Institute for Social Work Research Unit
Lindsley, O.R. (1964) 'Geriatric Behavioural Prosthetics' in R. Kastenbaum (ed.), *New Thoughts on Old Age*, Springer, New York
Lum, L.C. (1977) 'Breathing Exercised in the Treatment of Hyperventilation and Chronic Anxiety States', *Chest, Heart and Stroke, 2*, pp. 6–12
Mintz, J., Sener, J. and Jarvick, L. (1981) 'Psychotherapy with Depressed Elderly Patients: Research Considerations', *Journal of Consulting and Clinical Psychology, 49* (4), pp. 542–8
Murphy, E. (1983) 'The Prognosis of Depression in Old Age', *British Journal of Psychiatry, 142*, pp. 111–19
Myers-Pearce, D. and Goodglass, H. (1978) 'The Effects of Cueing on Picture Naming in Aphasia', *Cortex, 14*, 178–84
Patterson, R.L. and Jackson, G.M. (1980) 'Behaviour Modification with the Elderly', in *Progress in Behaviour Modification*, volume 9, Academic Press, New York, pp. 205–39

Pattie, A.H. and Gilleard, C.J. (1976) 'The Clifton Assessment Schedule — Further Validation of a Psychogeriatric Assessment Schedule', *British Journal of Psychiatry, 129*, pp. 68–72

Selvini-Palazzoli, M., Cecchin, G., Prata, G., *et al.* (1978) *Paradox and Counterparadox*, Jason Aronson, New York

Sholomskas, A.J., Chevron, E.S., Prusoff, B.A., *et al.* (1983) 'Short-term Interpersonal Therapy IPT with the Depressed Elderly — Case Reports and Discussion', *American Journal of Psychotherapy, 37* (4), pp. 552–66

Skelton-Robinson, M. and Jones, S. (1984) 'Nominal Sysphasia and the Severity of Senile Dementia', *British Journal of Psychiatry, 145*, pp. 168–71

Sparacino, J. (1978) 'An Attributional Approach to Psychotherapy with Aged', *Journal of the American Geriatrics Society, 26, 9*, pp. 414–17

——— (1979) 'Individual Psychotherapy with the Aged: A Selective Review', *International Journal of Ageing and Human Development, 9*, pp. 197–220

Spy, T. (1984) 'Counselling in Alzheimer's Disease — the Impossible Task', *Psychologists Special Interest Group in the Elderly Newsletter, 13*, pp. 8–13

Squire, L.R. (1982) 'The Neuropsychology of Human Memory', *Ann. Rev. Neurosci. 5*, pp. 241–73

Walker, S. (1982) 'An Investigation of the Communication of Elderly Subjects', M. Phil thesis, University of Sheffield

Watzlawick, P. and Coyne, J.C. (1980) 'Depression Following Stroke: Brief Problem-focused Family Treatment', *Family Process, Inc., 19*, pp. 13–18

World Health Organization (1978) *International Classification of Diseases*, 9th edn, WHO, Geneva

2 DYNAMIC PSYCHOTHERAPY WITH THE ELDERLY

Peter Hildebrand

'It doesn't seem to me to be superfluous to give a warning to beginners: psychoanalytic technique has undergone profound modifications since its early beginnings' (Freud, 1914). The occasion for this interesting remark was an important paper on psychotherapeutic technique entitled 'Remembering, Repeating and Working Through'; a topic which is central to the whole question of psychotherapy, the relation of the past to the present and the best ways of interpreting and working with psychological problems.

For the non-specialist reader, it is worth emphasising that these words of Freud are as true today as they were over 70 years ago. Psychoanalysis and its major therapeutic derivative, dynamic psychotherapy, are becoming as fluid and as changing in their techniques as they have ever been. Theoretical emphasis in the past has centred successively on catharsis, reconstruction, the lifting of infantile amnesia, analysis of defences and character analysis. Each in turn became the centre of therapeutic interest and therapeutic work. In more recent times, analysts have studied the widening scope of analysis, problems of identity, the borderline syndrome, narcissism and transitional space as the foci of therapeutic theorising. I would argue that today we are beginning to see the reconsideration of the developmental viewpoint in metapsychology as central to the next few years with considerable concomitant effects on the possibility of psychology with a wider range of patients.

In a recent paper on this topic, I suggested that we were 'moving towards a psychodynamic lifespan developmental psychology with a major corollary, the existence of phase-specific critical periods as individuals age'. It was also pointed out that 'psychoanalytic theorists have far too uncritically accepted a hypothesis of continuous psychic and psychosomatic development, with a rising curve of growth from birth to adulthood, a long refractory period and then a terminal stage of psychic deficit and social withdrawal preliminary to dying and death itself.' I have argued that though this was 'a familiar model', it was also an oversimplified one and that recent evidence in the field of development suggested that psychic and somatic function in the second half of life was far more complex and less regular than had been supposed up to this point (Hildebrand, 1982).

This evolution of the focus of psychoanalytic and psychotherapeutic thought has been part of the emergence of lifespan developmental psychology associated principally in psychoanalytic theorising with the work of Erikson (1981), supplementing and extending Freud's original developmental scheme which ended essentially with early adulthood. At the same time changes in therapeutic understanding have led to a contemporary recognition of the centrality for therapy of object — and self — relations with their emphasis on the creative power of continually changing relationships rather than concentrating entirely on very early experiences. Theorists today are moving towards considering the vicissitudes and history of object relations across the lifespan.

These developments have been welcomed by workers in the field of ageing as they contrast strongly with the earlier approach towards older patients, which was typical of Freud and his colleagues. Freud himself laid down in lectures which he gave in 1904 that 'psychotherapy is not possible near or above the age of 50, the elasticity of the mental processes on which the treatment depends is as a rule lacking — old people are not educable' (Freud, 1905). The present author has argued elsewhere that the reason for this dictum, given the highly dynamic intellectual world in which Freud lived and where he was in contact with many intelligent and elastic older minds, might be due to his seeing disorders of sexual life as being uniquely pathogenic for neurosis. Hence he took the easy but mistaken steps of identifying mental activity such as cognition and memory with sexual activity, so that if in terms of sexual life a gradual slowing down of gonadal activity led to the menopause in woman and loss of sexual potency in men, he could infer that the same would be true of mental activity and that cognition too would become rigid and inelastic after the age of 50.

I suggested that Freud was so fascinated with his own discoveries that he made this assumption without considering the weight of evidence against his hypothesis and dealt with the question as if it were a mere technical, self-evident detail (Hildebrand, 1985). Sadly, what was only a rule of thumb for an emerging psychotherapist became a rigid operating rule and in Great Britain the official institution governing psychoanalysis, the British Psychoanalytic Society, has until this year refused to accept patients over the age of 40.

At the same time, psychodynamic institutions such as The Tavistock Clinic, London, either for reasons of inanition or because the question had not been properly thought through, until recently also routinely rejected patients over the age of 40 as being unsuitable for dynamic psychotherapy. The influence of these conventions was so widespread that a survey of the literature will show only a few papers on psychoanalysis with older patients before the 1970s, and with the honourable exception of the Group for Geriatric Psychiatry in Boston, very few analysts had reported analytic work with patients in the 'third age' (Myers, 1984).

The first influential voice in Britain was that of King who published her 'Notes on the Psychoanalysis of Older Patients' in 1974. In this landmark paper, King identified some of the pressures which she felt operated as sources of anxiety and concern during the second half of life and which therefore led some individuals to seek psychotherapeutic help in later years. She summarised these pressures as:

1. The fear of the diminution or loss of sexual potency and the impact this would have on relationships;
2. The threat of redundancy or displacement in work roles by younger people and awareness of the possible failure of the effectiveness of their professional skills, linked with the fear that they would not be able to cope with their retirement and would lose their sense of identity and worth when they lost their professional or work role;
3. Anxieties arising in marital relationships after children have left home and parents can no longer use these children to mask problems arising in their relationships with one another;
4. The awareness of their own ageing, possible illness and consequent dependence on others and the anxiety this arouses in them;
5. The inevitability of their own death and the realisation that they may not be able to achieve the goals they set for themselves and what they can achieve and enjoy in life may be limited, with consequent feelings of depression and deprivation.

In the next few years, King developed her ideas further although she never organised any formal teaching or seminars around her work with older patients. In particular, she made the important observation that 'middle-aged and elderly patients may be functioning within a number of different time scales. These may include a chronological time scale or unconscious process which is paradoxically timeless'. She concluded that the developmental phases which most often need to be worked through in analysis in later life are those of puberty and adolescence, the analyst being experienced whatever his age as a significant adult from the phases of the patient's life-cycle (King, 1980).

King's views have been influential and have radically changed the attitude of psychodynamic therapists to older patients in this country. The major difficulty of her theory is that it implies a covert diminution of the achievements of adulthood and a lack of recognition of the existence of late-life developmental phases and phase-specific problems. Fortunately, this is an area which has begun to be researched exhaustively in the United States (Greenspan and Pollock, 1981). In addition, the work of the Chicago School, particularly Neugarten (1979) and her colleagues Gutmann (1977) and Cohler (1980) as well as Levinson at Yale (1978) has enlarged understanding of the normal psychology and psychopathology of older adults in Western culture. For example, Gutmann (1977) suggests, on the basis of extensive cross-cultural studies that in society, males in the age range 35 to 54 are mainly characterised by a stance of active mastery. They are invested in production and competition, and they strive to acquire control over the resources upon which their security and the security of their dependents is based. In the pursuit of these goals they rule out much of their capacity for tender feelings, for sensuality and for dependence, while giving priority to agency over community. By contrast, older men in the age group 55 and over are more diffusely sensual and they can become particularly interested not in what they can produce but in that which is produced for them: good, pleasant sights and sounds and uncomplicated supportive social contacts. In effect, the older men reverse the priorities of the younger males and orient themselves towards community rather than agency.

Gutmann says: 'Women age psychologically in the reverse direction, even in normally patriarchal societies like the one in which we live. Women become more aggressive in later life, less affiliative and more managerial or political. Unlike the easy-going older men, the older women become less interested in community and more turned towards agency.' Thus over time and across gender lines, Gutmann suggests that a massive transcultural gender shift seems to take place. During the post-parental years, he says, the husband who used to support his wife both physically and emotionally now becomes more dependent on her as a kind of maternal authority; in short, 'each sex becomes something of what the other used to be' (Gutmann, 1977).

Gutmann assumes that late-onset disturbances reflect older people's inability to assimilate — that is, to transform into newer executive capacities — the potentials that are released in the post-parental period of the life-cycle. Many men, like adolescents, are frightened by the emergence of a new feminine side to their sexual nature so that they produce severe reaction formations against threats from an emerging feminine side of self. In the same way, many older women are profoundly troubled by the emergence of a hitherto closeted competitive masculine and aggressive component of the self.

It would seem sensible, therefore, to glance briefly at sexual function in the elderly in this context. There has long been a view that later life is asexual with a gradual decline in sexual potency in men and women, leading to a cessation of satisfactory sexual relationships in later life. But as Colarusso and Nemiroff (1980, 1985), basing their thinking on the key research of Masters and Johnson (1966), have argued, this picture of an asexual old age is both physiologically and psychologically a myth. They point out that among the myths which have been exposed recently is the notion that the menopausal syndrome in women is caused by oestrogen deficiency. They suggest that it is likely to be much more psychologically based, occurring in those women with an exaggerated response to phase-specific developmental events such as loss of fertility, ageing of the body and the loss of the mothering function.

A second myth is that postmenopausal women cannot enjoy sex because of the physiological and psychological effects of oestrogen withdrawal. They say that, in fact, oestrogen depletion is only one factor, and a reversable one at that, determining the sexual capacity of the elderly woman. In their view, her attitude towards sexuality is determined partly by what is expected and allowed by society and partly by the availability of a sexual partner whose presence is the most important factor determining the presence or absence of a gratifying sexual life. A third myth they discussed is that a decrease in testosterone levels is responsible for the decline in sexual functioning in older men. Having reviewed the evidence and pointed out that the male menopause (so-called) is not caused by significant changes in plasma-testosterone levels, they suggest that the case is at best not proven as the relationship between sexual function and hormonal level is at present not known. In support, they quote Masters and Johnson (1966) in their seminal study:

> The fear of performance reflecting cultural stigmas directed toward erective inadequacy was that associated with problems of secondary impotence. These fears were expressed, under interrogation, by every male study subject beyond 40 years of age, irrespective of reported levels of formal education. Regardless of whether the individual male study subject had ever experienced an instance of erective difficulty, the probability that secondary impotence was associated directly with the ageing process was vocalised constantly. The fallacy that secondary impotence is to be expected as the male ages is probably more firmly entrenched in our culture than any other misapprehension . . .

> In most instances, secondary impotence is a reversible process for all men regardless of age, unless there is a background of specific injury or physical trauma (pp. 203–4).

Thus, it may be said that for the great majority of the aged, sexual function may continue normally until extreme age and in some individuals can continue into the 90s. In my own thinking I have come to the conclusion that as we age, sexuality becomes less a matter of discharge of hormonal tensions and far more the expression of what Butler and Lewis (1978) have described as 'the opportunity for the expression of passion, affection and loyalty; affirmation of the value of one's body and its functions, a means of self-assertion and affirmation of life, the pleasure of being touched and caressed, the defiance of the stereotype of aging and a continuing search for sensual growth and experience'. This is true for women equally as for men and there seems to be positive evidence suggesting not only that women over 40 want more in the way of sexual relationships but the relationship should not only be with their partners or peers but optimally with younger men. Moreover, masturbation in older women, which does not fall away to the extent which it does with men, is both healthy and life-enhancing. On the available evidence, the sexually deprived out-group in our culture are divorced, separated, single and widowed women whose sexual needs and problems are not viewed with as much sympathy as those of the older man, whose needs have been always better and more easily catered for by society.

In sum, where there is time, physical fitness and expectation, later life is a period when people can allow themselves the pleasure of sexual and sensual exploration, when for the elderly, genitality and pre-genitality merge together to produce not an amorphous mass but rather a dialectic exchange far richer than for the young person (Hildebrand, 1982).

Another important area in working with older patients is the notion of the individual's own death. There is a good deal of evidence to suggest that as well as the primal fantasies of birth, intercourse and generation, there is also in all of us a genotypic fantasy of one's own death (Hildebrand, 1983). Freud himself felt that this was a step he could not take. In his view, there could be no notion of death in the unconscious because there was nothing negative there and he got round the problem by positing a death instinct with a continual drive towards rest and nothingness. But as I have argued, so much of Western literature, so much of Western thought, has to do with death that the evidence seems overwhelming for the notion of a primary fantasy to do with one's own extinction and that of one's objects. While I am not prepared to espouse

Jacque's (1965) view of the mid-life crisis as being a reaction to the notion of death and personal extinction becoming central at the age of 37, I do feel that for many of the older patients, their personal death and the deaths of those close to them, whether parents, spouses or children, form a major preoccupation often unspoken and hard to express in words, which the therapist has to recognise and help the individual to cope with.

There are many ways in which people do this. Pollock (1981) has argued that the later periods of life should be seen as a time of mourning for what one has and has not achieved. In his view, there is a mourning process which is carried out throughout the second half of life where one's deficiencies and difficulties are taken up, reworked and grieved for. This, for him, is a normative process since none of us can achieve perfection, and one which is conducive to the gradual achievement of serenity in old age. Unless such a process is initiated and carried out by the individual either by himself or in conjunction with some form of help giving institution, rage and despair are turned against the self and we anticipate only too easily the depressive breakdowns of later life.

Given this theoretical approach towards understanding the problems of later life, psychotherapy with the elderly becomes a real possibility. In my experience, such therapy can take two forms — reminiscence or major psychotherapy. For many older people, as Cohler and Carnie (1980) have pointed out, reminiscence becomes a more important way of reorganising and understanding their lives and working through problems which are incomplete as they age. They say:

> As a consequence of increased awareness of the finitude of life, both men and women become increasingly absorbed with self and somewhat less patient with demands on time and energy which increasingly are experienced as in short supply. They are concerned with the realisation of their self, with reworking the present, the understood story of the past into a story of a life of some significance and coherence which becomes a primary task during later middle age, so that ability to mourn goals not attained and attainment of increased acceptance of the finitude of life without despair are signs of a relatively successful resolution of conflicts associated with this transformation. Across the second half of life there is increased concern with issues of reminiscence and introspection which may require time and energy now less available for the broad range of investments in social relations characteristic of younger adults. Time and effort are needed in order to sort out hopes, goals and disappointments and to grieve past disappointments, making possible successful adjustment to old age.

When we talk about their lives with older people we find this process to be helpful in understanding and adjusting to the problems of retirement, loss and approaching death, which is so characteristic of this later time of life.

There is an easy transition to formal psychotherapy here. In the workshop that I have conducted for the last ten years in the Adult Department of the Tavistock Clinic, we have interviewed and worked with many elderly patients. Our oldest patient, whom I shall describe below, was 84 when first seen, while the majority have been in their 60s and 70s. Our patients are seen once a week for 45 minutes for approximately 15 sessions, though some have been treated for two years or more. The therapy is normal face-to-face therapy using all the mechanisms of transference organisation and transference analysis (Hildebrand, 1981).

This workshop is unusual in that we feel psychotherapy with older patients is not only possible but effective. Silberschatz and Curtis (in press) in their important paper on research into the psychodynamic process in the treatment of older patients, say that there is little convincing evidence in the research or clinical literature to support the view that older adults can be treated effectively by psychodynamic psychotherapy, in their view. The reason for this is that psychotherapy generally focuses on a patient group that is unrepresentative both of the older population and of those likely to be seen in the psychotherapist's office. There is very little about the self-sufficient, independently functioning older adults who are, of course, far more representative of their age group than those generally written up. They point out that where older patients have been seen for psychotherapy, the recommendation has usually been for some combination of pharmacological treatment together with supportive work. They also make the point that the problems cited, such as insomnia, retirement problems, the empty nest and so on, are treated as if they were normative across the adult group whereas, of course, while being phase-specific these phases can vary widely between individuals, and they advocate a case-specific approach while they overcome some of the inherent weaknesses of the ordinary clinical trials and methodology (Silberschatz and Curtis, in press).

This, of course, chimes with our experience in many ways (Hildebrand, 1982). Older people should be credited with greater ego strengths. After all, they have been there, in the way a 25- or 30-year-old has not. They have been hardened and tempered by life and, where their defences have not cracked, they seem to have a good deal of capacity to delay gratification, allow problems to resolve and to take the long view. Moreover, they often have much greater self-reliance than do younger people and can be left to get on with things by themselves.

This leads to another point, one which is important in the cost-conscious world of today. Older people can use briefer experience of therapy than younger people, partly because as Dr Johnson once said, 'the prospect of execution concentrates a man's mind wonderfully'. Older patients do not have the time to hang about contemplating their navels, they want to get on with things — but different things. In an unpublished paper, Gutmann has reanalysed Malan's (1978) Tavistock sample of brief therapies and shown that, while the younger males in the sample were preoccupied with Oedipal themes, the older males, with whom better results were obtained on the whole, were involved more in questions of dependency and independence. Younger men presented with problems of unresolved struggles with dominant fathers, while older men had to face the problem of the newly aggressive wife while they were beginning to explore their own dependent wishes.

These problems of dependence for the older male and aggression for the older female are equally immediate and equally crucial in their resolution. Depressed older women are less depressed about the loss of their procreative function, the emptiness, the husband's disinterest or the pain of widowhood; their real losses are more apt to be internal. They are based on losses of self-esteem, provoked by developmental advances which relocate the inner life around unacceptable needs and identifications. These are focal internal issues which are reversible and treatable but, unfortunately, as with the older male, they are too easily ignored by therapists in favour of concentration on trying to support people through the loss of external figures or physiological functions such as menopause.

Another major problem for the therapist with older patients is of course that of transference and counter-transference. In my view there are few difficulties on the whole if therapist and patient are contemporaries, certainly no more than when a young psychotherapist might be working with an attractive patient of the opposite sex. As many analysts have pointed out, the ordinary transference modalities apply and the therapist of whatever age can easily become a parental figure, an internal object for the patient. What is perhaps less clearly recognised is that therapists, particularly young therapists, become in the transference the son or daughter of the patient and are invested in the usual way with idealised or denegrated feelings or attitudes. He or she is treated as the repository of hope and fears, shames or delights and aspirations or guilt, not only in terms of the past but also the future. It is the future, moreover, which may or may not include the older patient for whom personal death is a far more concrete reality than for the younger person. In a way, the therapist can also become the idealised child who will be the guarantor of the immortality of the patient and hand on to posterity the good aspects which each individual wishes to see preserved (Carney in Colarusso and Nemiroff, 1985).

I would like to conclude this chapter by giving some clinical examples of the problems which I am treating. In many ways the dynamic psychotherapist might best limit his attention to the phase-specific problems of the elderly. I consider that it is probably less productive to try and work through life-long problems with which people in their 60s and 70s are still struggling, although excellent examples of such work have been reported in the literature, for example, the analyses conducted by Segal (1981) and Sandler (1978).

In my view, the optimal use of psychotherapeutic intervention with older patients is those areas where people are struggling with immediate problems to do with mourning, loneliness, loss of sexual potency, the problems of retirement and facing up to the reality of a life-long marriage which is no longer satisfying. A group of patients for whom such brief psychotherapy is extremely helpful are those who are suffering from pathological mourning, where the loss of a spouse with the attendant guilt, the ending of a relationship and the inability to cope with unexpressed emotion means that the surviving partner is locked into a situation where therapeutic help can be affective very quickly. For example, consider the case of Mr T, a working class man from London, whose wife died suddenly after an illness lasting four years: he found it difficult to accept the situation and experienced severe depression. He cried a lot, smoked too much and wanted some help to get himself back together again. After 37 years of a good marriage in which all their activities centred around one another, he had to cope with a wife dying of a malignant melanoma, criticising himself and feeling guilty because he had not done enough about her illness earlier and because he might have had her operated on and perhaps saved her life. The patient suffered from poundings in his chest and irritability; in addition, he felt empty, unhappy and unable to leave the house or begin new social relationships. His father had died young and he felt himself to be a survivor. We felt that he had a problem of acute pathological mourning and it was suggested that he have 15 sessions with a woman therapist. Within a few weeks he began to come out of his depression, revealed that he had actually taken up with another woman and was having frequent and satisfying sexual intercourse with her. He began to be able to appraise himself, he was able to go back to work and eventually after 10 sessions left the therapy saying he no longer needed help and was now well and able to maintain his relationships. He shall shortly be followed up to see if this improvement has been maintained.

A second striking case was Mrs T, a large, smiling lady in her early 60s who had been widowed for about six years when she first came to see me. She was referred by her general practitioner who said that she had always been a very active, extroverted lady who had coped with everything that had happened to her. However, recently, partly precipitated by a complaint at work that she talked too loudly, which she put down to her being fairly deaf, she suddenly admitted to being depressed. She revealed to the GP that she had had a very deprived childhood, an unhappy marriage and was having major problems at work. Her general practitioner decided to refer her for therapy and I saw her myself in consultation.

When she entered the room she told me that a screw was missing in her spectacles and that she needed some help getting things right. She was quite deaf which made interpretative therapy somewhat difficult. I had the feeling that she desperately needed to engage my attention, demanding eye contact continually and watching me very closely. She said it was odd that she had been able to cope all life and had suddenly become one who could not cope. She felt vulnerable, stupid, ready to cry at the drop of a hat, and felt she just rabbited on — as indeed she was rabbiting on with me. She said she had a theory that because she couldn't necessarily hear what the other person was saying, she had to fill up the void, the empty space. I wondered aloud if what she was wanting was to be assured that the other person was still interested in her, but she refused this idea. She said that over-talkativeness was her method of becoming interesting. She felt that she needed to press conversation in order to capture and keep the attention of others. She reflected a bit and then said, 'I suppose really underneath I am panic stricken about stopping' (talking), which I thought was quite a good interpretation of her behaviour.

She also talked about her childhood and wondered why she had to be so overactive, particularly when her father had been so too. She recalled very little of her mother who had died of tuberculosis when she was eight. Her mother had been diagnosed as tubercular when she was three and spent most of her time thereafter either being nursed at home and somewhat inaccessible to Mrs T or else in sanatoria. After her mother's death, her father had lived a very loose life with lots of mistresses, so a childless aunt had brought up Mrs T because she felt it was the right thing to do. This lady was very strictly nonconformist and Mrs T had had to fight her about everything. Nevertheless, she had felt so obligated and grateful to the aunt that she had never been able to really express her anger. I said that perhaps recognition was only halfway to getting things better and that she felt still halfway there, still full of rage and anger and indignation at what had happened to her.

She then told a long story about having wanted to play the piano as a child and having done so and applying to the local conservatory. She had understood that she had been accepted but had never been actually sent a letter confirming her place. She waited for weeks. Two or three years later she said to her aunt that it was strange that she thought she had been offered a place but that they had never actually written to her to confirm it. Whereupon her aunt replied, 'Oh yes, they did. When the letter came I opened it and decided it wasn't the right thing for you, that you would be wasting your time and so I threw the letter on the fire'. Mrs T did not touch the piano for the next four years.

We talked more about herself and the ways in which she always had to cope, keeping her family when her husband was out of work and I pointed out that she did not feel that she could be of any value really to anyone. This was at the end of the consultation and within a moment or two, while she had not agreed with my thought, she asked if she was the right sort of person to have psychotherapy, whether she was just swinging the lead, so that I interpreted that she was asking me the same question, that is, could I value her, which brought her up short in her tracks. She wept a little and then apologised for using my tissues; I said again that it was as if she did not feel entitled to use whatever was available, and that perhaps this was the issue that had to be understood and worked with in the therapy.

I saw Mrs T for 15 sessions on a weekly basis and the interviews were videotaped with her permission. She began by presenting a very bright, competent front and talking about how she had always been the child who was expected to look after others. She had had to be responsible for herself from a very early age and as a result had never been able to explore dependency, closeness and loving feelings. She had married a man considerably older than herself, a rather feckless professional man, and so once again she had to be the prop for the marriage. He had died some six years earlier and she had not any relationships with men since his death. She revealed that she had been carrying on an affair with a mutual friend during the last few years of his life. She had in fact taken the friend to live with them with her husband's consent but he had died of multiple sclerosis three months after her husband had died suddenly from a stroke.

I was therefore taken aback somewhat when she announced in the course of the first session that she had 'taken up an offer', that is, that she had started an affair with somebody whom she knew and while physically this was very rewarding he was a rather boring man in other respects, but that she felt it was something of importance to her. I felt perhaps it was a way of avoiding the transference with me by involving herself at this point with a man outside the therapeutic relationship and put this to her, which she vehemently denied, of course. But there was a very clear thread of material to do with dependence running through the sessions at this early stage of the therapy.

By chance, she lost a screw from her glasses when she had gone to get a cup of coffee before coming to see me, and she described with some vivacity how people had clustered around to try and help her find it. When I said that that indeed was what perhaps she was looking for in the therapy — the opportunity to be dependent — she treated my observation with great hilarity. However, while she was pouring scorn on the transferential implications of what she was doing, it very quickly became clear that she was beginning to explore the possibilities of working even in a brief way with me through the major questions of her life, that is, the difficulties which had arisen following the early loss of her mother, the need to deny her dependency wishes and her inability to get close in an undemanding way to other people.

It rapidly became obvious that Mrs T had a basically depressive character structure and that she defended herself against her losses all her life by quite a deal of hypomanic behaviour. We worked with her problem in the transference over the next few weeks and she was gradually able to articulate the great anger which she had felt at the unhappiness of her childhood and the way in which she had been treated by her father and by her aunt. Following this, she was able to use the sessions to begin to talk much more freely about her mother, her early memories of her and her need to gain her attention as rapidly as possible and hold it for the few minutes that it was possible for a very ill woman to attend to her. It also became clear that the reason for her asking for help was the recognition that she might have to spend the rest of her life alone and that she had no way without some professional help of coming to grips with the losses which she had carried with her all this time. While she had been able to defend successfully earlier on, by this point in her life the same defences which had been so effective were now becoming counterproductive.

It should not be thought that all of Mrs T's relationships were poor.

She had had two children, with whom she got on relatively well. By the fourth session she had revealed that her second child, a daughter, was in fact not her husband's child although she had never told this to anyone before. She found herself being able to become more intimate with her daughter and grand-daughter and to treat their relationship as one much more between equals, rather than one in which she had to do all the giving. She could let her daughter care for her and establish greater mutuality between them than had ever happened before. She became more understanding in her relationship with her son and got much closer to him.

At the same time as we worked on the problems of anger and what to do with it, she was able to see that there was nothing wrong in exerting herself at work and making her presence felt, and that her staff and colleagues were in no way upset or frightened if she really stated quite clearly what she wanted or refused to follow what had been demanded of her. The tie between us strengthened as she tested out these feelings in the transference and she and I worked very hard on all of these matters until the end of the therapy, which was close to Christmas. She was able to mourn that she had had only a short therapeutic experience and tried to attribute it to the fact that she was not worth more. It was pointed out that this was indeed not the case but that in view of the shortage of therapeutic time, I could only offer people 15 sessions and that then they had to manage by themselves. We both could be sad about the limitations of this particular method and she had a brief burst of quite hypomanic activity; but this subsided to be replaced by genuine sadness as the therapy ended.

For many years it has always been the author's practice to try and evaluate psychotherapy, not at the time of termination when transference affects are extremely strong, but by follow-up months or years later. Mrs T has been seen twice for follow-up, once 18 months after the therapy ended and then another a year later. When she came to see me 18 months later, she brought with her an extraordinary story. She told me that just the night before coming to see me her son had telephoned and said might he come round to see her. When he did so, they chatted about old times and the family and he asked if she had any family photograph albums. She produced this and among the photographs was one of herself when she was about five, her aunt and her mother. The little girl had her arms around the neck of both women and was laughing wholeheartedly. The reason for this was that her mother, who had all her teeth removed as part of the attempted therapy of her tuberculosis, had replaced the lost teeth with mock teeth made of orange peel and as a child Mrs T had obviously found this quite hilarious. She said it was very strange that as she was explaining this to her son, she suddenly burst into tears and then apologised to him. He had said that it was perfectly all right, that she was welcome to cry, and that he understood. Probably because of her therapy sessions, she was able partly to work through some of her mourning for her lost and loved mother and come more to terms with it by sharing it with her son.

Apart from this episode, Mrs T said that at work she was now very successful and no longer had any difficulties, and was able to assert herself and to work appropriately in her executive role. There were no more complaints and everybody was very happy with her and her behaviour. Other aspects of her life were going well and she had received several honours in her particular field. As far as her daughter was concerned, she recently visited her and they talked at some length about their relationship. That evening her daughter had come to her room and said that, indeed, she did have difficulties in getting close to Mrs T, but that she understood these much better now. Her mother agreed and asked her daughter to try to be closer to her, although that was not essential, but also to allow her to be closer to her grand-daughter, whom she felt needed their relationship. The only major part of her life which was not satisfactory was the sexual one and she had realised that she might indeed have to stay on her own and make do as a single person. The sexual relationship which she had grabbed for when she first began therapy had soon ended because there was no genuine satisfaction in it, but she was reconciled to the loneliness and also to the advantages of being single and did not feel hard done by.

We parted on good terms, and an arrangement was made to see her a year later, when to my pleasure and surprise, she said that things were continuing to go well with her both at work and in her relationships with her children but that, most importantly, she had begun soon after seeing me 12 months before a relationship with a widower some years older than herself, whom she had known for some time. Although they are very different, they can particularly support one another because he, too, has experienced major losses in his life, having lost his mother at an early age and his wife having died of cancer some years before. The two of them get on well and spend weekends and a couple of nights a week together and Mrs T is extremely happy. She says that her sexual life is wonderful ('In fact, I don't know where he gets the energy from'), and that she feels that she has 'reached port' at last, and is living a rewarding and stable life, which seems to have the possibility of enduring. She was very grateful for the therapy which had indeed changed many things for her. Without it she doubted whether she would have come to the security and harmony which she now possessed.

The last patient to be described here will be referred to as Gloria. She was 84 when she was referred to the clinic by her general practitioner, who said that she had made a suicidal gesture, slashed her wrists and was asking for help with the problem of her infatuation for her 33-year-old lodger and lover. Gloria talks easily, though at times she is difficult to understand, as she is toothless in her lower jaw. She has never seen a therapist before. She is not senile or confused and indeed seems to be very much aware of what is going on in life and is able to present a coherent picture of her problem. She has been married six times and says that she has had no difficulties ever in her life in capturing men. She has had an interesting career having been, among other things, a film actress, a journalist, a writer and a dealer in used cars. At present she is retired and works as an artist living in her own home near the clinic in London.

The presenting problem was that for the last five years she has had a sexual relationship with her lodger, 'Joe'. She has represented herself to him as being 20 years younger than she actually is. Joe, she says, is a passive homosexual who looks after her, cooks for her and with whom she had an extremely good sexual relationship including orgasm for the first time in her life in heterosexual intercourse. Her history is very complex and will not be described at any length. She is American, comes from a distinguished famliy in New England, was brought up after her parents' divorce by an aunt and uncle and was seduced by the uncle at the age of 12. She is somebody who has to capture her audience and, indeed, she has no difficulties in doing this. She is extremely bright, sensitive and interestingly still has the remnants of past beauty in a very faded way.

Neither I nor the consultant psychiatrist who saw her at my request in view of her suicidal gesture, felt that psychotherapy could do very much for her, but partly because of her age and partly because she was an interesting person, I agreed to take her on for a limited contract. She was not the easiest of patients, as she was extremely narcissistic, needing vast supplies of admiration and praise in order to feel that life was worth living. She was therefore devastated when Joe left her. Interestingly, she quickly found another young man, Bill, to whom she sold some pictures, who fell in love with her and whom she managed to go to bed with. She says this has not continued but she does get from him the sorts of admiration that she is actually looking for.

I was able to help her work through her rage at the loss of yet another of the important people in her life and link with it all the other losses which she has surmounted in her 84 years. Among the other steps which she took after she came to grips with her fury and managed to get Joe out of the house, was to advertise for a new partner and indeed took several trips round England to see if the men who replied were in fact suitable for her. They were not, although she knew very well what she wanted. She thought a young man in his 50s, rather like me, she said, would do her very well. In fact, on various occasions she told me that I would be an ideal choice and could well meet her needs. She seemed sad when I pointed out that our relationship did not allow for that particular solution of her difficulties. I have talked with Gloria about herself and her situation — which for the average middle-aged person might seem pretty desperate. But she is not in the least bit frightened by it and, in fact, sees herself as being very lively, very energetic and full of ideas. She considers that she is not doing to die, and that there is always going to be somebody to look after her because there always has been. She thinks she is immortal and to prove it she often brings in books showing both clips from her early film successes and genealogies of her family which she can trace back to distinguished English forebears and the Norman Conquest.

For her, the denial of death is central and providing she can maintain that denial, capture people and use them to feed her narcissism, she is quite sure that everything will be all right. Indeed, she is extraordinarily lively and her capacity to live out and act out this world and to get people to play the game with her is most impressive. I have never been able to discover that she is in any way telling untruths about herself and her life: in fact, everything she claims to have done is true. Her situation is now stable.

I have tried to show that recent contributions from colleagues in Britain and the United States are leading towards a developmental psychology of later life which is much more real, which is age-appropriate and not based on deficit and loss, but much more directed towards the major questions of the second half of life. As suggested, Freud based his developmental psychology on infantile sexuality and emphasised the fact of loss of sexual potency in later life which more recent research has in any case shown to be greatly overstated. It is now known that there are many major factors which can and will be met by the competent therapist which enable psychologists to help patients when they come with psychological problems in their 60s, 70s and 80s. My own view as a psychoanalyst and a psychotherapist is that I also have a considerable function as an organiser: I can help older people to organise their problems in the transference, whether it is the emergence of aggression in older women and passivity in older men, whether it is coming to terms with loss of cherished aspects of the self, as Pollock (1980) has so elegantly and eloquently pointed out, whether it is the failure of a lifelong sexualised defence against anxiety or whether it is the contemplation of one's own death and what one leaves behind which is of importance to the individual.

It may well be that therapists have even more to learn from publishing and discussing not merely successes, but also failures. I could cite three cases of men who have been impotent for most of their lives with whom I have undertaken fairly brief psychotherapeutic interventions in the hope of enabling them to change and to take advantage of the possibilities which new relationships with kind and loving women were offering them. In each case, this has turned out to be impossible; the fear and secondary gain from their relationships has been such that the men have been unable to change. From my point of view I do not regard this as failure because I have been able to see with them the whole value from the point of view of the clients' lifetime scenario as they have written it for themselves — keeping women, keeping sexuality, keeping children at bay. As Kingsley Amis pointed out in *Jake's Thing*, there comes a time when the establishment of a personal sense of safety is perhaps more important than the fulfilment of sexual wishes, no matter how dominant and driving these may have been in earlier years; it is very clear that this is of considerable importance to some of the older men with whom I have worked.

In conclusion, I have tried to show how a greater understanding of the development problems of later life has led to the emergence of a dynamic psychotherapeutic approach with older people which has the potentiality for them to explore, to come to grips with and hopefully to resolve the difficulties which everyone must encounter in later life.

References

Butler, R.M. and Lewis, M.L. (1978) *Sex After Sixty*, Harper and Row, New York

Colarusso, C. and Nemiroff, R. (1980) *Adult Development*, Plenum, New York

——— (1985) *The Race Against Time*, Plenum, New York

Cohler, B. (1980) *The Course of Life. Psychoanalytic Contributions Towards Understanding Personality Development* (eds. S. Greenspan and G. Pollock(3 vols), National Institute of Mental Health, Bethesda

Cohler, B.J. and Carnie, J.K. (1980) 'Developmental Contributions and Adjustment in Adulthood: Social Relations, Morale and the Transformation from Middle to Late Life' in N. Miller and G. Cohen (eds.), *The Psychodynamics of Ageing*, IUP, New York

Erikson, E.H. (1980) 'Elements of a Psychodynamic Theory of Psychosocial Development' in S. Greenspan and G. Pollock (eds), *The Course of Life: Psychoanalytic Contributions towards Understanding Personality Development* (3 vols), National Institute of Mental Health, Bethesda

Freud, S. (1905) *On Psychotherapy*, Standard Edition 7, Hogarth, London

——— (1914) 'Remembering, Repeating and Working Through', Standard Edition 12, Hogarth, London

Greenspan, S. and Pollock, G. (1981) *The Course of Life: Psychoanalytic Contributions towards Understanding Personality Development* (3 vols.), National Institute of Mental Health, Bethesda

Gutmann, D. (1977) 'The Cross-Cultural Perspective: Notes towards a Comparative Psychology of Ageing' in J.E. Brun and W. Schue (eds), *Handbook of the Psychology of Ageing*, Van Norstand, New York

Hildebrand, H.P. (1981) 'Transference Organisation and Transference Neurosis', paper presented at San Francisco Psychoanalytic Society

——— (1982) 'Psychotherapy with Older Patients', *Brit. J. Med. Psychol.*, *55*, 19–28

——— (1983) 'The Unconscious in Later Life', Chicago, October (also published as 'Scene Originaire-Mort' in *Temps, Vieillissement, Society*, Proceedings of the 2nd Congress of International Association of Gerontologie Psychanalytique, Paris, November, 1982)

——— (1985) 'Psychoanalysis and Ageing', invited paper presented to the Chicago Psychoanalytic Society, April

Jacques, Elliot (1965) 'Death and the Mid-Life Crisis', *Int. Journal of Psycho-Analysis*, *46*, part 4

King, P.H.M. (1974) 'Notes on the Psychoanalysis of Older Patients', *J. Anal. Psychol.*, *19*, 22–37

——— (1980) 'The Life Cycle as Indicated by the Nature of the Transference of the Middle Aged and Elderly', *I.J.P.A.*, *61*, 153–60

Levinson, D.J., Darrow, C., Klein, M. *et al.* (1978) *The Seasons of a Man's Life*, Ballantine, New York

Malan, D.H. (1978) *Towards the Validation of Dynamic Psychotherapy*, Plenum, New York

Masters, W. and Johnson, V. (1966) *Human Sexual Response*, Hemdale, London

Myers, Wayne A. (1984) *Dynamic Therapy of the Older Patient*, Aronson, New York and London

Neugarten, Bernice L. (1979) 'Time, Age and the Life Cycle', *Am. J. Psych.*, *136*, 887–94

Pollock, George J. (1980) 'Ageing or Aged: Development or Pathology' in S. Greenspan and G.H. Pollock (eds), *The Course of Life: Psychoanalytic Contributions towards Understanding Personality Development* (3 vols), NIMH, Bethesda

Sandler, A.M. (1978) 'Problems in the Psychoanalysis of an Ageing Narcissistic Patient', *J. Geriatric Psychiatry*, *11*, 5–36

Segal, H. (1981) 'Fear of Death — Notes on the Analysis of an Old Man' in *The Work of Hanna Segal*, Aronson, New York

Silberschatz, G. and Curtis, J. (in press) 'Research on the Psychodynamic Process in the Treatment of Elderly Persons'

3 ISSUES IN THE THERAPEUTIC USE OF REMINISCENCE WITH ELDERLY PEOPLE*

Peter Coleman

Changing Attitudes to Reminiscence

The study of ageing, gerontology, has witnessed many changes in the last 20 years. One of the most remarkable has been the change in attitude by gerontologists themselves towards reminiscence as a healthy rather than an unhealthy activity of elderly people. An almost totally negative view to talking or thinking about the past has been replaced by a much more positive one. This turnabout is most graphically illustrated in the career of Robert Havighurst, a developmental psychologist and one of the pioneers in the study of social and psychological processes in ageing. At the end of the 1950s he was advising elderly people to avoid reminiscence (Havighurst, 1959). A little over ten years later he was researching the benefits of reminiscence (Havighurst and Glasser, 1972).

It is important to remember just how negative views were. The situation is graphically described by Dobrof, who was working in New York in the 1960s:

> I was then a very junior social worker on the staff of a home for the aged. I remember well being taught by our consulting psychiatrists and the senior social work staff about the tendency of our residents to talk about childhood in the shtetls of East Europe or arrival at Ellis Island or early years on the lower East Side of New York. At best, this tendency was seen as an understandable, although not entirely healthy, preoccupation with happier times, understandable because these old and infirm people walked daily in the shadow of death. At worst, 'living in the past' was viewed as pathology — regression to the dependency of the child, denial of the passage of time and the reality of the present, or evidence of organic impairment of the intellect. It was even said that 'remembrance of things past' could cause

---

* Some of the material in this chapter has appeared in previous publications, i.e. Coleman (1984, 1985).

> or deepen depression among our residents, and God forgive us, we were to divert the old from their reminiscing through activities like bingo and arts and crafts (Dobrof, 1984).

Even if sympathetic and seeking to be 'understanding', the attitude to reminiscence was demeaning. Many textbooks, for example, associated reminiscence with mental deterioration. The following example is from a textbook published in 1968:

> Elderly people, as is well known, spend an increasing amount of time talking and thinking about the past. It seems natural that as they feel out of the run of things, they should turn back to the days when life was more rewarding and enjoyable, and when events had a deeper impact on them. When the future holds little, and thinking about it arouses thoughts of death, interest will turn regressively to earlier years. Still, in most persons who become very old, the defect is more profound. The person becomes unable to recall events and lives more and more in the remote past, as if a shade were being pulled down over recent happenings, until nothing remains except memories of childhood. This type of memory failure depends on senile changes in the brain and is perhaps the most characteristic feature of senility. We do not properly understand why earlier memories are retained while more recent happenings are lost (Lidz, 1968).

It is true that the formulators of 'disengagement theory' (Cumming and Henry, 1961) saw increased reminiscence as one manifestation of the process of ageing, and since their intent was to put forward disengagement as a normative process, reminiscence appeared in a more reasonable light. But the subsequent backlash against the thinking typified by disengagement theory — and in particular the research which demonstrated that the greater part of the withdrawal from involvement with the outside world shown by elderly individuals, was forced upon them rather than initiated by them — tended to confirm the original negative connotations given to reminiscence.

It is often an oversimplification to attribute changes in attitudes within a particular field of study to a particular individual's contribution. (Indeed, Buhler in Vienna had written, already in 1935, of reminiscence as an inevitable part of the ageing process resulting from the individual's need to substantiate his life in the face of loss of ability.) But a new interest in reminiscence was clearly awakened by a striking paper published by Butler in 1963, entitled 'The Life Review: An Interpretation of

Reminiscence in the Aged' (Butler, 1963). I remember very well the excitement felt when first reading this article a few years later.

Quoting his own clinical experience as well as a wide range of literary authorities, Butler made out a case for viewing reminiscence as a normal activity in old age, that the life review was indeed a process that people may have to undergo if they are to come to terms with their lives as they have lived them. Dobrof, quoted above, testifies to the influence this single article had on attitudes to the elderly: 'In a profound sense, Butler's writings liberated both the old and the nurses, doctors and social workers; the old were free to remember, to regret, to look reflectively at the past and try to understand it. And we were free to listen, and to treat rememberers and remembrances with the respect they deserved, instead of trivialising them by diversion to a bingo game' (Dobrof, 1984).

Butler's article was followed by a number of other important contributions to the understanding of reminiscence. McMahon and Rhudick (1964) published a study of veterans of the Spanish-American war. They were struck by how well adjusted this particular group of men was, and also by the extent of reminiscing they displayed. Reminiscence, therefore, did not seem to be a negative sign, but on the contrary closely related to freedom from depression. They observed that the reminiscences of these men tended to be of a story-telling nature, intended to be entertaining and/or instructive, and McMahon and Rhudick related this to anthropological studies on the role of old people in primitive societies in preserving and handing on traditions. They also noted that the reminiscers tended to exaggerate the value of the past in comparison with the present, claiming 'to have seen the best'. They suggested that reminiscence could play a significant role in the face of the losses of role and function in old age, in preserving self-respect by investing in the image of oneself as one had been, and stressing its importance.

Lewis (1971) took this idea further in an experimental study in which elderly people's expressed opinions were challenged in an authoritative fashion. Elderly people who were classified as 'reminiscers' on the basis of their conversation habits were shown to react differently to 'non-reminiscers'. Both groups had initially been asked to describe themselves as they used to be and as they were now. Whereas there was no different at the outset between 'reminiscers' and 'non-reminiscers' in the degree of relationship they indicated between their past and present views of themselves, after being threatened in this way, the 'reminiscers' reacted by making their present self-concept much more consistent with their past self-concept. Lewis interpreted this identification with the past as a strategy, or 'defence', reminiscers used to deal with current threats to a sense of worthiness of self.

Butler, McMahon and Rhudick, and Lewis expressed some of the most influential ideas about reminiscence, and their articles are often cited by the more recent proponents of 'reminiscence therapy' in individual casework and groupwork settings, in hospitals, residential homes and day-care establishments. However, it is rarely acknowledged that a number of subsequent studies which followed up their seminal work and tried to show in a rigorous way that reminiscence was related to individual adjustment, produced disappointing results.

Lieberman and Falk (1971), for example, explored the function of reminiscence in three samples of elderly people: those who were living in their own homes; those who were waiting to enter homes for the elderly; and those who had been living in such institutions for some time. They found that those who were in the waiting situation were considerably more involved in reminiscence than either of the other two samples. But when they investigated whether degree of reminiscence was related to subsequent adaptation to the stress of moving, no relationship was found. Similarly, negative results on the adaptive value of reminiscing were reported in a study of my own, which sought to discover whether there was a relationship between talking and thinking about the past and measures of present life satisfaction and freedom from depression, either in general or at some level of loss (physical or social) that had been incurred in recent years (Coleman, 1974). Havighurst and Glasser (1972) did identify an associated pattern between high personal–social adjustment, positive effect of reminiscence and high frequency of reminiscence, but their study was not able to clarify the direction of causation. Taken altogether, as many studies seem to have found no evidence for the adaptive value of reminiscence as have found positive evidence (Merriam, 1980; Merriam and Cross, 1982).

Thus, reminiscence therapy cannot be said to stand on a very solid base, and recent commentators, notably Merriam (1980) have been led to criticise simplistic thinking about reminiscing and its value. Talking or thinking about the past may serve various functions, and one must try to be more discerning in one's observations. Also, reminiscence may mean different things to individuals in different situations. For example, a frail, disabled, elderly person may learn to appreciate thinking back on past memories in a way yet inconceivable to a younger, active person. In a study of 300 adults aged from 18 to 90 years, Merriam and Cross (1982) showed that older adults more frequently experienced feelings of satisfaction and well-being with reminiscence than did other age groups. Moreover recent work on 'differential gerontology' (for example,

Thomae, 1976) has taught that one must no longer expect to find common laws of social or psychological ageing. Whether a person stands to gain from reminiscence will depend on his past history as well as his present needs. Therefore, more detailed analysis of individual cases seems to be called for, using diverse samples of elderly people.

Functions of Reminiscence

It is important to note that even in the first writings on reminiscence, quite a divergence of views was expressed on the function reminiscence might play in old age. Butler (1963) stressed that the life review was a normative process in later life, prompted by the realisation of approaching death. It was 'characterised by the progressive return to consciousness of past experience, and, particularly, the resurgence of unresolved conflicts'. He stressed, as have later writers (for instance, Kaminsky, 1984), that the life review is not necessarily easy to recognise. It can appear fragmentary with key themes occurring in dream material as well as in conscious daydreaming and more purposeful thinking. Typically, ordinary daily occurrences may trigger thinking on associated events in the past.

Ingmar Bergman's film *Wild Strawberries* is quoted both by Butler (1963) and Erikson (1978) as an example of the process of life reviewing. This is the story of an egocentric professor who becomes aware of his failings by a process of dreams and of conscious recollection of family relationships and his place within them, and as a result is led to seek reconciliation with his estranged son and daughter-in-law. However, Butler is careful to stress that the outcome of the life review is not necessarily positive. The individual may remain obsessed with events and actions he regrets, finds no solution and no peace, and develop chronic feelings of guilt and depression. It is also possible that the individual may 'block' the life review process altogether, succeed in avoiding certain thoughts and reject the past. This might be a successful way of avoiding a negative outcome, particularly if the individual has plenty of present interests, but it denies the potentiality of growth inherent in the life review process.

Close similarities can be seen between the concept of a normative life review and Erikson's earlier notion of the achievement of integrity as the final task of life, first set out in his book *Childhood and Society* (1950). Indeed, Butler's theory may be regarded as an extension of one of the key notions in Erikson's last stage, as it suggests a process whereby 'acceptance of one's one and only life cycle' is or is not achieved.

McMahon's and Rhudick's (1964) observations on how much time the veterans they interviewed devoted to talking about the past led them to speculate on a number of other uses of reminiscence: 'the maintenance of self-esteem in the face of declining physical and intellectual abilities; coping with grief and depression resulting from personal losses, finding means to contribute significantly to a society of which older persons are members; and retaining some sense of identity in an increasingly estranged environment'. They also explicitly linked their ideas to the life cycle theories of Erikson, by saying that the adaptational significance of reminiscence can best be understood in the light of Erikson's view that identify formation is a lifelong task.

The close link between reminiscence and preservation of identity is made by a number of other writers (Castelnuovo-Tedesco, 1978; Zinberg and Kaufman, 1963). 'Reaching out to share recollections with others may be motivated by the need to convince oneself of a continuity between the past and present' (Carlson, 1984). A similar point is made by Blythe: 'One of the reasons why old people make so many journeys into the past is to satisfy themselves that it is still there' (Blythe, 1979). The past represents a platform of security which may give strength and effort to continue.

However, maintaining a sense of identify is quite a distinct idea from the life review. Indeed, McMahon and Rhudick (1964) dispute the implication of Butler's view that all individuals feel a need for self-justification at the end of their lives, and rather go to the other extreme by denigrating this function as characteristic of 'obsessive-compulsive subjects who, we may suspect, have been reviewing their past behaviour in the same judgemental and evaluative way all their lives', that is, it is evidence of a lifelong and ongoing pathological process.

For McMahon and Rhudick, if there is an ideal use of reminiscence it is the one traditionally ascribed to older men in primitive societies, as bearers and transmitters of their culture's stories and traditions. They describe their 'best-adjusted' group, quite simply, as storytellers, 'recounting past exploits and experiences with obvious pleasure in a manner which is both entertaining and informative'. Moreover, these storytellers seemed to have little need to depreciate the present or glorify the past, as did other members of their sample. Rather their reminiscing is a happy instance of behaviour serving both personal ends and social goals: 'The older person's knowledge of a bygone era provides him with an opportunity to enhance his self-esteem by contributing in a meaningful way to his society' (McMahon and Rhudick, 1964).

It has to be admitted that the storytelling function of the old has become devalued in modern societies, both because of the fast-changing nature of society which has appeared to make the past seem less relevant, and because of the development of many other means of preserving and communicating information. Nevertheless, the recent growth of interest in oral history has done something to reverse this trend. It has led to a revaluing of the memories ordinary individuals possess of the times they have lived through. The memories of the oldest generations have come to appear especially valuable, with the realisation that the possibility of collecting records of experiences of a whole era, such as the Edwardian period before the First World War, dies with them.

When I first began to research the functions of reminiscence in the late 1960s, I took care to try to distinguish between the two types of reminiscence, 'life review' reminiscence, as described by Butler, and 'informative' or 'teaching' reminiscence, as described by McMahon and Rhudick. I also included basic assessments of the amount of conversation individuals devoted to past events and of the extent to which they said they thought about the past. As already mentioned, there was no evidence that 'simple' reminiscence *per se* was related to adjustment in general or at some particular level of social loss or physical disability, and this has also been the finding of a number of other studies.

But the more particular measures of the individual's conversations about the past did produce interesting results. 'Life reviewing', defined in terms of questions or statements about the kind of person the individual had been in his life and why he had done the things he had, did seem to be adaptive for those individuals who were also dissatisfied with their past lives. Likewise, 'informative' reminiscing, defined in terms of communication of historical facts or attitudes to the world based on past experience, also seemed adaptive, at least for the men in the author's sample (Coleman, 1974). These findings convinced the author of the value of trying to be more specific in describing the meaning or function of reminiscence.

Attitudes of Elderly People to Reminiscence

If one wants to know what elderly people are doing when they reminisce, one can do worse than ask them directly. Of course, it is likely that their attitudes will reflect to some degree the attitudes of society as a whole, but it is also interesting to observe what variations there might be in attitude and what implications, if any, these have for other aspects of the individual's life.

Through the 1970s I have carried out three studies in which either as a main or subsidiary part of the research, elderly people were asked about the past and their reminiscences. The smallest study (in numbers), but the most intense, has been a longitudinal study of elderly people living in sheltered housing schemes in London, which was started in 1969 (Coleman, 1986). The main aim of this study at the outset was to explore the adaptive value reminiscing might have. A sample of elderly people living alone in 16 sheltered housing schemes spread throughout five London boroughs was interviewed. In total, 68 people were approached and, of these, 51 were included in the original data analysis — those from whom a complete set of data had been collected. Elderly people living alone in sheltered housing were consciously selected because of the ease of interviewing, but also because it was judged that they would have experienced considerable loss in their lives (for instance, bereavement, separation from their old environment) such as to provide a good background for discerning any beneficial role reminiscence might play in helping adjustment to loss.

Over a period of two years, each person was interviewed on average six times each. Many notes were kept of these conversations. One or two hours of conversation with each individual were tape-recorded and transcribed. A series of standardised questionnaires and interview formats were used for rating health, change in social roles and morale. It included the attitude to reminiscence questionnaire that Havighurst had then recently developed (Havighurst and Glasser, 1972). Over the succeeding years, these individuals were visited whenever I was in London. In 1980 and 1981, exactly ten years after the original data collection, the same interviewing schedules were deliberately repeated with the eight remaining survivors.

The second study was a survey of elderly people living in the Dutch city of Nijmegen in the Netherlands, in which I was involved as a member of the gerontological centre there. A large number of people were interviewed (455) and some questions on reminiscence were included in the questionnaire. The third study was aother large-scale community survey of elderly people living in Southampton (n = 366) in 1977 to 1978, in which questions on reminiscence were also included. Table 3.1 shows the answers to particular questions that were asked in all three studies. The answers reveal a varying attitude to reminiscence according to the phrasing of the questions. Thus, whereas only a quarter to a third of the elderly people interviewed say they 'live in the past more and more', two-thirds to three-quarters say they 'like to think about the past'. The

Table 3.1: Attitude to Reminiscing Among Elderly People Over the Age of 65 Observed in Three Studies

	Survey of elderly people living in Nijmegen (The Netherlands) 1974–75 (N = 455)	Survey of elderly people living in Southampton (England) 1977–78 (N = 336)	Elderly people living alone in sheltered housing in London (England) 1971 (N = 51)
Like to think about the past	68%	78%	47%
Lives in the past more and more	36%	25%	–
Prefers to think on the future than the past	52%	42%	51%

former statement has a negative connotation in society, and it was therefore not surprising that those who assented to it were more likely to be depressed and to have low morale. The latter statement, on the other hand, was found to have a much more positive connotation, and indeed assent to this statement was correlated with high morale. When asked to choose between thinking about the future and the past, the split was almost 50–50 in all three studies.

Attitudes for and against reminiscing were most evenly balanced in the London study, in which a lot of other data was collected on these individuals' attitudes to reminiscence, including objective conversation ratings and observer's ratings. A consideration of all the data seemed to bear out Lewis's point (1971) that it makes sense to speak of 'reminiscers' and 'non-reminiscers'. A substantial number said they enjoyed thinking about the past and thought it a good and helpful thing to do, whereas an equally substantial number did not enjoy it and thought it a pointless and useless thing to do. It was interesting to explore the sources of these differences.

In order to gain insight into people's attitudes, however, it is important not only to describe their content but also the reasons underlying them, and it was clear that not all those who reminisce did so for the same reasons, and the same applied to those who did not reminisce. Whether people reminisced or not was not in itself associated with whether they also expressed a sense of well-being. But there was an association between well-being and the reasons for reminiscing and not reminiscing. Thus, reminiscing could have a positive or negative association, depending on the individual's attitude to what he was doing. 'Living

Table 3.2: Types of Attitude to Reminiscing and Subsequent Adjustment Among Elderly People Living Alone in Sheltered Housing in London 1970–71

Group 1: Reminisces to a great or some degree, and values reminiscence (N = 21)	Maintained mainly high morale; only four people in group became depressed, all in the face of severe disability or illness
Group 2: Reminisces, but finds reminiscence disturbing (N = 8)	Psychological disturbance intensified for most of group; two people showed some significant resolution of problems with their life histories
Group 3: Does not reminisce at all or reminisces little; no point or purpose (N = 16)	Maintained mainly high morale; only three people in group became depressed
Group 4: Does not reminisce because depressing; contrast between past and present life too great (N = 6)	All remained or became depressed/ maladjusted

in the past' for most people tended to reflect a negative activity, whereas, 'liking to think about the past' reflected a positive one.

Looking carefully at all the data from the London study, including most importantly what people actually said about their own reminiscing, it made sense to divide the group into four regarding their orientations towards reminiscence (Table 3.2).

The first is a large group of individuals who indicated that reminiscence played an important and positive part in their lives. The characteristic the past had for all of them was that of a treasured possession, even with and sometimes because of its difficulties. Significantly, a number said that they could and would like to write a book. For that reason they were particularly interested in the book they thought I would write about them. It included individuals for whom the past in general was seen as preferable to the present (one said it had 'more common humanity') and therefore they were grateful they had lived in an earlier period. Most were not concerned with this comparison, but simply gained a great deal psychologically from remembrances of happy times and achievements (concerning, for example, childhood, family life, collaboration at work and responsibilities fulfilled).

Most were remarkably well-adjusted but few, if any, had had easy lives. They referred a lot to coping with surviving and learning from difficulties. One woman described experiencing her life now as 'a pattern, all rolled out behind her'. From her own description of changes she had experienced in herself, she appeared to have been through a period of life review, and only comparatively recently to have become 'reconciled' to all the difficulties she had encountered in her life: a drunken father who beat her mother; nursing her son, who was born with deformed kidneys, until he died at the age of 15; and caring for her husband too, in his last years, with terminal cancer. Her life, she said, had had much sadness, but what she remembered now was the love. It had become a source of wisdom. She felt she knew now what was important in life. She saw things clearly at last. As a result, old age was a happy time for her and she felt very peaceful. Although one must be careful in interpreting retrospective information about an individual's psychological development, this account is most suggestive of a successful life review process.

Four people, although expressing positive attitudes to reminiscence, indicated that it was of little help in the face of their present difficulties. Three of them had severe problems with their health: one had much pain from a carcinoma of the stomach; one was largely incapacitated by a stroke; one was losing her eyesight rapidly. The fourth member had a history of depressive reactions to loss and had been treated for depression with ECT after losing her husband two years previously, but still felt very depressed.

The second group is particularly interesting because they could be called 'compulsive' reminiscers. They reminisced a lot although it made them feel bad about their past lives to a significant extent. They were dissatisfied with their lives as a whole or had significant and troubling areas of regret. They could not repress their memories. Interestingly, they were a significantly younger group than the rest of the sample, with no one over the age of 78. Their reminiscences were really suggestive of difficult life reviewing. A number had noticeable psychological problems. One man had married late in life, quarrelled with his wife over the upbringing of their children and had struck a daughter who had been promiscuous and had himself been taken to court as a result. Eventually, his wife separated from him on grounds of mental cruelty: it drove him mad to think back on it, but he could not help it. Another had served a prison sentence for theft: he said he had to do it to support his wife and family and still greatly resented that whole episode in his life. His friends had not looked after his wife and family, as they had promised him when in prison, and she had died soon after his release. He was 'always thinking about her'. He argued with himself over what had happened and what he had done. He just sat and thought and some of his thoughts were 'terrible'.

Some had troubled memories of wasted chances, failures to marry or to make more of a success of their working lives. Others were still worried by things that had happened to them and permanently affected their lives. One lady born in Belgium, whose father was a well-established concert pianist had lost her home in the First World War and fled with her parents to London. Her mother had died soon afterwards. She had never recovered the same standard of life. Her thoughts about the past were full of episodes of 'man's cruelty to man', and she said she would rather not have lived. All members of this group were maladjusted to a greater or lesser extent with their lives in old age, and in retrospect may have benefited from active psychosocial intervention.

The third group is the most heterogeneous. They saw no general value in reminiscence. The majority had found other ways of coping with life. Certainly, and this is important, they seemed no less well-adjusted than those in the first group. Some had striking life histories to tell. But they did not feel any need to dwell on them further. This is a noteworthy distinction. A number of writers have referred to the importance of acquaintance with the individual's life history to understanding their needs in their present situation (Johnson, 1978). They have also stressed the individual's need to explain himself by describing his past history to an interested hearer. Indeed, a number of people in this group spoke a great deal about their past lives when I *first* met them. They seemed to want to tell their life story to indicate how they had become the way they were. One stressed his Quaker upbringing, and the brutalising experiences of the First World War. Another analysed carefully the events of his life, and how bad health and accidental events had intervened to prevent his being the success he could have been. But fundamentally their analyses were more dispassionate than those of the previous groups. Life in the present (or future) was important, not the past. There was no point in reminiscence, or as the last man put it 'no LSD' (pounds, shillings and pence!).

There was an interesting subgroup of three women whose previous lives had been very restricted, being tied down by their husbands and/or work responsibilities. They now very much enjoyed the hobbies and handicraft interests they had developed. They appreciated old age as a time they could at last devote to themselves: they had no need at all for looking back.

The fourth group indicates another important distinction. These were people who, like the previous group, did not reminisce and did not want to reminisce, but, like the second group, their relationship with the past was an uneasy one. They had to avoid reminiscing because it made them feel depressed. This was not because there was anything to regret in the past; on the contrary, the past had been fuller and happier, and the contrast with the emptiness of the present made them more sad than they need be. Unlike the third group, they could not find present interests which formed on adequate substitute for their past lives, and the past was a source of depression instead of being a comfort, as with the first group. Three of the six were men who had recently lost their wives and could not come to terms with living alone.

The striking point to emerge from looking at the sample as a whole is that those who displayed consistency between their attitudes to their memories and their actual degree of reminiscence were better adjusted than those who displayed inconsistency. This helps to explain why reminiscence *per se* is not likely to be related to measures of adjustment. Those who had a positive attitude to reminiscing and actually reminisced were by and large well-adjusted. Those who saw no point in reminiscing and so did not reminisce were likewise well-adjusted. On the other hand those who could not bear to reminisce, although their memories were happy, tended to be depressed. And those who could not avoid reminiscing — although their memories were painful — were troubled people.

The same people have been followed up over a period of more than ten years, so it is possible to analyse what happened to the members of each of the above groups. The results of this analysis are also shown in Table 3.2. A general point to stress about these longitudinal data is that, consistent with other longitudinal studies on interests and attitudes, a considerable degree of stability was evident in these elderly people's attitudes to reminiscence. Changes, if any, are subtle and gradual rather than striking.

Briefly expressed, the large group of those who reminisced, valued their memories highly and found them helpful in coping with life in old age, and appeared to adapt well to the vicissitudes that faced them. Only one person became depressed and this because of her sharply deteriorating memory (she died one year later). They maintained positive attitudes to reminiscence. For one man, his experiences in the First World War had remained in the forefront of his mind. His was a reflective interest which included a striking measure of sympathy for the German enemy. His continued involvement was such that at the age of 93 he obtained a new book that had come out on the battle of the Somme. The woman mentioned earlier who had had a worrying life continued to draw lessons from it: 'Love and friendship were the most important things in life. One should not be too busy.' She had been too busy, she said, and she had later regretted it. The evidence on this group is so consistent that one can suggest with some confidence that the positive value given to reminiscence seemed to indicate a good prognosis.

Of the four people who initially said they valued reminiscence but found it insufficient in coping with personal difficulties, three were already in very poor physical health and all died within a couple of years. The remaining lady lived another 12 years. By then she had overcome the loss of her husband and had high morale. The past continued to be very important for her. Thus she had become indistinguishable from the other members of the first group. Given her degree of physical frailty and initial level of depression, it seemed in retrospect remarkable that she lived so long. Although one cannot generalise from this one case, it suggests that a positive value given to reminiscing can be indicative of survival even when the individual does not have the means to adjust to the immediate losses confronting her.

The second group is particularly interesting since it seems to exemplify the life review process. Five of the eight died within two years. From the evidence collected, it was clear that two at least showed increasing psychological disturbance. According to the reports of wardens and neighbours, they had become alcoholics and did not look after themselves. One had become labelled a 'nuisance'. By contrast, the other three survived a long time (two long enough to become case studies in 1981). Two made significant changes in attitude: the Belgian lady who had come to London as a refugee mellowed in her attitudes to life and in particular her attitudes to her past life became more accepting. On one occasion she said she was glad she had been a girl and so had been able to look after her father in the disasters that befell him. She took pleasure in showing photographs from his concert tours in Europe. When she was last seen a few months before she died, she spoke very serenely: she could hardly believe her father had been dead so long, and she said he had been a very good companion. Although her outlook on the world was still pessimistic, it was kinder.

Of the two men who survived more than ten years, one was much less critical of himself ten years later. He no longer regretted his lack of a good career or his not getting married. He said that he had not been the type for such a responsibility. He was fortunate in that he maintained good health. The other man, by contrast, did not resolve regrets of a similar nature. In fact, in 1981 he probably felt them more acutely. Health seemed to be a crucial difference. Ten years later the second man was severely disabled by angina and cancer and felt very lonely: he greatly missed not having a family. A comparison of these two cases is instructive and shows the importance of interacting physical, social and psychological factors.

Of the people who discounted the importance of reminiscence, the interesting question is whether they were able to adapt to the vicissitudes of old age as well as the reminiscers. The answer seems to be that they were. One of the 16 was 'lost' when he moved out of his housing complex, but of the remaining 15, 12 remained well-adjusted until their deaths. Three became depressed and, of these, two did so in face of considerable disability. The rest maintained much the same attitudes. They had found successful ways of coping with old age which did not involve reminiscence. Nearly all had plenty of outside interests and they did not feel any need to look back.

From the evidence available on the six people in the final category, who in 1971 did not like to reminisce because of the contrast with their present situation, five were at that time clearly depressed. The sixth was not and is interesting for that reason. She entertained me well and seemed to be content, although signs of nervous tension were noted. The warden said that she concealed her true feelings about her only daughter who had largely broken off relationships with her for reasons which were unclear. In the circumstances, her avoidance of reminiscence seemed to be a significant indicator of maladjustment, of pain on remembering happier times. She was not seen again, but on the warden's account and that of neighbours, she became increasingly worried and nervous and had hallucinations. She died one year later in a psychiatric hospital. The other five retained the same negative attitudes to their present life and an avoiding attitude towards reminiscence. Three lived a considerable time and the stability in their attitudes was striking. One man was still making the same incipient but insufficient moves to find a new wife in 1981 as he was in 1971. He and some of the others might have benefited a great deal from a therapeutic intervention, such as could be provided in a group work setting.

Implications for Therapy of a Differential View of Reminiscence

A close attention to elderly people's conversations reveals a rich variety of content and function in their reminiscences (Coleman, 1986). In addition, negative attitudes to thinking or talking about the past are themselves revealing and take different forms. It therefore seems unhelpful to stress any one perspective on reminiscence or non-reminiscence to the exclusion of others.

What is essential is that any helping individual, professional or otherwise who is considering using reminiscence as a means of therapy, should try, before making any specific intervention, to understand from the elderly person's perspective his/her life history and circumstances. The same applies to any offer of practical help: one should consider beforehand what the likely benefit is going to be. The distinctions drawn in the previous section between types of attitudes to reminiscence are admittedly crude, but they do offer a framework around which to consider various approaches to therapy, using, or rather avoiding reminiscence, as the case may be.

In those who already reminisce readily and have a positive attitude to memories of their past lives, these memories constitute strengths which can be tapped in the face of difficulties. But the links between past and present can be broken. The stresses and strains of old age may be so great that they disrupt the person's sense of continuity between past and present. Reminiscence then can come to seem irrelevant to the present situation. Thus, although reminiscence occurs naturally and spontaneously in many elderly people, there can be times when an outsider does need to promote it. For example, it may be the task for a social worker to remind an elderly client that he or she has met crises before, and has struggled and persevered. Such an interpretation of one's life history can serve as a powerful motivation to try and cope with the new demands of the present.

Of course, a social worker may initially know little about the individual's past, but the very activity of exploring it with the individual concerned will likely help them both to understand better the situation they are now in. At the least the client should feel that the social worker has a better appreciation of him/her as an individual. The social worker may be able to spot ways in which the individual has coped in the past which can be used again. Information collected also from others about the client's previous life may be useful to the social worker in challenging an elderly person's depressed view of himself and the world, and to help him reach a more positive view of his current efforts.

Moreover, it is not only that people may 'forget' about their own individual histories; they may also have adopted from society at large a general attitude to what has happened in the past as irrelevant, uninteresting or of no further value. Individuals in a group setting such as a long-stay hospital or residential home may have done worthwhile and interesting things in their lives and may have contributed to society in various ways, but may need encouragement to re-evaluate these things — perhaps by the act of having to tell others about them. It is in such circumstances that the various forms of group reminiscence therapy, around particular themes and/or using visual and other aids (objects, pictures, slides and so on) are most helpful in stimulating memories and the sharing of experiences. A skilled leader is needed who can search beneath self-effacing attitudes and elicit important memories, and not allow the more talkative and assertive individuals to dominate conversations. Fortunately, the recent growth of interest in oral history has made the collection of reminiscences about past events and ways of life a truly valued contribution to society, and reminiscence work in an institutional setting can be given a similar status.

But such creative reminiscing needs to be distinguished from a brooding on the past, such as was shown by people in the second group in the study described. Their thoughts were often dominated by regretful memories about things they wish they had or had not done in their lives, or about sad things that had happened to them and their families. Short-term counselling offers a number of possibilities for helping such individuals. Again, it is important to be clear about what one is dealing with. One needs, for example, to try and develop a sense of how justified or rational the person's accusations are. Many individuals may have a tendency to blame themselves and feel guilty for past events for which they really had little or no personal responsibility, especially if they are depressed. Also, they may feel profoundly unlucky in a way which makes luck appear as something directed against them personally rather than a random occurrence.

Beck (1976) writes of the 'depressogenic error of generalization' whereby selective negative thinking is projected into the past. Various techniques have been suggested for countering such thinking by cognitive therapists; for example, 'disattribution' which involves teaching the client to stop attributing all blame to himself by recognising the role played by fate and others in events (Rathjen, Rathjen and Hiniker, 1978); or rational disputation of thoughts (Ellis, 1974) which encourages people to appreciate and then modify the way irrational beliefs about events often determine their feelings about things that happen to them; or by simply changing the forms of attention and seeing that there were positive things in the past as well as negative, and attending to them for a change. Some therapists specialising with the elderly, as Sherman (1981), regard such types of 'cognitive therapy' as being especially relevant to the elderly. Circumstances in old age may not easily be changed, but it is possible to be more hopeful about changing an elderly person's perception of them.

However, it should be very naive to think that all problems with a difficult 'life review' can be solved in these ways. A person's sense of guilt may be well-founded. As Sherman himself points out, where actual wrong has been done to someone and that person is dead, the wrong has to be accepted, not disputed. To do this would tend to make matters worse by making the client attest to his or her guilt all the more, as well as reducing confidence in the counsellor. One should listen to the client carefully, hear him out fully and completely, provide the necessary catharsis and then help to move him from a sense of guilt to a sense of forgiveness.

The importance of the help that can be provided by religious practices, as the Christian confession, cannot be denied, and it would be foolish to omit religion from a discussion of forgiveness, and also of the healing of tragic and hurtful memories (Linn and Linn, 1974). Jung is one of the very prominent psychologists who have openly acknowledged the psychological value of religion. It was vital, he held, for clergy and psychotherapists to join forces, and he was urging this more than 50 years ago (Jung, 1933). Indeed, Jung was fond of saying that all of his patients had fallen ill because they had lost contact with their religious traditions, and that they recovered only inasmuch as they regained a religious outlook. Jung had a profound respect for the myths, symbols and rituals of religious tradition, seeing the symbol as a bridge between the conscious and the unconscious. Unfortunately, a mutual antipathy between psychologists and religious thinkers has existed for so long that psychotherapy and spiritual guidance are rarely discussed in the same context. But at last the beginning of a change of attitude is now evident on both sides (see, for example, Leech, 1977; Bergin, 1983).

The life review, as described by Butler (1963) and later writers (for example, Kaminsky, 1984) should be seen as a natural activity, perhaps especially but not exclusively related to old age (Molinari and Reichlin, 1985), and one that needs respect. One would benefit from more descriptive material on the courses life reviews can take. A number of individuals in my study had seemed to have been through such a process, and it is important to stress that people do not necessarily want or benefit from the help of a counsellor in 'putting their house in order'. For some it may be an entirely private matter. But for those with deep feelings of regret and dissatisfaction, it may be vital that they are not left alone with their thoughts. Creative use can also be made of negative reminiscences, and writing an autobiography for a small group of interested others or for a therapist is better than sitting around and brooding about past events.

It must also be admitted, however, that there is some danger of overemphasising intrapsychic aspects in discussing the situation of elderly people. Neither psychology — nor religion, for that matter — concerns itself only with what happens within the individual. Each person has a need to be connected with the world at large, and a crucial problem of old age, apparent especially in modern western societies, is the isolation and loss of role and purpose in society which many old people can feel. Also, the supports and expressive outlets that one might have been able to rely on in family and at work to maintain adjustment in one's life may be gone. Of all the classical psychotherapists, Adler has perhaps the most to say about loss of self-esteem in old age (Adler, 1956). Feelings of uselessness or inferiority present the individual with a challenge to overcome from childhood onwards, and the key for Adler is the acquisition of '*Gemeinschaftsgefühl*', usually translated as 'social interest', that is, taking into account the well-being of other people.

Many negative phenomena in old age, as hypochondriasis and prejudiced views, may reflect fears about loss of identity and inferiority. Bringing a person to a less egocentric view of life and to develop interest in the happiness of others may be the best way of combatting such feelings. Therefore, rather than staying with the individual in his morbid thoughts about the past, it may be much more profitable to try to encourage an orientation to the world around him, to develop social interests and contacts. Again, it must be stressed, judgement is required as to whether reminiscence is a productive or counterproductive activity, and whether some other intervention might be called for.

In those who deny the importance of reminiscence to them — the third group in my study — one should not lightly dismiss their view as (over) defensive. Most of the people interviewed who came into this category had very understandable reasons for not reminiscing. They were too busy with other things they preferred to do. Some had been provided with opportunities they had not had earlier in life and wanted to make the most of them. If help does need to be offered to such people, it surely makes more sense to help them to continue with their chosen way of life and special interests — for example, find ways of transporting them to their old clubs or provide special aids to compensate for disabilities — rather than to say they should sit quietly and contemplate their past. In addition, some, especially perhaps the very old members of society, may well have been through a period of life review and feel no need to retrace their steps. Sufficient for them the issues of the day.

The final group in the same study were those who tried not to reminisce although they said that their past lives had been very happy. The reason for their avoidance was because, they said, it was too painful to reminisce. It made them more sad than they need be. All these people were depressed when first spoken to, or subsequently became so. All had been bereaved or had suffered another important loss (for example, severe disability or separation from a previously close family) and had not come to terms with these changes. In retrospect, it seemed evident that the inability to reminisce had reflected their inability to overcome these losses, and perhaps resulted from their failure to grieve satisfactorily. The same link between reminiscence and grieving has also been made recently by Pollack (1981) and Castelnuovo-Tedesco (1980). Reminiscence, they observe, may be functionally analogous to the grieving process. Like the work of mourning, reminiscence involves a reorganisation of one's relationship to the lost other. Reminiscence, too, can involve obsessive recounting. It can appear to reflect self-absorption. In some it can also result in a failure to give what has been lost. Indeed, in those who never give up wishing for the return of the past, reminiscence may not be pleasurable because they are unable to detach themselves from and freely enjoy their memories of the past, as memories.

This outcome may occur most where people have become very dependent on past relationships and roles for their idea of themselves. Worden views highly dependent relationships as especially difficult to grieve (Worden, 1982). He cites the research of Horowitz and colleagues who suggest that a person who has a highly dependent relationship and then loses the source of that dependency experiences a change in self-image from that of a strong person, well-sustained by the relationship with a strong other, to the pre-existent structure of a weak, helpless waif suplicating in vain for rescue by a lost or abandoning person (Horowitz *et al.*, 1980).

In the particular people I interviewed this may well have been an important factor. The three men who had all been bereaved gave indications of having lived very much for their wives. The three women who came into this category had, because of relocation or disability, lost the close links with family and friends and colleagues in a voluntary welfare organisation that had been the focus of their lives. At the least, it seems plausible to suggest that persistent inhibited or painful reminiscence, of the kind these people showed, is a good indicator of the need for grief therapy.

Therefore, proper consideration of reminiscence raises many other issues of importance in old age, and it seems right that increasing attention is being given to it. The main point here, however, has been to emphasise that one cannot make simple generalisations about the value of reminiscence. Each person needs to be considered in a special way. Whether reminiscence is a positive or negative factor in their lives, whether they can be helped with reminiscence which disturbs them or causes them pain, whether reminiscence should be avoided or stimulated, are all questions which call for a careful appraisal. Certainly, memories can be a source of great creativity, and this is an important point to stress, but elderly people should be offered many other possibilities as well to express themselves. Research on the value of formally stimulated reminiscence — for example, in institutional settings — should take a differential view, paying due attention to each individual's life history and circumstances.

Reminiscence and Mental Deterioration

The previous view that reminiscence was related to or even caused mental deterioration has been turned on its head. Now, reminiscence is seen as the 'new' means of preserving mental functioning in old age. A number of recent papers have pointed to the benefits of organised reminiscence in psychogeriatric institutions both to patients and staff (Kiernat, 1979; Lesser, Lazarus, Frankel, *et al.*, 1981; Norris and Abu El Eileh, 1982; Cook, 1984). Although most of the evidence is of an anecdotal nature rather than quantitative, it is consistently positive. The writers point to improvements as increased participation in discussion and more spontaneity on the part of elderly people (stressed both by Cook and by Norris and Abu El Eileh), greater socialisation before and after the sessions and even higher self-esteem and behavioural improvements.

The nurses and other staff involved have been said to benefit from knowing the elderly people better and, as a result, being able to form closer relationships with them. Other valuable spin-offs are referred to (for example, the formation of activity programmes based on the interests expressed in the groups). Evidence has also been collected that structured reminiscence exercise leads to improvement in cognitive functioning as measured by the Raven Standard Progressive Matrices (Hughston, 1976). At the least, activities involving reminiscence seem to be an eminently suitable means of attracting and maintaining the engagement of many elderly people.

Comparison with the enthusiasm expressed for reality orientation comes readily to mind. As Woods and Britton point out in their recent text (Woods and Britton, 1985), research on the benefits of reminiscence in institutions for the elderly will now probably mushroom and researchers should take notice of the lessons emerging from the previous research on reality orientation.

However, there is some danger that this association will lead, at least as far as mentally deteriorated elderly people are concerned, to an exclusive concern with the 'cognitive' and 'activity' benefits of reminiscence therapy, and a neglect of the broader issues of the relationship between reminiscence and psychological adjustment that have been the focus of this paper. Yet these same issues, such as maintenance of identity, present themselves as much with people suffering from dementia as with mentally intact elderly people, perhaps even more so. For example, one often needs to look beyond the immediate content of the reminiscence towards its meaning for the individual. Reminiscence may be a means of communicating feelings which, if expressed directly, would be difficult to handle both for the elderly person and the people who care for them. One illustration of this is talk about parents. Elderly people, and elderly women in particular, seem to reminisce a lot about childhood (Coleman, 1986). But why do confused elderly people speak so often about their parents as if they were alive? Does this tell us something about their sense of security and need for roots (Miesen, 1982)? In recognising reminiscence as a valuable activity for mentally deteriorating elderly people, one should not thereby become insensitive to what is said. Nor should one assume that reminiscence activities will suit everyone equally.

Postscript

As a final point, the extent of individual variation in orientation to reminiscence should be stressed again. Some people put a very high value on memories as their most treasured possessions. For others, the past is gone and unimportant. The psychoanalyst Schachtel has written colourfully of the conflict between the requirements of the present and the delights of recollection, and how this is reflected in literature (Schachtel, 1959). For the ancient Greeks, Mnemosyne, the goddess of memory, was the mother of all the Muses and hence of all art. But a contrasting picture is presented by Ulysses, who had to bind himself to the mast to escape the lure of the sirens' call. Proust renounced ordinary life entirely in order to achieve 'remembrance of things past', and argued that events and personal experience can only properly be understood and appreciated in retrospect, in remembrance. To Henry Ford, on the other hand, is attributed the short but effective quote 'History is bunk!'

The development of such a value orientation deserves analysis in its own right. At which point in the life span does it emerge, and how stable is it over time? It should be noted that the value an individual places on his memories of past experience is different from being satisfied with one's past life. It is also different from the affective quality of one's memories. It is rather an evaluation of the importance of memories to the individual as a personal possession. Presumably, everyone values their personal memories to some degree as a bedrock of personal identity, but some put more value on them than others.

References

Adler, A. (1956) *The Individual Psychology of Alfred Adler*, ed. by H.L. Ansbacher and R.R. Ansbacher, Harper and Row, New York

Beck, A.T. (1976) *Cognitive Therapy and the Emotional Disorders*, International Universities Press, New York

Bergin, A.E. (1983) 'Religiosity and Mental Health: a Critical Re-evaluation and Meta-analysis', *Professional Psychology: Research and Practice, 14*, 2, pp. 170–84

Blyth, R. (1979) *The View in Winter: Reflections on Old Age*, Allen Lane, Harmondsworth, London

Butler, R.N. (1963) 'The Life Review: An Interpretation of Reminiscence in the Aged', *Psychiatry, 26*, pp. 65–76

Carlson, C.M. (1984) 'Reminiscing: Toward Achieving Ego Integrity in Old Age', *Social Casework: The Journal of Contemporary Social Work*, February, pp. 81–9

Castelnuovo-Tedesco, P. (1978) 'The Mind as a Stage: Some Comments on Reminiscence and Internal Objects', *International Journal of Psychoanalysis, 59*, pp. 19–25

——— (1980) 'Reminiscence and Nostalgia: The Pleasure and Pain of Remembering' in S.I. Greenspan and G.H. Pollack (eds), *The Course of Life: Psychoanalytic Contributions toward Understanding Personality Development, Volume III: Adulthood and the Aging Process*, US Department of Health and Human Services, Washington DC, pp. 115–27

Coleman, P.G. (1974) 'Measuring Reminiscence Characteristics from Conversation as Adaptive Features of Old Age', *International Journal of Aging and Human Development, 5*, pp. 281–94

——— (1984) 'The Value of Reminiscence in Adaptation to Old Age. Longitudinal Case Studies over Ten Years' in D.B. Bromley (ed.), *Gerontology: Social and Behavioural Perspectives*, Croom Helm, London, pp. 195–205

——— (1986) *The Ageing Process and the Role of Reminiscence*, John Wiley, Chichester

——— (in press) 'The Past in the Present. A Study of Elderly People's Attitudes to Reminiscence'. *Oral History. The Journal of the Oral History Society*

Cook, J.B. (1984) 'Reminiscing: How it can Help Confused Nursing Home Residents', *Social Casework: The Journal of Contemporary Social Work*, February, pp. 90–3

Cumming, E. and Henry, W. (1961) *Growing Old: The Process of Disengagement*, Basic Books, New York

Dobrof, R. (1984) 'Introduction: A Time for Reclaiming the Past' in M. Kaminsky (ed.), *The Uses of Reminiscence: New Ways of Working with Older Adults*, The Haworth Press, New York

Ellis, A. (1974) *Humanistic Psychotherapy: The Rational-Emotive Approach*, McGraw-Hill, New York

Erikson, E. (1950) *Childhood and Society*, Norton, New York

——— (1978) 'Reflections on Dr Borg's Life Cycle' in E. Erikson (ed.), *Adulthood*, W.W. Norton, New York

Havighurst, R.J. (1959) 'Social and Psychological Needs of the Aging' in L. Gorlow and W. Katkovsky (eds), *Readings in the Psychology of Adjustment*, McGraw-Hill, New York

——— and Glasser, R. (1972) 'An Exploratory Study of Reminiscence', *Journal of Gerontology, 27*, pp. 235–53
Horowitz, M.J. *et al.* (1980) 'Pathological Grief and the Activation of Latent Self-Images', *American Journal of Psychiatry, 137*, pp. 1157–62
Hughston, G.A (1976) 'The Effects of Two Educational Interventions on the Cognitive Functioning of Older People', doctoral dissertation, Pennsylvania State University, University Park, Pa37 (5)
Johnson, M. (1978) 'That Was Your Life: A Biographical Approach to Later Life' in V. Carver and P. Liddiard (eds), *An Ageing Population*, Hodder and Stoughton, Sevenoaks
Jung, C.G. (1933) *Modern Man in Search of a Soul*, Routledge and Kegan Paul, London
Kaminsky, M. (1984) 'Transfiguring Life: Images of Continuity Hidden Among the Fragments' in M. Kaminsky (ed.), *The Uses of Reminiscence. New Ways of Working with Older Adults*, The Haworth Press, New York
Kiernat, J.M. (1979) 'The Use of Life Review Activity with Confused Nursing Home Residents', *American Journal of Occupational Therapy, 33*, pp. 306–10
Leech, K. (1977) *Soul Friend. A Study of Spirituality*, Sheldon Press, London
Lesser, J., Lazarus, L.W., Frankel, J. *et al.* (1981) 'Reminiscence Group Therapy with Psychotic Geriatric Inpatients', *The Gerontologist, 21*, pp. 291–6
Lewis, C.N. (1971) 'Reminiscing and Self-concept in Old Age', *Journal of Gerontology, 26*, pp. 240–3
Lidz, T. (1968) *The Person: His Development Throughout the Life Cycle*, Basic Books, New York
Lieberman, M.A. and Falk, J.M. (1971) 'The Remembered Past as a Source of Data for Research on the Life Cycle', *Human Development, 14*, pp. 132–41
Linn, D. and Linn, M. (1974) *Healing of Memories*, Paulist Press, New York
McMahon, A.W. and Rhudick, P.J. (1964) 'Reminiscing: Adaptational Significance in the Aged', *Archives of General Psychiatry, 10*, pp. 292–8
Merriam, S. (1980) 'The Concept and Function of Reminiscence: A Review of the Research', *The Gerontologist, 20*, pp. 604–9
——— and Cross, L. (1982) 'Adulthood and Reminiscence: A Descriptive Study', *Educational Gerontology, 8*, pp. 275–90
Miesen, B. (1982) 'Ouder-oriëntatie in de Ouderdam', unpublished report, Department of Social Gerontology, University of Nijmegen, The Netherlands
Molinari, V. and Reichlin, R.E. (1985) 'Life Review Reminiscence in the Elderly: A Review of the Literature', *International Journal of Aging and Human Development, 20*, 2, pp. 81–92
Norris, A.D. and Abu El Eileh, M.T. (1982) 'Reminiscence Groups', *Nursing Times, 78*, pp. 1368–9
Pollack, G.H. (1981) 'Reminiscences and Insight', *Psychoanalytic Study of the Child, 36*, pp. 279–87
Rathjen, D.P., Rathjen, E.D. and Hiniker, A. (1978) 'A Cognitive Analysis of Social Performance' in J.P. Foreyt and D.P. Rathjen (eds), *Cognitive Behaviour Therapy: Research and Application*, Plenum Press, New York
Schachtel, E.G. (1969) *Metamorphosis*, Basic Books, New York
Sherman, E. (1981) *Counseling the Aging. An Integrative Approach*, The Free Press, New York
Thomae, H. (ed.) (1976) *Patterns of Aging*, Karger, Basel
Woods, R.T. and Britton, P.G. (1985) *Clinical Psychology with the Elderly*, Croom Helm, London/Aspen, Rockville, MD
Worden, J.W. (1982) *Grief Counseling and Grief Therapy*, Springer, New York
Zinberg, N. and Kaufman, I. (1963) 'Cultural and Personality Factors Associated with Aging: An Introduction' in N. Zinberg and I. Kaufman (eds), *Normal Psychology of the Aging Process*, International Universities Press, New York

4 REALITY ORIENTATION IN THE CARE OF THE ELDERLY PATIENT WITH DEMENTIA — THREE CASE STUDIES

Ian Hanley

To some, the evidence for reality orientation (RO) as a viable and effective approach to the management of psychological disturbance in the confused elderly is unconvincing (Powell-Proctor and Miller, 1982; Britton, 1983). The purpose of this chapter is not to describe further the approach, seek to reiterate the theoretical perspectives that underpin it or to criticise the often unimaginative efforts to apply and evaluate it. To attempt to do these things might only serve to confuse the issues further. Rather than take a panoramic perspective this chapter will seek instead to focus in on some case studies that have applied the principles of RO to the problems presented by individual patients. In doing this, it is hoped the reader will be able to view RO from a different perspective.

A number of introductory points need to be made. First, dementia is a very general term used to describe a number of distinct disease entities which, in turn, cover extremely heterogeneous groups of patients. Simple classification by degree of dementia, useful as it is for some purposes, tends to lead into oversimplifying the condition. It is surely unreasonable to apply a psychological treatment such as RO 'off the peg' to a group of dementia patients and expect to get results of any clinical significance to the individual. It would not be attempted, for example, in applying psychotherapy with younger people, the uniqueness of the individual is automatically accepted in this context.

Why are we reluctant to look closely at the individual with dementia? Partly, perhaps, because this is in some ways an onerous task that involves a style of assessment on which little has been written. The establishment of a personal relationship in the assessment and treatment of the dementia patient can be achieved, however, and some would go so far as to advocate the use of modified psychotherapy with dementia patients (Solomon, 1985). Another reason might be the 'rising tide' perspective which can be so prominent in one's thinking — because the numbers involved are large, one tends to think of dementia patients as a *group*. Third, dementia patients tend to have in common a number of psychological deficits. This means greater attention is paid to the similarities between patients rather than to the differences. However, as Hodge (1984) clearly demonstrates, when detailed behavioural analysis and neuropsychological assessments are conducted, the conclusion is that not only do a diversity of problem behaviours exist, but so too does a diversity of causal explanations for these behaviours.

At the risk of being oversimplistic and perhaps uncharitable, the arguments against RO run roughly as follows:

1. Attempts to 'orientate' patients by offering verbal learning sessions have shown only limited gains in acquisition of new information and no behaviour change. (Why should one expect behaviour change at all with such an unimaginative interpretation of RO that makes no effort to address behaviour directly and personally?)
2. RO is demeaning, intrusive and treats the elderly patient like a child.

In the present author's view, RO is a multifaceted approach, comprising much more than the simple rehearsal of information. However, where efforts have been made to apply a more elaborate strategy in the context of patients' daily activity (24-hour RO), no evidence has been presented to show that this was actually delivered. The reader is referred to Chapter 7 for further consideration of the issues involved in changing the way care is 'delivered'.

In a previous paper (Hanley, 1984), at least four strands to the RO approach were identified:

1. Presentation of new information in a variety of formats including routine communication and special learning groups;
2. Correction of confused behaviour;
3. Prompting, rehearsal and reinforcement of adaptive behaviour;
4. Provision of memory aids as prostheses for memory problems.

All four can obviously be applied skilfully in the context of a therapeutic relationship that conveys positive attitudes, feelings and expectations to the patient. Such sensitive application dismisses the second point of criticism.

In earlier work I have tried to explore the relationship between these four components, focusing in particular on points three and four (Hanley, 1981; Hanley and Lusty, 1984) which have received scant attention in the literature. It is becoming clearer that it is somewhat artificial to seek to separate them.

The cases examined here have not been highly selected. Hopefully, they are a fair reflection of my clinical experience with RO over the past couple of years. No claims are made, however, for the generalisability of the findings. The hope is that they might help to revive interest in RO applied creatively to case management of patients with dementia — not simply applied as an unimaginative experimental exercise.

Case 1: Mrs S

Mrs S was an 84-year-old patient who had been admitted to a medium dependency psychogeriatric ward some nine months previously. She had a five-year history of being increasingly forgetful, isolated and unable to look after herself. The diagnosis supported by EEG examination and neuropsychological investigation was of senile dementia. This was moderately advanced according to the criteria of the Clifton Assessment Procedures for the Elderly (CAPE) on which the patient scored C on the scale A–E.

A 30-item personalised memory and orientation test was constructed from the patient's records, information from relatives and so on. It contained items of personal current and personal past information, together with items of current non-personal orientation. Initial assessment of Mrs S on this instrument revealed that she was unable to give correct answers to more than seven items (Figure 4.1, week 1).

As classroom RO, that is, rehearsal of information in the setting of a small group, has been repeatedly shown to produce only modest and time-limited gains in orientation, it was decided to attempt a different approach that might allow Mrs S greater access to relevant past and present information. As mentioned above, RO advocates the use of memory aids in the patient's environment. This is consistent with principles of information recall through cued and recognition procedures which greatly enhance performance of dementia patients. Previous research by the writer has shown that signposts accompanied by behavioural training produced a sizeable and relatively durable improvement in the ability of spatially disorientated patients to find places in the ward environment (Hanley, 1981).

It was decided to test the effectiveness of a diary as a memory aid for the set of 30 items in the Personal Orientation Questionnaire (POQ). Table 4.1 shows the design of the study. Although Mrs S presented no behaviour problems in the ward, it was felt that she, like many dementia patients cared for in institutional settings, was overly passive and disengaged from her surroundings. With the overall intention of

Figure 4.1: Subject's Daily Orientation Score During Baseline and Experimental Phases

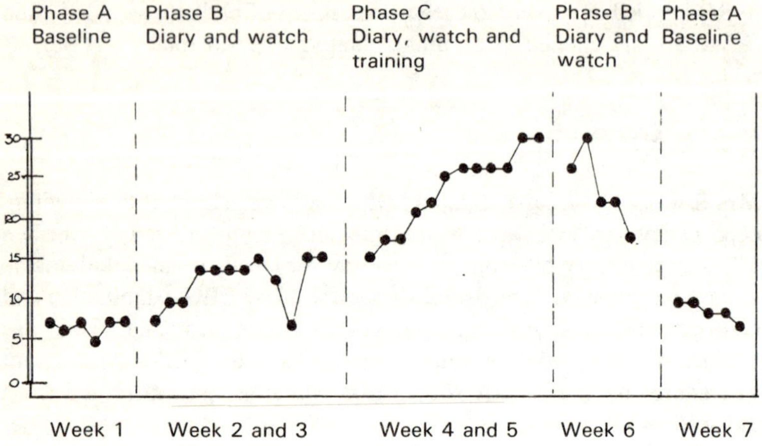

Table 4.1: Design of Study

Baseline (A)	No diary or training
Phase B	Diary containing personal information and daily appointments provided; no training
Phase C	Diary and training
Phase B	Diary only; training withdrawn
Baseline (A)	Diary withdrawn

improving her quality of life, it was decided also to attempt to train purposive behaviour, deficits in which are well-established in dementia. This was to be attempted by providing her with three scheduled daily appointments for interesting activities, such as having her hair done (she used to be a hairdresser), visiting the experimenter for coffee and so on. These appointments were written in the diary the day before. The answers to the 30 POQ items were also arranged across several pages of the diary.

Throughout the treatment, Mrs S was seen daily (except Sunday) and the POQ was administered. Correct answers were not provided as the intention was to measure the effectiveness of the diary alone, complementary training to use the diary, but not information rehearsal. In future purely clinical application of this approach, it would be advisable to include routine provision of correct answers to enhance responding and facilitative therapeutic interaction during treatment. During phase B the diary was presented to Mrs S and she was shown once only at the

Figure 4.2: Subject's Daily Appointments Scores During Baseline and Experimental Phases

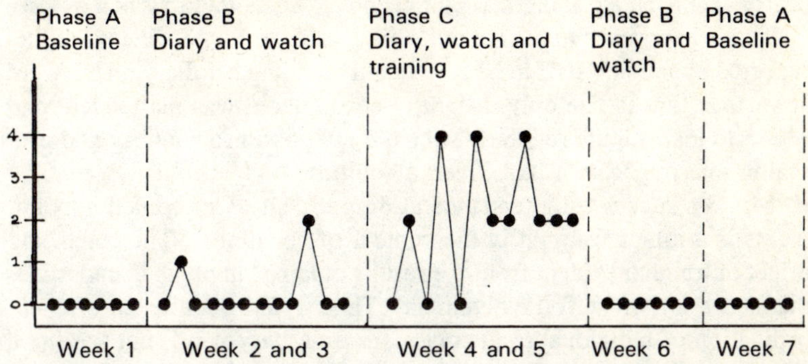

beginning of the phase how to use it to answer questions and attend appointments. If she failed to use the diary subsequently she was not reminded during phase B.

During phase C, however, she was actively trained to make use of the diary. This involved a five-minute training period at the end of each day's session. Mrs S was asked to look at the diary and answer each question incorrectly answered during the session, for example, 'Mrs S, the answer to the question about your brother's name is on page 2 of your diary. Look at page 2 and tell me the answer'. She was also taught to use the diary to keep appointments. This involved reminding her about each failed appointment after ten minutes had elapsed and asking her to look at her watch and diary. The activity was then carried out.

Figure 4.1 shows Mrs S's scores on POQ over the period of the study. The final plateau of 30 reached at the end of phase C is the test ceiling and represents an increase of 23 points over baseline. Although some improvement is noticeable in phase B (diary only), this is small and irregular compared with the cumulative increase in score evident through phase C. Figure 4.2 shows the daily appointments scores (maximum: three appointments × two points = six points) over the course of the study. During phase A, Mrs S consistently failed to respond. During phase B, only 1/36 appointments were kept. When training was introduced in phase C, 12/36 or 33 per cent of appointments were kept.

These results suggest that dementia patients such as Mrs S with preserved reading ability can be successfully taught to use a diary to respond to demands on their orientation and memory for personal information. As there is a clear upper limit to the amount of information dementia patients can successfully retain, the learning of such a simple set of skills, that is, those involved in using a diary or notebook, gives the patient access to a much larger store of information. This can have practical clinical advantages as will become evident in discussion of Case 2. Such an approach appeared quite acceptable to Mrs S. She was often reported by nursing staff to be seen quietly reading her diary on the ward at various times. The only difficulty encountered was the tendency of Mrs S to lose it quite regularly. She did not possess a handbag and providing one might well have been a solution.

Mrs S's successful attendance at 33 per cent of scheduled appointments is a minor triumph in the context of her illness. The enhancing effect of training evident from the results obtained in phase C underlines the necessity of staff involvement. This would require careful co-ordination of individual treatment plans on a busy ward, but the small amount of time involved is surely cost-effective when this approach is used with selected cases.

Case 2: Mrs B

Mrs B is an 83-year-old patient with a moderately advanced dementia (grade C on CAPE) resident in a medium dependency ward. She had entered care one year before, following the death of her husband, John, who had been supporting her at home. She had been first admitted to a local authority home for the elderly, but was soon referred on to the psychogeriatric assessment unit after her behaviour became disturbed and difficult to manage. This disturbance took the form of episodes of confused behaviour. She became agitated, insisted that John was still alive, and made efforts to strike out at staff who prevented her from leaving the home. After three months in the assessment unit she was placed in a long-stay ward. No improvement had occurred in her behaviour and she was considered unsuitable for return to the old people's home.

In the long-stay unit, as in the assessment unit, Mrs B continued to express the desire to 'go home' and regularly referred to John as being still alive. Occasionally, she would have brief lucid periods when she remembered his death. These were accompanied by obvious grief and distress. Although gravely disorientated, Mrs B showed little impairment in her memory for remote events that had occurred before the onset of the dementia. Her language function was intact, as were her social skills, and she required only minimal assistance with activities of daily living.

A decision on how to handle Mrs B's confusion over the loss of her husband needed to be made. Following the suggestions of Church (1984), who has reported a similar case, Mrs B was asked during one of her lucid spells whether or not she wanted to remember the events that had overtaken her. Quite clearly and unambiguously she stated that (1) she wanted to remember that John was dead; and (2) she wanted staff to correct her if she became confused.

Notwithstanding the complex ethical issues involved in consent to psychological treatment (see Chapter 10), Mrs B's clearly expressed view was taken as evidence of her consent and she became the subject of a single case study. The main purpose of this was to test the effectiveness of a reality orientation treatment plan based on (1) correcting her confusion over the loss of her husband; and (2) providing her with a memory aid in the form of a notebook which listed some 20 items of personal information, including a number of items related to the death of her husband, for example, the date of his death and the name of the church yard in which he was buried. The notebook also included a picture of Mrs B standing by the gravestone.

The approach taken to correcting Mrs B's confusion was similar to that suggested by Holden and Woods (1982), namely allowing time for the therapist to deal sensitively with the feelings expressed by Mrs B when presented with the information that John was dead. Arie (1978), among others, has noted the intensity of the emotions experienced by memory-disordered dementia patients hearing such information 'as if for the first time'. Church (1984) has described this sort of approach as an adaptation of grief therapy for the dementia patient.

Following the successful use of a diary as a memory aid with Case 1 (Mrs A), it was decided to extend the treatment plan for Mrs B (and two other patients not presented here) to investigate the effects of placing a large reality orientation board prominently on the ward and teaching the patients to make use of it for general orientation.

Three phases were involved in the study, which is to be reported in detail elsewhere (Hanley and Hogg, 1986). The data collected on a daily basis throughout was her response to (1) a 19-item orientation questionnaire; and (2) the set of 20 items of personal information to which answers were made available in her notebook. Care was taken to disguise the questioning as far as possible by embedding the procedure in a conversational interaction with Mrs B. This type of approach was considered less distressing to Mrs B than a straight 'question and answer' approach.

The first baseline phase lasted one week and took place before Mrs B was given her notebook and before the reality orientation board was put up. During the whole of the second phase, which lasted three weeks,

Mrs B had the notebook and the reality orientation board was situated on the wall of the dayroom where the treatment was conducted. The therapist made reference to each memory aid once only at the beginning of this second phase.

During the third phase, which lasted three weeks, a treatment plan was carried out that involved reminding Mrs B to use the RO board and the notebook. The data-gathering interview followed the same order throughout the study, namely a block of orientation questions was asked first, followed by a block of personal information items. The reminding procedure adopted in the third phase involved: (1) taking Mrs B over to the board after the orientation questions had been asked, having her read material off the board and informing her that the board was there of help her memory for this information; and (2) having Mrs B locate and open her notebook, after the personal questions had been asked, read the information contained in it and discuss items of interest.

This procedure was adopted daily irrespective of whether Mrs B referred to the board or the diary during the course of questioning. Her use or otherwise of the board and diary was noted for each item in each session. Furthermore, during the third phase Mrs B was corrected on the items relating to the death of her husband, her feelings were shared and time was taken to talk with her a while about John. Once weekly during this phase she was taken to visit the grave.

Figure 4.3 shows Mrs B's performance on the total of orientation items across the three phases of the study. Figure 4.4 shows her response to the total of personal information items and Figure 4.5 her response to the specific items concerned with John's death.

The results for orientation show that this improved only during the final phase of the study. The data on use made of the board indicated that it was only during this phase that she acquired the skill to use the board to answer the questions. The results for personal information are very similar, but data on the use of the notebook indicated that the improvement was *not* related to increased use of the notebook. This suggests that Mrs B learnt the items of personal information without the need to use the notebook during questioning. It is likely that these items, which were not new information, but rather related to events that had occurred before her illness, were acquired by a relearning process based on the correction/rehearsal procedure itself. This was not sufficient for the orientation material which were all items of *new* information and which she answered correctly only through using the board.

Figure 4.5 demonstrates a major change during phase 3 in her awareness of John's death and his place of burial. On 11 of the 15 days

Figure 4.3: Mrs B's Orientation Scores During Baseline and Treatment

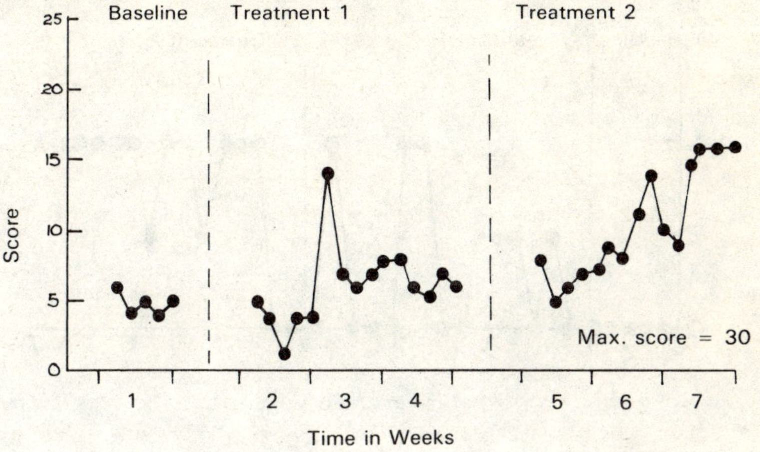

Figure 4.4: Mrs B's Personal Information Scores During Baseline and Treatment

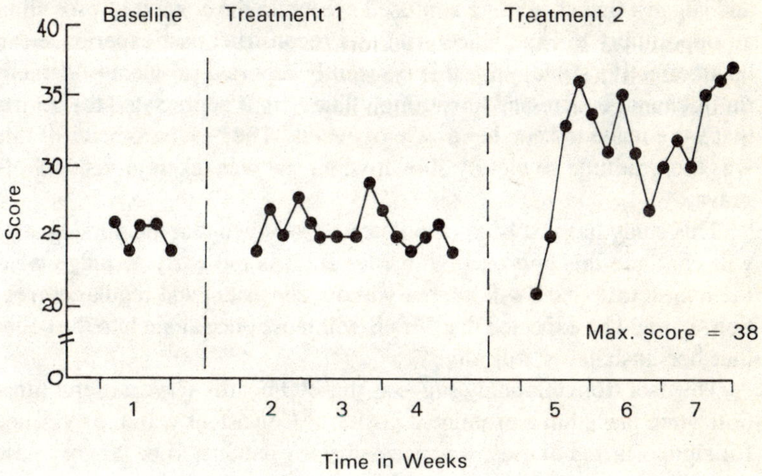

Figure 4.5: Mrs B's Scores on Two Items Related to the Death of Her Husband During Baseline and Treatment

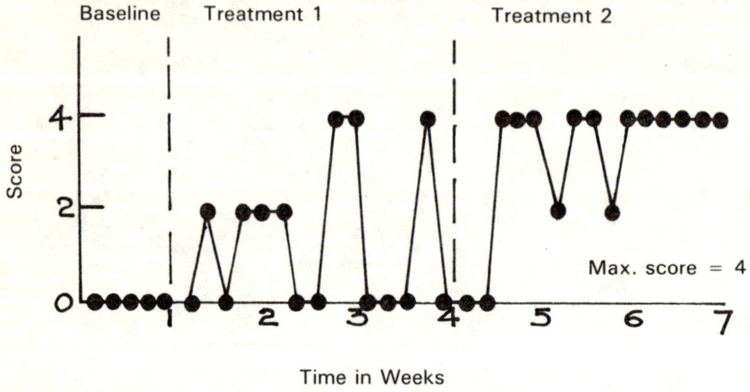

both these questions correctly compared with three out of 15 days in phase 2. On the five days of baseline, she had made no correct responses to these questions. These results clearly replicate those of Church (1984) and suggest that correcting confused speech in the context of providing an opportunity to experience grief and reconstruct past experience can be an effective strategy for this frequently reported problem of dementia. It cannot be stressed too strongly that Mrs B appreciated the efforts that were made to keep her aware of events. The best barometer of this was the gratitude so clearly shown when she was taken to visit John's grave.

This study has just been completed. It is hoped that the nursing staff will continue this approach with Mrs B. It is too early to judge what the long-term effects will be, but without consistent and regular correction, it might be expected that Mrs B will lapse once again into the belief that her husband is still alive.

The data from this study suggests that RO boards serve a useful function when placed in a prominent position. Consistent with the evidence for signposts and diaries, it is necessary for patients to be taught to use the board as a memory prosthesis.

Case 3: Miss M

Miss M is an 85-year-old patient in the long-stay unit of a psychogeriatric hospital. She suffers from severe dementia as assessed by CAPE (grade E). The presenting problem that led to her referral for psychological treatment was frequent double incontinence. Medical checks had revealed no urinary tract infection or other treatable condition and the pattern of the incontinence was not consistent with a diagnosis of bladder hyper-reflexia, stress incontinence or urge incontinence.

Miss M urinated on the linoleum floor covering at the foot of the staircase in the large Victorian house where the ward was situated. This continued to occur even though the nursing staff had introduced a two-hourly toileting regime. The specificity of the spot where Miss M urinated was such that the floor covering became saturated, started to rot and created a pervasive smell of urine on the ward. About one square yard of floor covering was lifted to let the flooring dry beneath. She also dropped small balls of faecal matter over the gate positioned at the front of the stairs. Although suffering from a senile dementia of the Alzheimer's type, the absence of any incontinence in other parts of the ward was not consistent with an explanation of the problem as simply due to cerebral impairment.

On interview Miss M denied the problem, stating that it must be 'the dogs that did it'. When asked to point out where the ladies' toilet was situated (directly off the sitting room where she was seated) Miss M pointed out through the window to the garden area. She stated that there was no toilet in the building. She was also unable to point out other parts of the ward, such as the dining room and the four-bedded dormitory where she slept.

When Miss M's history before admission was reviewed it was discovered that she had spent most of her life in a remote rural area some 70 miles from the hospital. She had lived most of her adult years in a simple farm cottage and worked as a shepherdess until her retirement. This involved long periods out of doors, herding sheep in rough hill grazing areas. Although it was not known whether or not her cottage had an inside toilet, it would certainly have been the case that Miss M, during working hours, would have gone to the toilet out of doors.

It was striking to note that the area in which Miss M was incontinent on the ward was close to the barrier which blocked off the stairway to prevent the frail patients climbing the stairs to the unused top floor of the building. Beside this barrier was a large potted house plant. It required little imagination to see the similarities between the spot where

Miss M was incontinent on the ward and the sort of place she would have used on a hillside in Southern Scotland. In this area dry stone walls or dykes provide the only cover. 'Historical' factors have been noted before in cases of incontinence among mentally frail elderly patients. Lodge (1979) noted that some elderly patients at Carlton Hayes Hospital in England would go out of the assessment ward into the garden area and then come back and be incontinent of urine on their return. These patients had all lived in houses with outside toilets. They would wander into the grounds, presumably looking for the toilet, and on not finding it be incontinent of urine on their return.

One possible interpretation of Miss M's incontinence, albeit in part conjectural, was that somehow she was confusing her current environment in hospital with her circumstances prior to admission several years before. Moreover, she had manifestly failed to learn to negotiate the hospital environment. She did not appear to have a 'map' of the spatial and functional characteristics of the hospital ward. It often seems that the patients with dementia who most confuse past and present are those whose memory for remote events is relatively unimpaired, but whose memory for current reality, dependent as this is on new learning ability, is grossly impaired.

As mentioned earlier, it has been demonstrated (Hanley, 1981) that patients with severe dementia can learn to negotiate a hospital environment when trained to do so through a combination of prompting, rehearsal and reinforcement. This learning decays rapidly after training is withdrawn unless large signposts are introduced to act as aids to orientation. Svensson (1981) has also shown how dementia patients may sometimes perceive symbols better than words. This suggests that to be maximally effective signposts should contain both.

Applying reality orientation to Miss M's situation led to the following programme being established:

1. The two ward toilets were clearly signposted with large symbol and word signs;
2. Miss M was prompted to use the toilet hourly, that is, asked if she would like to use it;
3. Minimal assistance was provided to help Miss M find the toilet herself. She was 'cued' where necessary to find her way, for instance, 'Actually, its just across from the big window', and praised for using the toilet correctly;
4. Each trip to the toilet was followed by a ward 'walkabout' during which other areas were identified.

The goal of this programme was simply to ensure that Miss M learnt what appeared to be the 'missing link' in her continence chain — to find the toilet. Incontinent episodes were charted throughout. Within a week of starting the programme the frequency of incontinence had reduced considerably. After two weeks incontinence had stopped and now, one year later, remains so. The programme was discontinued after two months, except for two-hourly toiletting reminders. The lino has been replaced and the ward smells sweet again.

Comments

With the exception of Case 3, which required immediate psychological intervention, the treatments involved were investigated formally through single case study methodology (Hersen and Barlow, 1976). Salkovskis (1984) has suggested that this type of research is synonymous with applicable research in clinical settings. Even if easily applied, albeit methodologically suspect, designs such as the A/B design are opted for, this might constitute 'one enormous step forward that would greatly expand our data base' (Barlow, 1980). Although Barlow is not making specific reference to the investigation of psychological treatments applied to problems experienced by the elderly person with dementia, this view has much to commend it in this context.

As Hodge (1984) has pointed out, there are a multitude of pathways that can lead to many of the behavioural disturbances found in patients with this condition. If Hodge's argument is developed further, then not only is it well-advised to conduct detailed neuropsychological assessments and behavioural analysis, but this information must also be put to use in the construction of practical treatments. Single case study designs still offer the best tool to investigate the functional relationships involved between specific problems, specific treatments and outcome.

One major advantage of the single case approach, which is too often neglected by those investigators who have both eyes firmly fixed on scientific credibility, is that it can be deliberately idiographic, that is, take the client personally into account. Reality orientation, and the same must be true for other psychological approaches, is unlikely to fulfil its potential if implementation is rote and impersonal. As a multidimensional approach involving a number of general components, the goal must surely be to investigate the effectiveness of specific strategies, or combinations thereof, in the treatment of specific problems. The well-established reality of 'excess disabilities' in dementia should be remembered (Brody,

Kleban, Lawton, *et al.*, 1971).

Interventions, if made in a fashion that takes both the patient and the care-giver into account, might also have a positive knock-on effect on care-giver attitudes and behaviour. Modelling the application of RO-derived treatment plans in the three cases discussed in this chapter seemed to facilitate staff in adopting for themselves the procedures concerned. As mentioned earlier, one of the most common deficiencies in studies of RO has been the tendency not to document whether the patient actually 'got the pill', that is, was in receipt of an altered approach from staff.

The success of the treatment strategies applied in these three cases does not constitute sufficient evidence for the conclusion to be drawn that RO has universal value in the management of the problems treated. Considerably more work of this type needs to be done to develop additional creative strategies and apply them to a wider range of behavioural problems. It is reasonable to conclude, however, that worthwhile short-term changes in behaviour and orientation are possible and that the simplicity of the treatments involved may even make such interventions cost-effective. It is yet to be demonstrated whether these changes can be maintained in the long-term and whether systems of care can be engineered that allow these approaches to be used creatively and independently by those having most contact with patients.

Note: A range of visual aids designed to enhance orientation are available from Orientation Aids, Dalebank, Glencaple, Dumfries, Scotland.

References

Arie, T. (1978) 'Confusion in Old Age', *Age and Ageing, 7*, pp. 72–6

Barlow, D.H. (1980) 'Behaviour Therapy: The Next Decade', *Behaviour Therapy, 11*, 315–28

Britton, P.G. (1983) 'Psychological Services for the Elderly' in A. Liddell (ed.), *The Practice of Clinical Psychology in Great Britain*, Wiley, London and New York

Brody, E.M., Kleban, M.H., Lawton, M.P. *et al.* (1971) 'Excess Disabilities of Mentally Impaired Aged: Impact of Individualized Treatment', *The Gerontologist, 1*, pp. 124–33

Church, M. (1984) 'Some Aspects of Bereavement Counselling with Elderly People', *PSIGE Newsletter, 12*, pp. 6–9

Hanley, I.G. (1981) 'The Use of Signposts and Active Training to Modify Ward Disorientation in Elderly Patients', *J. Behav. Ther. and Exp. Psychiat., 12*, pp. 241–7

——— (1984) 'Memory Aids in Reality Orientation: A Single Case Study', *Behav. Res. Ther., 22* (6), pp. 709–12

Hanley, I.G. and Hogg, K. (1986) 'Further Studies in Reality Orientation', *Age and Ageing* (in preparation)

Hersen, M. and Barlow, D.H. (1976) *Single Case Experimental Designs: Strategies for Studying Behaviour Change*, Pergamon Press, New York

Hodge, J. (1984) 'Towards a Behavioural Analysis of Dementia' in I. Hanley and J. Hodge (eds), *Psychological Approaches to the Care of the Elderly*, Croom Helm, London/Methuen, New York

Holden, V.P. and Woods, R.T. (1982) *Reality Orientation*, Churchill-Livingstone, Edinburgh

Lodge, B. (1979) *What's Happening to Grandad?* MIND (National Association for Mental Health) Publications, Leeds

Powell-Proctor, L. and Miller, E. (1982) 'Reality Orientation: A Critical Appraisal', *Brit. J. Psychiat.*, *140*, pp. 451–63

Salkovskis, P. (1984) 'Psychological Research by NHS Clinical Psychologists: An Analysis and Some Suggestions', *Bulletin of the British Psychological Society*, *37*, pp. 375–7

Solomon, K. (1985) 'The Subjective Response of the Alzheimer's Disease Patient', paper presented at the 13th International Congress of Gerontology, New York

Svensson, T. (1981) 'Understanding of Symbols among Institutionalized Elderly', paper presented at 12th International Congress of Gerontology, Hamburg

5 PSYCHOLOGICAL CONSIDERATIONS IN THE DAY CARE OF ELDERLY PEOPLE

Victor G. Cicirelli and Ellen Browne

Although day care for the elderly has been in existence for many years, it has experienced major growth in the last decade. Yet many who work with the elderly are not well aware of the opportunities which are possible for care of the older client in the day care setting. This chapter will provide an introductory overview of the nature of day care and its place in a long-term care system, examine some current issues in the use of day care, present some findings from existing evaluations of day care and draw some conclusions about the strengths of day care and how it might be improved.

Adult day care is a programme of services and activities for functionally impaired elderly provided in a protected setting to which the elderly come for care, activities or therapeutic treatment during some part of the day (but less than 24-hour care) and from which they return to their homes in the community at night. The term 'adult day care' is applied to a variety of types of services and programmes differing in objectives, types of clients, and service setting (Weiler and Rathbone-McCuan, 1978). It serves those elderly who are unable to function independently in the community but who do not require full-time care in a nursing home or other institution.

Objectives of Adult Day Care

While specific objectives of a day care programme vary depending on the type of service provided, general objectives of day care are to maintain, restore and rehabilitate the individual as far as possible (National Council on the Aging, 1984). That is, day care programmes seek to maintain the level of functioning of the elderly client for as long as possible, preventing or delaying any decline, and restoring and rehabilitating functional abilities to the highest extent possible.

In addition, day care programmes seek to promote socialisation and peer interaction among the participants, to provide respite and support to home caregivers and to function as part of an integrated continuum of care. Overall, day care seeks to promote the highest possible level of independence for the individual. The emphasis of day care on a rehabilitative approach and one which is concerned with the whole person distinguishes it from the more custodial objectives of residential care or the traditional nursing home.

Place in an Integrated Long-term Care System

Day care does not exist as an isolated service, but as one of a variety of services in a continuum of long-term care services available to the elderly. Day care hospitals and day centres are an integral part of the British system of care, organised under the National Health Service. In the United States, the continuum of services is a loosely organised collection of services offered by government-sponsored agencies, voluntary organisations and proprietary concerns. In such an informal system, the place of day care is not clearly defined as it is in the British system.

Clark (1982) depicts a continuum of services for the elderly ranging from social services (for example, telephone reassurance, friendly visitors, congregate meal sites, chore services and so on) to various home health care services, to nursing homes and hospitals and finally to hospice care during the final stage of life. Depending on the type of programme offered, day care can be placed at various points along this continuum. Although at present services along the continuum tend to be more fragmented than integrated, many communities are now working on projects designed to co-ordinate the available care alternatives for the elderly.

History of Adult Day Care

While a detailed history of the day care movement is not possible here and is available to the interested reader from other sources (Brocklehurst, 1970; O'Brien, 1982b; Weiler and Rathbone-McCuan, 1978), a few points of this history will help to explain the differences between the development of day care in Britain and in the United States.

Adult day care has its roots in the psychiatric day hospital. Although the earliest day hospital was established in Moscow in 1933, and was followed by similar day hospitals for severely ill psychiatric patients in Britain and the United States in the 1940s, the first use of the day hospital for physically ill or impaired geriatric patients did not take place until the 1950s. By 1959, there were ten such day hospitals in operation in Britain.

Growth continued rapidly through the next decade, and by 1971 the day hospitals were integrated within the long-term health care system. Because the day hospitals emphasised treatment and rehabilitation (at least in theory), a second type of day care (the day centre) was established to offer socialisation and supervision rather than rehabilitation: such centres usually are operated by local authorities. By the 1980s, it was estimated that 40,000 elderly people attended some 1,000 day care centres and hospitals in Britain on any given day (Goupille, 1982).

In the United States, a few centres serving the elderly were established around 1957, but major growth of day care for the elderly did not take place until the decade of the 1970s and this growth is still going on. From a handful of centres in 1970, day care grew to more than 1,000 adult day care centres in 1984 (Mace and Rabins, 1984a). Some of these centres were funded through government-sponsored programmes, while others were established by community and voluntary organisations, and still others were established by proprietary concerns. Reflecting the variety of auspices under which the adult day programmes were organised as well as the specialised needs of the elderly they served, these centres represented a spectrum of different types. This contrasts with adult day care in Britain, which falls more easily into two main types.

Models of Day Care

Although several different typologies of day care programmes have been proposed (for instance, Weissert, 1976; Weiler and Rathbone-McCuan, 1978; Dix, 1982; O'Brien, 1982a), most can be conceived as existing on a continuum between two main types: the medical–rehabilitative model and the psychosocial model. These types roughly parallel the two major types in the British system, the day hospital and the day centre. The medical–rehabilitative model focuses on the use of treatment and rehabilitation to restore the patient's level of functioning. (To the extent that functional abilities can be rehabilitated, the patient may be able to continue an independent life in the community.) Typically staffed by registered nurses, with physicians and therapists consulted as needed, programmes focus on specific therapies and help with activities of daily living. The psychosocial model focuses on social interaction and activities which emphasise psychosocial well-being. Although a nurse is frequently in attendance, staff typically includes a social worker and a recreation worker.

To the extent that both rehabilitative therapies and social and recreational activities are present, an adult day care programme can be placed somewhere on the continuum between the two main types. Most adult day care centres in the United States are now of a mixed type, while in Britain there is a great deal more variation than the two main types would seem to suggest.

Populations Served by Adult Day Care

Broadly speaking, adult day care serves those elderly persons who are unable to function independently in the community and who would be at risk of institutionalisation without assistance. According to the National Council on the Aging (1984), the day care population can include those with physical, emotional or mental impairment who require assistance and supervision and those who need restorative or rehabilitative services. This can include those elderly recovering from an acute illness as well as those with chronic conditions for which support is needed. In addition to those with physical illnesses, day care can also serve those with psychiatric disorders, cognitive impairments and those who are socially isolated or whose social functioning has regressed.

One of the great values of day care is its ability to offer a variety of services and activities so that a programme can be tailored to meet the needs of specific clients. In spite of this, certain types of clients are generally excluded from day care: those who are too ill, those who are confined to bed, those with communicable diseases, those with active alcoholism or drug abuse, those with active psychosis or violent or unmanageable behaviour or those with uncontrolled incontinence or wandering (Mace and Rabins, 1984a; National Council on the Aging, 1984). However, these ineligibility criteria are somewhat flexible and depend on the size and expertise of staff, the physical characteristics of the centre, and on the number and types of other clients in the day care programme. Many centres now are admitting clients (at least on a trial basis) who formerly would have been considered ineligible. Yet, an adult day care centre, like the child nursery school, may be able to manage only a limited number of clients whose difficult behaviour or lack of basic functional abilities require a great deal of care.

Directly or indirectly, day care also helps to meet the needs of home care-givers of elderly clients (this includes family care-givers as well as care-givers in foster homes or group homes). At the very least, respite is provided. However, some day care centres also offer care-giver counselling and training and other care-giver support activities.

Trends in the Use of Day Care

Adult day care itself is a service for the elderly which is continuing to grow and gain acceptance as part of the long-term care continuum. Most patients and families would prefer to see the patient at home, but when this becomes impossible, they look for alternatives to institutionalisation (Kane and Kane, 1980). Day care is becoming increasingly recognised as an alternative which is desirable. In those few states in the United States in which community-based respite care is available under Medicaid, day care is one of the four most frequently requested services (Gibson, 1984). Thus, there are increases both in the number of centres and in the number of elderly using them. This is also true in Canada and many western European nations.

Parallel to the growth of day care is the growth of integrated long-term care systems which include day care as part of the system of care. In the United States, some of these have been demonstration projects under government or private foundation grants, in which a model system of care is established in a few selected sites to test the feasibility of the new system and to provide a guide for other communities to follow. Others have been local voluntary efforts.

A major trend in the use of day care has been the growth in the number of elderly with Alzheimer's disease or other forms of dementia who are in day care. Greene and Timbury (1979) reported a five-year growth of dementing elderly from 46 to 90 per cent of the clientele of a British geriatric psychiatry day hospital. Similarly, Mace and Rabins' (1984a; 1984b) survey of day care for dementing elderly in the United States found that 46 per cent of 980 adult day care centres to which they sent initial enquiries reported that they served demented clients (and this is surely an underestimate since it did not take account of non-responses). The number of centres dealing with dementia, particularly specialised centres, is increasing.

Another trend in day care is the development of services to support the family care-giver. Such activities as family counselling, group support and information and referral are all regarded as core services by the National Council on the Aging (1984). Mace and Rabins (1984a) found that 89 per cent of centres provided counselling, 86 per cent encouraged families to attend support groups, and 84 per cent met with families for planning or discussion of problems. However, only 51 per cent actually provided support groups as part of their programme. Since family care of the elderly day care client at home is essential to making the day care experience a successful one for that client, family support activities can help achieve continuity between home and centre as well as help care-givers with particular problems.

Issues in Adult Day Care

There are certain factors in the structure and operation of adult day care which have particular implications for the psychological well-being of the elderly people attending those centres. There has been a considerable disagreement with regard to some of these factors. Three of these will be discussed here.

Integration of Dementing Elderly With Other Clients

With the acceptance of dementing elderly into day care, there is a difference of opinion among day care professionals as to whether dementing elderly should be segregated in a separate facility for care or whether they should be integrated with other clients who are not cognitively impaired. Those favouring segregated care argue that elderly clients with dementia need special programmes and specially trained staff to deal with their unique problems. They need more space than other clients since they tend to be more mobile, require more staff time for their supervision and need secure physical facilities to curb wandering (Mace and Rabins, 1984a).

In integrated programmes, those with dementia may be shunted aside and ignored in centre activities. It is argued that it is unfair to cognitively unimpaired day care clients to subject them to bizarre or annoying behaviours of those with dementia. Some of these arguments may have some validity when the day care programme has a limited offering of activities, when the programme is rigidly structured for the group as a whole and when the ratio of staff to clients is low.

However, in a day care centre with an individualised programme tailored to the needs of each participant, well-qualified staff and suitable resources, there are a number of benefits possible in an integrated programme. First, there is a greater opportunity for stimulation, socialisation and learning within an integrated setting. There is some evidence that cognitively impaired elderly interact to a greater degree with 'normal' elderly than with other dementia victims in a day care setting (Lawton, 1980), although this may be due in part to relative numbers of normal and dementing elderly in the centre. Mace and Rabins (1984a; 1984b) found that 84 per cent of the centres reported peer friendships between demented clients; these were more common in centres with a higher proportion of demented elderly.

Another consideration is that placing clients who are only mildly demented in a segregated facility with more severely demented clients may be unfair to them if the programme does not offer sufficient stimulation. Also, the client and family may feel that there is a stigma attached to participation in adult day care expressly for those with dementia.

Finally, integration of elderly dementia victims into an adult day care group can provide some benefits for the other clients. Many elderly people have a need to help others and not merely be recipients of services (Cantor, 1975; Cicirelli and Browne, 1983; Kahana and Midlarsky, 1983). They want to feel useful and gain in self-esteem when they help others less fortunate. In a secondary way, cognitively unimpaired elderly can gain in self-esteem through social comparison processes as they see how well off they are compared to others with dementia (Kahana and Midlarsky, 1983). Helping interactions can lead to improved morale in the normal elderly as well as in the demented elderly, who receive greater help, attention and understanding and react with happier moods.

In the Mace and Rabins survey (1984a; 1984b), 76 per cent of the centres serving demented elderly had less than 50 per cent demented clients in their total enrolments. Although some of these centres separated cognitively unimpaired and demented clients, it is clear that integration is more common than segregation. Only a small number of centres specialised in elderly with dementia (for example, Sands and Suzuki, 1983). Some 57 per cent of the integrated centres reported that cognitively well clients had no trouble mixing with and accepting demented clients; centres commented that cognitively well clients were helpful in assisting demented clients with activities.

Although most centres had experienced incidents of wandering, agitation and combatitiveness on the parts of demented clients, they felt able to manage these behaviours unless a client had a high frequency of such behaviour or was unusually disruptive. Centres with high proportions of demented clients experienced a greater frequency of disruptive behaviour, due to the increased number of such clients and the fact that these centres accept clients whose dementia is more severe.

Thus, it has been demonstrated that integration of dementing and cognitively well elderly in day care can be successful. Clearly, much more research study needs to be done to determine the client ratios that are optimal, the kinds of activities and therapies that are best and the effects on both groups of clients.

Inclusion of Family Members

Although the importance of family involvement in geriatric day care programmes is recognised (for example, Dix, 1982; Rathbone-McCuan, 1976), the question of whether family members should be welcomed as visitors, participants and volunteers to the adult day care centre is one on which there are differences in views. Some centres actively discourage family members from attending the centre except on special occasions and for an initial visit. Centre staff believe that the clients function better when the home care-giver is not present and feel that some family members are over-anxious or place unrealistic demands on the client or the centre. Mace and Rabins (1984a) found that only 27 per cent of centres encouraged family members to attend. On the other hand, they found a positive relationship between client adjustment and the family's attendance at the centre. Some centres (for instance, Cicirelli and Browne, 1983) are quite open to family members, encouraging whatever level of family participation seems best for client and care-giver. Some family members have extreme attachment, as in the case of some elderly spouses, and continue to give each other reassurance in the day care situation. Other elderly care-givers themselves profit from the social stimulation which the centres provide. Helping clients and care-givers reach the best possible adjustment can be regarded as part of the general objective of providing support to family care-givers. If this can be achieved through care-giver participation in the centre, it may help to maintain the client in the community for a longer period of time.

Location of Adult Day Centres

Establishing a day care facility as part of a hospital or nursing home is a practice which falls within the accepted tradition of the British geriatric day hospital. Where the emphasis is on treatment and rehabilitation, the availability of professional staff and equipment, cost savings possible through use of existing space, ease of transition to and from hospital or nursing home care and similar reasons are advanced for situating adult day care in an institutional setting. However, arguments are also advanced for locating adult day care within separate facilities in the community. Among them are greater proximity and convenience within the client's community, lower costs for programmes with psychosocial emphases and easier integration with other community services. In addition, many clients and families are reluctant to use day care connected with a nursing home for fear of being identified with its residents (Nusberg, 1984). The more positive social image of a community-based facility can be an important psychological consideration in planning day care.

Problems in Evaluating Day Care

If adult day care is to take its full place in the continuum of health and social service programmes available to the elderly, then the effectiveness of the day care programme in attaining its objectives must be established. In the United States the importance of demonstrating programme effectiveness has been recognised to the extent that all federally funded day care demonstration projects must include an evaluation component.

However, the very nature of the day care programme itself makes any rigorous evaluation difficult if not impossible. A number of factors contribute to these difficulties in evaluation (Cicirelli and Browne, 1983; Weiler and Rathbone-McCuan, 1978). These include problems in finding an appropriate comparison or control group, small sample size and sample attrition, lack of suitable measuring instruments, wide range of client characteristics, lack of a clearly defined and standardised 'treatment' for all clients and varying degrees of client participation in the day care programme.

An ideal evaluation design involves the random assignment of potential programme participants into two groups, one receiving the programme and a control group which does not. Both are measured on outcome variables both before and after the experimental group receives the day care 'treatment'. Comparison of change for these two groups provides a test of the effectiveness of the programme. However, it is difficult to implement such a design in practice.

Few centres have waiting lists of potential day care users from which treatment and control groups can be randomly selected. Even when a random assignment can be made, not all of the experimental group actually enters day care since a sizeable percentage of the group typically decides not to go or drops out after only a few sessions. Thus, the remaining day care group is biased in some way due to this self-selection. In the case of control group clients, many go on to make other care arrangements over the course of the study. This means that the day care programme is being compared against a variety of other care arrangements, and makes any findings difficult to interpret. If day care or other services are withheld from potential users for the purpose of research, there is likely to be a negative effect, if indeed such a step can be justified on ethical grounds.

An attempt to find a suitable control group in the community through matching control group members with day care participants on certain key variables may be exceedingly difficult to do and result in groups which are biased on characteristics other than those used for matching. Some studies simply compare groups receiving various care alternatives, such as day care, home health care, alternative living services, nursing homes or family care (for example, Skellie and Coan, 1980; Weissert, Wan and Livieratos, 1980).

However, such groups differ at the outset in the degree to which their members are sick, frail or impaired; they may differ in other characteristics as well. For such reasons, one cannot consider such care alternatives as simple alternatives to one another. An elderly person may be able to profit from day care, yet not require either the intermediate or skilled nursing care found in an institution. Arling, Harkins and Romaniuk (1984) compared nursing home applicants with elderly who were already in day care in Virginia. Although the two groups were similar in most demographic characteristics, number and types of diseases and mental status, those seeking admission to nursing homes were distinguished by lower socioeconomic status, lack of a family care-giver, a greater degree of physical disability and sensory impairment and greater use of in-home and hospital services. This study clearly illustrates the difficulty of making valid comparisons between such groups.

An alternative to evaluation studies involving comparison or control groups uses day care participants as their own controls. This approach consists of measuring the participants before they begin the day care treatment and at intervals thereafter. If client change is observed with respect to the original or baseline measure, the change is typically associated with the day care experience. However, unless day care is subsequently withheld from the participants for a period of time and the measures are observed to return to baseline levels, one cannot rigorously infer that day care is the cause of the observed change.

In the practical situation, it is impossible as well as unethical to withhold day care from clients simply for purposes of evaluation. In any event, one cannot know just how much the day care clients might have changed spontaneously over the same period of time if they had not had day care. A further complication of evaluation studies of this type is that a true baseline measure cannot be obtained unless the evaluation is planned and instituted at the time the centre is established and clients first enter; yet the programme may still be in the formative stages at that time. If the desired changes are not detected, it may only be the result of a day care programme which was poorly implemented in its early stages.

Day care programmes themselves tend to be unstandardised and changing; frequently they are individualised for each client. This makes the 'treatment' difficult to specify or to hold constant over a long period of time for purposes of evaluation.

Measurement of change in the elderly is at best problematic. It is difficult, if not impossible, to find instruments which are capable of repeated administration and which are sensitive to change. Also, if there are cognitively impaired clients at the centre, instruments which are suitable for cognitively intact clients may be inappropriate or unusable for those with cognitive impairment. Use of ratings by staff members can be helpful since all clients can be rated, but rating instruments are subject to known problems of reliability and validity. Where direct testing or interviewing of clients is planned, clients may be unco-operative or unresponsive, or they may have hearing, visual or memory problems which make it impossible to validly administer a given test or self-report instrument.

Finally, most day care centres serve only a small number of clients and these clients attend for varying periods of time each day and for varying numbers of days each week. Thus, there is great difficulty in obtaining a large enough sample to apply statistical procedures which might otherwise be employed to deal with some of the variable conditions of the study.

Similar difficulties are encountered when attempts are made to evaluate outcomes over a larger number of centres. Unless a rigorous evaluation can be made at the centre level, amassing the results over several centres will not provide a valid overall evaluation. (Few existing evaluation studies provide results in a form suitable for the calculation of effect sizes so that techniques of meta-analysis can be applied. However, advanced analytical techniques would not compensate for the basic flaws in day care evaluation studies.)

In spite of the fact that day care evaluation studies have major inherent methodological difficulties, the little that is known about the effects of day care comes from such studies. Therefore, when such material is presented in this chapter, it is with the recognition that the findings are at best tentative. In the absence of more rigorous studies, these findings provide at least some indications of what happens when elderly people receive day care.

Costs of Day Care

A frequent argument advanced by proponents of day care is that it reduces costs of care for the elderly by postponing or substituting for the presumably more costly nursing home care. A number of studies have evaluated cost hypotheses, with the most extensive research into day care costs in the United States carried out by Weissert and co-workers (Weissert, 1976, 1978; Weissert, Wan and Livieratos, 1980; Weissert, Wan, Livierators and Katz, 1980; Weissert, Wan, Livieratos and Pellegrino, 1980). These studies first investigated 10 sites which had ongoing day care programmes involving approximately 300 elderly, and later studied approximately 1,900 elderly in a variety of projects. In the earlier study, costs of day care were compared to nursing home costs. In general, Weissert found that daily costs of day care exceeded those of nursing home care, but when data were corrected for the fact that day care clients used fewer days of care over the same period than did nursing home patients, a net savings of about 35 per cent of the cost of nursing home care could be realised by keeping patients in day care.

Critics attacked Weissert's findings from two sides, arguing on the one hand that Weissert's average day care cost was too high due to the inclusion of one centre with extremely high costs (reflecting a heavy emphasis on medical/physical rehabilitation), and arguing, on the other hand, that Weissert overestimated nursing home costs and underestimated the true costs of all care for the individual in day care (for example, Grimaldi, 1979). It is not relevant to this chapter to review the argument regarding costs. The point to be made is that day care cannot properly be regarded as a simple and less expensive substitute for intermediate or skilled nursing home care. In fact, day care and nursing homes do not serve comparable populations (in spite of the fact that day care clients may be deemed eligible for other facilities), and they provide different types of care. Grimaldi regards day care as an 'add-on' rather than a substitute for other types of care. As such, it should be justified on the basis of its contribution to the health, well-being and quality of life of its elderly clients.

Cost-effectiveness (or cost-benefits) studies of different types were carried out by a number of investigators (for example, Holmes and Hudson, 1975; On Lok, 1975; Rathbone-McCuan, Lohn, Levenson, *et al.*, 1975; von Behren, 1979; Weiler, Kim and Pickard, 1976; Weissert, Wan and Livieratos, 1980; Weissert, Wan, Livieratos and Katz, 1980; Weissert, Wan, Livieratos and Pellegrino, 1980).

Ideally, one would hope that the demonstrated benefits of day care would outweigh the costs of the programme, and that day care would prove to be more effective than alternative programmes in attaining certain desired outcomes and at less cost. However, findings of these studies were equivocal. In regard to costs, some of these studies found day care to be more expensive and others found it to be less expensive than alternative methods of care. Again, there were questions regarding comparability of populations in the different programmes, which costs should properly be included in making a comparison, which time periods should be compared and the representativeness of the sites selected for study. Most studies appeared to show some benefits from day care, in the form of improved functioning or feelings of well-being and contentment. However, the size of benefits decreased substantially when differences in demographic characteristics, health and care utilisation rates between elderly in alternative programmes were controlled statistically. Thus, the cost-effectiveness of day care is still far from settled.

The effect of day care on the participants' health and physical functioning, psychological and social functioning, and on family care-givers will be considered in the following sections of this chapter.

Effects on Health and Physical Functioning

Most evaluations of adult day care have attempted to determine the impact of the day care programme on the health and physical functioning of the day care clients. While some positive effects have been reported, the majority of findings have been equivocal. In the Weissert studies (Weissert, Wan and Livieratos, 1980; Weissert, Wan, Livieratos and Katz, 1980), the initial analysis indicated that day care users had improved functioning in activities of daily living, increased likelihood of survival and lowered likelihood of institutionalisation.

However, when effects of other variables were removed in multivariate analyses, the impact detected in the preliminary analysis did not hold up. At best, the impact of adult day care on clients' physical functioning appears limited (Palmer, 1985). Other studies showing little effect were those of Weiler *et al.* (1976), the On Lok project (On Lok, 1975) and Rathbone-McCuan *et al.* (1975). A recent two-year longitudinal study of adult day care in Canada (Chappell and Blandford, 1983) found no effects on survival or on medical claims and use of hospital services. By contrast, von Behren (1979) found some evidence of both maintenance and improvement of functional status.

Other studies (Cowen, 1971; Novicks, King and Spaulding, 1976) found that day care was effective in achieving certain short-term therapeutic goals. One can conclude from all this that where effects of adult day care on clients' physical functioning can be demonstrated they seem to occur early in the day care experience, after which the effects dissipate with time. Whether day care helps to maintain the functioning of elderly clients is difficult to demonstrate since one does not know what the trajectory of such patients might have been without day care. Although patients' families report client improvement in day care, it may be that they overestimate any effects since their own stress is reduced (McIntyre and Brink, 1983).

Effects on Psychosocial and Social Functioning

The most consistent positive effects of adult day care on its elderly clients are found in the area of psychological and social functioning. Weissert, Wan and Livieratos (1980) found that day care led to enhanced feelings of mental well-being and contentment among day care clients. Weiler *et al.* (1976) found that day care clients had improved emotional functioning and interpersonal relationships with family; von Behren (1979) found a decrease in depressive symptoms; Rathbone-McCuan (Weiler and Rathbone-McCuan, 1978) found greater involvement in family-related social roles. Chappell and Blandford (1983) found that day care was associated with increased life satisfaction, greater social integration, and increased participation in activities.

Demented elderly persons, too, were observed to show some improvements in the social area (Greene, 1984; Greene, Timbury, Smith *et al.*, 1984). Day care clients showed less agitation, less pacing and wandering, and more appropriate responses to social situations (Mace and Rabins, 1984a). In addition, they formed stable friendships with other clients and indicated that they were happy to be in day care. Interviews with care-givers (Cicirelli and Browne, 1984) revealed that many of these improvements also extended to the home environment.

Psychogeriatric day care serves elderly with such diagnoses as schizophrenia, affective psychoses, neurotic disorders, organic psychotic conditions and paranoid psychosis. Such elderly are recognised as chronically mentally ill and a high percentage has a history of previous hospitalisation for psychiatric treatment (Rinehart, 1984). While real improvement in long-standing mental problems is unlikely, one measure of success is the ability to maintain such clients in the community with the help of day care. Rinehart reported that about half the elderly enrolled attended day care consistently for a year or more. Somewhat similar figures have been reported by others (Mace and Rabins, 1984a). The British day hospitals, by contrast, attempt to treat more severely mentally ill elderly; once behaviour has stabilised, they are transferred to day centres to receive social support during maintenance in the community. About 50 per cent of the patients in the day hospitals are discharged as improved (Nusberg, 1984). However, many patients become dependent on the day hospital and tend to become permanent clients (Arie, 1975). Indeed, such dependency may be true of the day care population in general. Barresi and McConnell (1984) observed that dependency can create a condition whereby the elderly in day care have fewer worries, less emotional disturbance and a better outlook on life, but at the same time seem disoriented and out of touch with regard to everyday matters. However, it is not known whether day care fosters such dependency or simply attracts more dependent individuals.

If day care can be said to be a clear success, it is in the area of creating an improved quality of life for its elderly clients. Day care clients themselves seem to recognise this. When interviewed about their day care experience, social stimulation provided at the centre was regarded as the single most valuable aspect of the adult day care programme (Cicirelli and Browne, 1983, 1984).

Effects on Family Care-givers

Although a major objective of adult day care is to provide respite and support to the home care-giver, little research into the effects of day care on the family care-giver has been carried out. Reduced stress on the family care-giver was noted by McIntyre and Brink (1983) and by Mace and Rabins (1984a). Cicirelli and Browne (1984) reported on a more detailed interview of two groups of family care-givers: those caring for clients with dementia and those caring for clients with physical problems but without mental impairment. Both groups of clients reported experiencing many behaviour problems and care problems with clients at home. These problems were greater for care-givers of the demented; they also experienced a greater sense of burden.

Day care provided both groups of care-givers with some respite from care-giving, increased opportunity for work or for other activities and increased peace of mind knowing that the client was well cared for during the day. Some reported a sense of emotional release during the period when the client was in day care. Both groups reported that as a result of day care they felt in a better emotional state, felt better about themselves and found more time for housework and chores as well as for recreation and leisure.

Care-givers of clients with physical problems felt, in general, that day care had a more positive impact on their own lives than did care-givers of demented elderly. With regard to the effects of day care on the clients, care-givers of both groups reported that clients liked day care and looked forward to going (after an initial adjustment period when they resisted going). Care-givers felt that clients benefited from the day care programme, particularly from the social stimulation. They reported that clients were more active at home, were more relaxed, were in a better mood, slept better at night and increased social conversation with the family. Thus day care appears to produce changes which transfer to the home environment. Family care-givers, for their part, seemed to be committed to continue caring for the client at home with the help of day care. Although family care-givers did not rule out the prospect of eventual institutionalisation, it appears that day care is a viable alternative to institutional care for these family care-givers in the foreseeable future.

Although studies in the United States have generally found day care to have positive effects on care-givers, studies in Britain have yielded mixed findings. Levin, Sinclair and Gorbach (1984) found that day care services 'promoted the capacity of the supporters to continue to give care'. Also, improvements in care-givers of dementing elderly were observed to accompany therapeutic day care intervention with day care clients (Greene, 1984; Greene *et al.*, 1984). On the other hand, Newbigging (1981) found no relationship between frequency of day hospital attendance and care-giver morale. Similarly, Gilhooly (1984) found no relationship between day hospital care and care-giver well-being; this was surprising since most care-givers considered day care to be a great source of help. However, Gilhooly identified a variety of factors mediating this relationship as well as influencing care-giver preferences for institutional care (Gilhooly, in press), indicating that determining effects of day care on care-givers may be a more complex task than previously thought.

Obviously, as McIntyre and Brink (1983) suggest, care-givers may overestimate the positive benefits of adult day care for the client as well as themselves as the result of the reduction in stress which they feel. Since they have made the commitment to keep the client in day care, it is expected that care-givers would see more positive benefits in order to justify their decision. Nevertheless, it is important in itself that care-givers experienced less care-giving stress and perceived day care as offering positive benefits for them and the day care clients. Most elderly and their families regard family care as the most appropriate type of care and prefer to continue it for as long as possible. Other care-givers cannot offer either the extensiveness or quality of care given by a close family member (Johnson, 1979). Within such a family situation, day care is for many families a 'last-ditch effort' to keep the elderly person at home and avoid institutionalisation (Rathbone-McCuan, 1976). Thus, the extent to which family members feel that day care enables them to sustain their home care-giving roles is an important consideration in the continuation of such care.

Conclusions and Recommendations

Adult day care is a unique institution in the long-term care continuum because it appears to be able to satisfy so many different needs and objectives. It serves needs for short-term rehabilitative care as well as for long-term supportive care; it provides intellectual and social stimulation as well as satisfaction of dependency needs; it provides a therapeutic programme for the individual at the same time that it maximises the right of the individual to self-determination in the selection of activities and to be treated with respect and dignity; it frequently offers hours and days of attendance which are suited to client and family needs (at least in the United States); it offers respite to the family care-giver at the same time that it allows the client to keep family and community identity. Unless one takes the trouble to become familiar with the many types and aspects of day care and the great variety of programmes and activities which are available, it is difficult to appreciate the flexibility of the institution of day care in meeting so many needs.

To carry out so many objectives, it is essential for a day care centre to assemble both knowledgeable and dedicated staff who can relate to clients with sincere interest and concern. Because the day care centre works to promote the maximum possible independence and growth of the individual, there is a positive atmosphere and sense of hope about it which is communicated to staff. According to Peace (1984), day care enhances staff morale, because staff members experience a sense of progress in their patients' well-being. Most day care centres report at least some short-term improvement in physical and mental status. If, after a long stay in day care, the client ultimately declines in functioning, the same client may still be experiencing social gains through activities at the centre. Day care administrators can work to foster this kind of positive atmosphere and good staff morale by encouraging the recognition of client gains and planning activities designed to bring about such gains.

Psychologists or psychiatrists working with elderly clients in day care can provide more than specific therapy sessions; they can also make use of the general therapeutic value of the programme activities and social stimulation at the centre. (A depressed client can be encouraged to participate in activities which will increase interaction with others and a sense of purpose, for example.)

Continuity of care for the client is very important. To this end, client and staff transfers should be avoided as much as possible. Such changes disrupt the delicate social milieu at the centre. When social relationships with staff and peers at the centre are broken, they are not quickly replaced.

Integrated adult day care centres are flexible institutions serving a broad purpose; they have the ability to care for clients with physical illnesses and impairments, dementia, psychiatric problems and social isolation. However, there may be groups of clients whose needs in a particular area are so acute or whose behaviours are so difficult or disruptive that they cannot be cared for in an integrated setting. For such clients, centres specialising in the care of a specific type of client are needed; for instance, specialised day care for elderly with dementia.

One way in which day care can be made more effective is to work toward greater integration of services for client and family in order to maximise the transfer of gains from centre to the home environment. There is a need for frequent and open communication between care-giver and centre so that both can be aware of the client's needs, problems and best means of treatment. Centres also need to determine what other services the care-giver requires in order to continue to care for the client at home. Such services might either be provided to the care-giver by the centre or the care-giver might be referred to another existing service. To this end, efforts should continue to develop a well-integrated system of long-term care services to the elderly and their care-givers; adult day care services within such a system can more easily work to achieve optimal outcomes for the elderly day care clients.

References

Arie, T. (1975) 'Day Care in Geriatric Psychiatry', *Gerontologia Clinica, 17*, pp. 31–9

Arling, G., Harkins, E.B. and Romaniuk, M. (1984) 'Adult Day Care and the Nursing Home: The Appropriateness of Care in Alternative Settings', *Research on Aging, 6*, pp. 225–42

Barresi, C.M. and McConnell, D.J. (1984) 'Discriminators of Adult Day Care Participation Among Impaired Elderly', paper presented at the 37th Annual Scientific Meeting of the Gerontological Society of America, San Antonio, TX, November

Brocklehurst, J.C. (1970) *The Geriatric Day Hospital*, King Edward's Hospital Fund, London

Cantor, M.H. (1975) 'Life Space and Social Support System of Inner City Elderly of New York, *Gerontologist, 45*, pp. 23–7

Chappell, N.L. and Blandford, A. (1983) 'Adult Day Care: Its Impact on the Utilization of Other Health Care Services and on Quality of Life', paper presented at the 36th Annual Scientific Meeting of the Gerontological Society of America, San Francisco, CA, November

Cicirelli, V.G. and Browne, E. (1983) 'A Model for the Evaluation of Adult Day Care report to the Gerontological Society of America, Washington DC, September

——— (1984) 'A Continuing Evaluation of Older Adult Day Care: Longitudinal Evaluation of Day Care Clients and Assessment of Family Caregiver's Views', report to the Gerontological Society of America, Washington DC, September

Clark, A. (1982) 'Planning for Adult Day Care Within a Continuum of Long-term-care Services' in C.L. O'Brien (ed.), *Adult Day Care: A Practical Guide*, Wadsworth, Monterrey, CA, pp. 36–68

Cowen, L. (1971) 'Achievement of Specific Treatment Goals Through Day Hospital', *Psychological Reports, 29*, p. 1206

Dix, G. (1982) 'Implementation' in C.L. O'Brien (ed.), *Adult Day Care: A Practical Guide*, Wadsworth, Monterrey, CA, pp. 266–304

Gibson, M.J. (1984) 'Family Support Patterns, Policies and Programs' in C. Nusberg (ed.), *Innovative Aging Programs Abroad: Implications for the United States*, Greenwood Press, Westport, CT, pp. 159–95

Gilhooly, M.L.M. (1984) 'The Impact of Care-giving on Caregivers: Factors Associated with the Psychological Well-being of People Supporting a Dementing Relative in the Community', *British Journal of Medical Psychology, 57*, pp. 35–44

——— (in press) 'Senile Dementia: Factors Associated with Caregivers' Preference for Institutional Care', *British Journal of Medical Psychology*

Goupille, V.T. (1982) 'British Geriatric Day Hospitals: Implications for America' in C.L. O'Brien (ed.), *Adult Day Care: A Practical Guide*, Wadsworth, Monterrey, CA, pp. 181–94

Greene, J.G. (1984) 'The Evaluation of Reality Orientation' in I.G. Hanley and J. Hodge (eds), *Psychological Approaches to the Care of the Elderly*, Croom Helm, London/Methuen, New York

——— and Timbury, G.C. (1979) 'A Geriatric Psychiatry Day Hospital Service: A Five-year Review', *Age and Ageing, 8*, pp. 49–53

——— Timbury, G.C., Smith, R. *et al.* (1984) 'Reality Orientation with Elderly Patients in the Community', *Age and Ageing, 12*, pp. 38–43

Grimaldi, P.L. (1979) 'The Costs of Adult Day Care and Nursing Home Care: A Dissenting View', *Inquiry, 16*, pp. 162–5

Holmes, D. and Hudson, E. (1975) *Evaluation Report of the Moshulo-Montefiore Day Care Center*, Community Research Applications Inc, New York

Johnson, C. (1979) 'Impediments to Family Supports to Dependent Elderly: An Analysis of the Primary Caregivers', paper presented at the 32nd Annual Scientific Meeting of the Gerontological Society of America, Washington DC, November

Kahana, E. and Midlarsky, E. (1983) 'The Elderly Helper', paper presented at the 36th Annual Scientific Meeting of the Gerontological Society of America, San Francisco, CA, November

Kane, R.L. and Kane, R.A. (1980) 'Alternatives to Institutional Care of the Elderly: Beyond the Dichotomy', *Gerontologist, 20*, pp. 249–59

Lawton, M.P. (1980) 'Psychosocial and Environmental Approaches to the Care of Senile

Dementia Patients', in J.O. Cole and J.E. Barrett (eds), *Psychopathology in the Aged*, Raven Press, New York, pp. 265–78

Levin, E., Sinclair, I.I. and Gorbach, P. (1984) *The Supporters of Confused Elderly Persons at Home. Extract from the Main Report*, National Institute for Social Work, London

Mace, N.L. and Rabins, P.V. (1984a) *A Survey of Day Care for the Demented Adult in the United States*, National Council on the Aging, Washington, DC

——— (1984b) 'Day Care and Dementia', *Generations, 9*, pp. 41–5

McIntyre, E. and Brink, T.L. (1983) 'Families Over-predict Improvement of Elders in Day Care', *Clinical Gerontologist, 1*, pp. 94–5

National Council on the Aging (1984) *Standards for Adult Day Care*, National Council on the Aging Inc, Washington, DC

Newbigging, K. (1981) 'A Ripe Old Age: An Investigation of Relatives of Elderly Dependents with Dementia', report of an inquiry submitted in part fulfilment of requirements for British Psychological Society Diploma in Clinical Psychology

Novicks, L., King, B. and Spaulding, W. (1976) 'The Diabetic Care Unit. I. Development of an Index to Evaluate Diabetic Control', *Canadian Medical Association Journal, 114*, pp. 777–9

Nusberg, C. (1984) 'Health Care' in C. Nusberg (ed.), *Innovative Aging Programs Abroad: Implications for the United States*, Greenwood Press, Wesport, CT, pp. 61–86

O'Brien, C.L. (1982a) 'Program Development' in C.L. O'Brien (ed.), *Adult Day Care: A Practical Guide*, Wadsworth, Monterrey, CA, pp. 233–50

——— (1982b) 'The History of Adult Day-care Programs' in C.L. O'Brien (ed.), *Adult Day Care: A Practical Guide*, Wadsworth, Monterrey, CA, pp. 145–80

On Lok (1975) 'Evaluation Study of On Lok Senior Health Services Demonstration Project', California Department of Health, On Lok Senior Health Services, San Francisco, CA

Palmer, H.C. (1985) 'Adult Day Care' in R.J. Vogel and H.C. Palmer (eds), *Long-term Care: Perspectives from Research and Demonstrations*, Aspen Publications, Rockville, MD, pp. 415–36

Peace, S. (1984) 'Mental Health' in C. Nusberg (ed.), *Innovative Aging Programs Abroad: Implications for the United States*, Greenwood Press, Westport, CT, pp. 87–114

Rathbone-McCuan, E. (1976) 'Geriatric Day Care: A Family Perspective', *Gerontologist, 16*, pp. 517–21

Rathbone-McCuan, E., Lohn, H., Levenson, J. *et al.* (1975) *Cost-effectiveness Evaluation of the Levindale Adult Day Treatment Center*, Levindale Geriatric Center, Baltimore, MD

Rinehart, B.H. (1984) 'Day Care for the Psychogeriatric Population: What Works and for Whom?' paper presented at the 37th Annual Scientific Meeting of the Gerontological Society of America, San Antonio, TX, November

Sands, D. and Suzuki, T. (1983) 'Adult Day Care for Alzheimer's Patients and their Families', *Gerontologist, 23*, pp. 21–3

Skellie, F.A. and Coan, R.E. (1980) 'Community-based Long-term Care and Mortality: Preliminary Findings of Georgia's Alternative Health Services Project', *Gerontologist, 20*, pp. 372–9

von Behren, R. (1979) 'Adult Day Health Services', Final Report, Section 1115, Project No. 11-P-903549/01, California DHS

Weiler, P.G., Kim, P. and Pickard, L.S. (1976) 'Health Care for Elderly Americans: Evaluation of an Adult Day Health Care Model', *Medical Care, 14*, pp. 700–8

Weiler, P.G. and Rathbone-McCuan, E. (1978) *Adult Day Care: Community Work with the Elderly*, Springer, New York

Weissert, W.G. (1976) 'Two Models of Geriatric Day Care: Findings From a Comparative Study', *Gerontologist, 16*, pp. 420–7

——— (1978) 'Costs of Adult Day Care: A Comparison to Nursing Homes', *Inquiry*,

15, pp. 10–19

——— Wan, T.T.H. and Livieratos, B.B. (1980) 'Effects and Costs of Day Care and Homemaker Services for the Chronically Ill: A Randomized Experiment', *NCHSR Research Report Series*, NCHSR, Hyattsville, MD, February

——— and Katz, S. (1980) 'Effects and Costs of Day-care Services for the Chronically Ill', *Medical Care, 18*, pp. 567–84

——— and Pellegrino, J. (1980) 'Cost-effectiveness of Homemaker Services for the Chronically Ill', *Inquiry, 17*, pp. 220–43

6 SELF HELP AND FAMILY SUPPORT GROUPS

Rachel Filinson

The importance of self-help as a social service delivery strategy has become increasingly salient (Gartner and Riessman, 1977; Pancost, Parker and Froland, 1983; Silverman, 1980). Self-help groups have proliferated to reach various populations and fulfil multiple needs. While it is unclear to what extent the elderly have availed themselves of appropriate generic self-help groups, one is in a better position to evaluate the self-help modalities which have evolved specifically for the aged constituency and their families (Hess, 1976). In this chapter, the literature on self-help among the elderly and their families is examined, the diverse models are described and evaluations of the effectiveness of alternative self-help approaches are assessed.

The growth of self-help among the elderly can be attributed to a number of factors. First, the elderly are more at risk than other age groups of succumbing to chronic illnesses for which the chances of rehabilitation and recovery are slim. They seem also more prone to neglect by a medical establishment in which geriatrics has only recently become a specialty. Self-help groups have enabled those afflicted with chronic illness and their families to exchange coping strategies, to educate themselves about the nature and behavioural ramifications of their disease, to bolster their social supports and to mobilise politically in demands for funding of research and care.

Second, the elderly, due to limited resources and a determination to remain independent, tend to shun seeking formal medical and social assistance to the full extent of their needs. In particular, the elderly have been found to be resistant to traditional forms of mental health care delivery (Szwabo and Thale, 1983), although they are more vulnerable to depression and suicide than younger cohorts. Self-help groups, with the alliance of professionals, have been an inexpensive and flexible means of training in behaviour modification, problem-solving and self-care techniques outside a conventional health care setting. In addition, group activities have had therapeutic effects through the build-up of self-esteem and an enlargement of social networks of the involved individuals.

Third, the contribution of the family to the well-being and care of the elderly has been thoroughly documented, but the number of elderly who can continue to rely on this source is diminishing. The imbalance of an expanding aged population and shrinking care-giving population, the reported loneliness and isolation experienced by many elderly recipients of 'intimacy at a distance' (Ward, 1978), the immense burdens shouldered by many families providing care to an elderly relative (Cantor, 1983) and the lack of family oriented styles of interventions with the elderly (Kuypers and Trute, 1978) reduce the traditional reliance and pose serious problems.

Lopata (1978), for instance, in her study of widows, has argued that in contrast to bereaved women in less-developed countries, such as India, American widows experience a paucity of formal and informal supports because of the fragmented, voluntaristic aspects of modern social organisation. In the same vein, Kamerman (1981) has pointed out that the absence of a deliberate family policy in the United States and the United Kingdom, based on the assumption that government interference would further endanger the already fragile family bonds, has deprived families of the financial and emotional support they need in caring for older relatives. Self-help groups have demonstrated they can fill some of the gaps left by a 'hands-off' family policy practised in a privatising society. Self-help has provided a compensatory social support network for the elderly and as collectivities have been organised for family members of the elderly, they have offered a forum for sharing experience, for working out solutions to care-giving dilemmas and for acquiring information about assistive formal services.

The factors mentioned above — the increasing number of chronic diseases; disillusionment with bureaucratised medical and social service systems; the declining availability of formal service under conditions of fiscal austerity; and a desire to recreate a lost sense of community in an alienating society — have fostered the development of self-help groups for the non-elderly as well (Wollert and Barron, 1983). Nevertheless, these forces are of particular relevance to the elderly who find themselves in a kind of social vacuum due to a succession of crucial losses. In addition, there is evidence that age segregation promotes informal support among the elderly (Ward, 1979). Hence, although the needs of the elderly are similar to those of other subgroups in the general population in many respects, the effectiveness of self-help groups may be heightened by the age congruence of its members.

Self-help is defined very broadly for the purposes of this paper, incorporating overlapping concepts of self-enrichment, mutual help and peer support. It will not be limited exclusively to formally organised, self-sufficient groups with purely grass roots origins but will refer as well to groups facilitated and organised by professionals, informal mutual help networks, educational self-care initiatives and non-reciprocated assistance to aged peers by the elderly themselves. The decision to define self-help in the broadest possible terms as active engagement by elderly to improve the quality of their lives and the lives of other elderly persons stems from the diffuse and complex character of this phenomenon. First, evidence pointing to the relative significance of informal support systems in sustaining the elderly in the community (Wenger, 1982) precludes a focus on only formal self-help strategies as it would mean that neglect of the predominant pattern of assistance among the elderly.

Second, many self-help groups serving the elderly, while independent of institutional support, have originated under professional auspices. Thus, to differentiate groups according to the presence or absence of professional involvement makes administrative but not sociological sense. Third, on the assumptions that the elderly cannot profit from educational experiences in later life (Owen, 1981), cannot function in the psychotherapeutic milieu of a group (Cohen, 1984) and cannot add on to their social networks to the same degree as younger age groups (Lakin, Bremer and Oppenheimer, 1983), even with professional intervention, self-care educational programmes and other professionally led groups have been deemed inapplicable for the elderly. Evidence, to be reviewed in this paper, shows that elderly can effectively participate in educational programmes. While such groups are typically not signified by self-help in the vernacular, particularly when there is a professional leader, many do have a self-help component in that they attempt to teach skills and techniques which enable greater self-reliance and independence. Furthermore, in content and format, many of these groups come close to the mutual-help support group model used in elderly self-help groups.

Finally, it has been argued that the formation of the elderly as a crucial subgroup of the electorate has transformed them into welfare clientele. The dependent status of this group is exacerbated by limited participation of the elderly in the planning and implementation of aging policy (Schram, 1979). Contrary to this opinion, the elderly have not been solely the recipients of assistance determined and provided by formal or non-elderly informal sources (Bowles, 1976). By considering the aid provided by aged peers to the elderly as a form of self-help, it is intended to legitimise the view of the elderly as benefactors, not only as beneficiaries of help. Consequently, the definition of self-help has been stretched to signify help provided by a group (the aged) for consumption within the same group, rather than self-help on an individual basis only.

This chapter is organised into four sections, reflecting four basic types of self-help. As will be shown, these types of self-help can be used coterminously and do sometimes merge in their features. In the first section, support groups and educational self-care groups for the elderly are discussed. Since many groups function in both an educational and social support capacity, it is not feasible to consider these groups separately. The second section focuses on self-help techniques directed toward families caring for dependent relatives. As family members typically play an integral role in the care of elderly relatives, areas of common concern which have encouraged self-help groups among the elderly have likewise promoted groups for care-giving relatives. The third section deals with peer counselling and other formally organised support systems of older adults by elderly para-professionals. In the final section, informal and natural helping networks of aged peers are examined.

Self-help and Self-care Groups of the Elderly

In a 1979 review of self-care and self-help groups among the elderly (Butler, Gertman, Oberlander, *et al.*, 1979), it was claimed that there were not many groups specifically geared to the aged. More recently, however, Haber (1983) has reported that the number of gerontological mutual help groups is growing. Haber goes on to suggest that these groups have advantages over traditional professional help in that they provide multifaceted support, offer accessible, reliable, decentralised services, strengthen community networks and bring various perspectives to bear on a problem. A substantial number of informal accounts from participants and professional advisors have corroborated the merits of self-help.

On the negative side, self-help groups have been criticised for diverting attention from larger social issues (Butler *et al.*, 1979). Some observers have warned that inappropriate application of group intervention may be harmful to participants (Lieberman, Yalom and Miles, 1977; Strupp and Hadley, 1977), especially those without adequate psychological defences or accurate expectations (Galinsky and Schopler, 1977). Simons (1984) has cautioned that types of interactants in the social network are not functionally substitutable. Consequently, while groups may enhance positive self-esteem, they cannot compensate for loss of family and friends who are the primary sources of assistance, intimacy and security. Simons' (1984) data reveal, for instance, that group participation of elderly persons without spouses may actually augment feelings of loneliness.

The evidence is not so much contradictory as it reflects the considerable differences among self-help groups and the reliance on clinical reports for assessment of group effectiveness. Groups vary in terms of their scope of organisation, degree and type of professional involvement, structure, goals and targetted populations. Semantics make appraisal of self-help groups even more difficult since groups similar in content or format have been referred to by different names — mutual help group, change group, support group, self-care group and self-help group.

Moreover, short-term subjective assessments of group performance have been more readily available than longitudinal objective evaluations. The bulk of literature on self-help groups has consisted of descriptions of single, locally organised, professionally influenced self-help projects, frequently without an evaluative element altogether. While evaluations are missing or have methodological defects, a meta-analysis of the research must necessarily concentrate more on common themes and process styles across groups than on their comparative effectiveness or long-term consequences. The latter aspects of self-help groups require further investigation before any synthesis is attempted.

Professional involvement in self-help groups of the elderly is a logical starting point in discussing groups since it usually affects other facets of the group such as method of recruitment, setting, duration, group process, thematic content and evaluations of the group. (Groups which have professional impact are also, of course, ones most likely to be reported in published form.) Gwyther (1982) states that self-help groups are not antagonistic to professional commitment but are in fact outright conducive, allowing professionals to expand limited institutional services to the community. The whole process of self-help formation and functioning changes the attitudes of both sides because the group departs from the stigmatising, traditional model in the human services in which clients are regarded as pathological and dependency is fostered by the mode of treatment.

The roles of professionals in the development and maintenance of self-help groups have been multiple. They have identified need (Lucks, 1981), enlisted and screened potential members (Pilisuk and Minkler, 1980), led group sessions (Gray, 1982), prepared educational materials (Nahemow, 1981), arranged programmes (West and Ernst, 1981), acted as consultants for independent groups (Armstrong and Warner, 1982; Office for Senior Citizens and Handicapped, 1981), developed training modules (Butler *et al.*, 1979; Mellor, Rzetelny and Hudis, 1981) and more generally served in an advisory capacity. While all of these functions can and have also been assumed by lay group members, many involved professionals maintain a number of obstacles on the way to disengagement from group activities. Attrition — often regarded as a healthy sign that group members have accomplished their goals and chosen to terminate their membership — hinders group continuity without the cohesive effects of professional input. Furthermore, comparative studies of group processes of young and old age cohorts have indicated that the elderly depend more on the active, directive leadership provided by a professional than their younger counterparts (Richardson and Lowman, 1980; Weiner and Weinstock, 1979).

While the advantages of professional involvement for participants are well-documented, the question of professionalism in dealings with self-help groups remains unsettled. Age bias on the part of professionals can undermine their contribution to the group (Troll and Nowak, 1977). Furthermore, the coverage of potentially distressing topics such as disability and death, and the intrusion of these issues in the smooth running of the group require a professional who has adequately resolved these concerns in private life (Klinger-Vartabedian, 1982; Cooper, 1984). Unfortunately, studies of the effects of professional profiles on groups are not available.

Groups with professional collaboration are often the formal continuation of a professional–client relationship in an ambulatory clinic setting (Reifler and Eisdorfer, 1980), residential setting (Dutro, 1983; Hawkins, 1983) or in hospitals (Weiner and Weinstock, 1979). As a result, the institutions with which professionals are affiliated have become the venue for group meetings. In other cases, although group members are unknown to the professional before start-up of the group, they have been contacted through community agencies, churches (West and Ernst, 1981; Haber, 1983), senior centres (Feldman, 1982; Lakin *et al.*, 1983) or other organised groups (Jackson, 1980; Zgliczynski, 1982). In effect, members are not representative of the elderly population and are more likely to be self-selected individuals who are open to group involvement and professional assistance.

The description of an unsuccessful endeavour to initiate a self-help group through professional intervention in the Tenderloin district of San Francisco (Pilisuk and Minkler, 1980) clearly illustrates that this strategy cannot be applied in every setting nor for every population. An initial attempt by professionals to form a self-help group of hotel dwellers in the Tenderloin failed despite the common institutional background of the targetted members. Public health nurses were able to stimulate dyadic relationships based on shared interests between hotel residents. An activities club, with many features of a self-help group, eventually emerged from the network of dyads but without professional tutelage.

Some groups described in the literature have restrictions placed on the membership due to the experimental interests of the professional bringing the group together. It is impossible to assess the extent to which research activities of professionals involved in founding groups influence their composition. Available evidence suggests that, in general, self-help groups attract a heterogeneous cross-section of the elderly population in terms of race, income, occupation and education. Groups tend to be predominantly female, reflecting the unbalanced sex ratio in older age.

In professionally established groups, the trend has been towards a time-limited structure, with an orientation to accomplish agreed upon goals over a set time period. Self-perpetuating groups, which are often spin-offs from groups formed by professionals, are more likely to have open, revolving membership and their direction and focus change as group composition alters. Groups intended to provide sharing and mutual support in regular sessions — whether professionally led or not — tend to have limited membership to optimise interaction.

The main source of variety among professionally led groups of the elderly are the approaches applied. Evidence suggests that older adults can profit from group work as they have been seen to be more willing to use group processes, to share experiences with other group members and to act as positive reinforcers to other group members (Lakin *et al.*, 1983; Richardson and Lowman, 1980). Some groups with professional leadership have utilised psychotherapeutic techniques including role play, life review, remotivation and reminiscence (Szwabo and Thale, 1983) to address the mental health needs of the group. However, psychotherapeutic group methods have required some modification to accommodate elderly participants. Therapy is offered at a slower pace, behavioural rather than insight-oriented therapy is emphasised (Richman, 1979), active leadership is provided and, in general, a less psychologically sophisticated framework is used.

SAGE (Senior Actualisation and Growth Encounter) is one of the best known examples of a psychotherapeutic group programme for the elderly. As with many programmes in the psychotherapeutic mode, it does not fit easily into the classical self-help mould because of extensive professional involvement and the didactic nature of the group. The organisation was started by a care-giver who had discovered techniques that helped her cope with her aged mother. The group has been developed by lay and professional workers with the assistance of various grants. Therapy consists of a mixture of procedures and activities including 'group therapy, encounter groups, Zen, biofeedback, meditation, and various physical programs' (Lieberman and Gorash, 1979, pp. 283–4) with relaxation components. Meetings are formal, structured and led by professional leaders trained in group methods. Informal relationships between members outside group meetings are encouraged, but their formation is not a central objective of the group.

SAGE, like many groups with psychotherapeutic content, has not been designed only for the relief of psychological stress. It also seeks to tackle the developmental tasks of the latter half of life. These tasks include dealing with physiological decline and one's own mortality, maximising independent functioning and retaining and expanding social networks. Educational approaches, blended with or separate from traditional psychotherapies, have been utilised in self-help groups to accomplish developmental goals. Professionals have played a significant role in the preparation and presentation of educational material.

Instructional methods have been adapted in groups for the elderly to take into account learning strengths and weaknesses in old age (Josephs, 1978). Older adults have been found to learn better when they can pace themselves, when tasks are concrete and meaningful and when conditions for learning are not threatening (West and Ernst, 1981). They are also more likely than younger age groups to externalise their problems and to believe they cannot change their environments. Consequently, the lecture-style format is inadequate for elderly self-help groups in most areas and when applied, has to be supplemented with approaches that provide environmental incentives for learning. In other words, the learning capacity of the elderly has to be capitalised upon in relation to the setting in which they function. Educational techniques used in older groups tend, as a result, to feature simulation of problem-solving skills rather than merely the transmission of topical information (Petersen, 1979).

It should not be thought that the application of psychotherapeutic and or didactic approaches characterise the majority of self-help groups or of group sessions, though accounts of it saturate the literature in the area. Many groups or group sessions are devoted to the sharing of experience, the development of *affinal* bonds between group members, the exchange of information and the offerings of mutual support — and in pursuing these goals, they do not follow any recognised techniques in psychotherapy or education. These informal and spontaneous activities constitute the backbone of the self-help movement, in particular, of that portion which has reduced or eliminated professional involvement. Such groups perform psychotherapeutic and educational functions for their participants as well as augment social networks among members in a way that more structured group organisations cannot. Information about this faction of the self-help movement is primarily anecdotal, however.

The approaches used in group activities — whether structured or unstructured — correspond to the main preoccupations of self-help groups for the elderly. Maintaining emotional health, acquiring a positive outlook on ageing, promoting self-sufficiency and enlarging social networks have been cited as the major underlying objectives of self-help groups for the aged. Against the background of these general goals, self-help groups have handled a broad array of issues narrower in scope. The focus ranges from grief (Parkes and Weiss, 1983, p. 250; Ray, 1983), health promotion (Craven, 1984; Harper, 1980; Rainey, 1980; Washington University, 1982) and life-threatening illnesses (McCarthy, 1980) to citizen participation (Jackson, 1980), food delivery for elderly (Lidoff and Abbott, 1983; Pilisuk and Minkler, 1980) and unemployment and retirement (Gray, 1982; Pearce, 1978). Self-help groups have displayed immense creativity in diversifying their strategies to effectively address specific issues. Telephone therapy, utilising a conference call system, for example, has enabled blind elderly to participate in self-help groups (Evans and Jaureguy, 1982), while groups serving widows have relied on a one-to-one outreach of group representatives to the newly bereaved before integrating initiates into small, homogeneous discussion groups and plenary, educational sessions (Lucks, 1981).

Rigorous evaluative studies can be applied essentially only to groups which have delineated concrete and well-defined problems. Assessment consists of an examination of changes in stated objectives which can be ascribed to the influence of group experience. The typical evaluation scheme is an experimental design in which standardised tests are administered before and after group participation to measure the changes in the dependent variable and group impact is assessed by comparisons with a control group. Variables measured are as diverse as self-help group goals.

Researchers have investigated the effects of group participation on health status, health care utilisation, morale, locus of control, sociability, execution of daily functions, employment and knowledge of and attitudes toward ageing. Findings from experimental studies have been mixed and are not as uniformly favourable as those obtained from concomitant subjective evaluations by participants, leaders and observers. Evaluative studies, while limited to professionally led, time-limited groups with clear-cut goals have a more general significance by identifying what aims can be considered achievable in a group setting. The studies also clarify under what conditions positive changes can be expected. An assessment of SAGE, for instance (Lieberman and Gourash, 1979), revealed that the group did not stimulate new relationships nor were far-reaching changes in attitudes about health and illness attained. The researchers conclude that groups for the elderly may be unrealistic if, like SAGE, they strike for further growth among older adults instead of concentrating on adaptation to the inevitable cognitive, physical and social losses accompanying old age.

To reiterate, because of the fluidity of self-help groups and their idiosyncratic character, an analysis at present could hardly result in generalisable conclusions. Since groups have been adapted to suit local community conditions and specific populations, it may not be valid to extrapolate findings from the evaluative studies so far reported and apply them to other settings. The overall impression derived from those studies is instructive, however, in that it underlines the important contribution professionals can make at all levels of group operation, although professional involvement and self-help are conventionally viewed as mutually exclusive. Moreover, while certain goals of a general nature have repeatedly emerged among self-help groups, it appears that the type of problems that can be addressed by the self-help strategy is limitless.

Self-help Groups for Care-givers

Support groups for care-givers indirectly serve the same purpose as groups for the elderly, that is, sustaining and enriching the lives of independent older adults. Their mission is to relieve care-givers of some of the burden they carry in order to fortify supporters in their care-giving efforts and prolong the period of informal care. In this way, they enable the elderly to remain in the non-institutional settings they prefer. (Support groups have also been formed for care-givers of the institutionalised elderly.)

The parallels between these two kinds of groups (care-givers and groups for the elderly) extend to their central themes, organisation and professional collaboration. The therapeutic and educational objectives of support groups for care-givers overlap in many areas with those of self-help groups for the elderly (see, for example, the description by Brahce, Silverman and Leon, 1981, of the 'As Parents Grow Older' programme). Group participants become acquainted with the ageing process, learn problem-solving and stress management techniques, acquire information on formal supportive services, share common experiences and gain social contacts through group membership (Cohen, 1983; Mellor *et al.*, 1981). The approaches are equally eclectic, ranging from professionally facilitated topical presentations, group counselling and instruction in applied skills to informal, unstructured cathartic discussion sessions. The impetus for the formation of care-giver support groups, as with self-help groups for the elderly, has often come from professionals who have organised groups (cf. Fuller, Ward, Evans *et al.*, 1979; Hammond and Bonney, 1983; Orr, 1982; Sanchez, 1984), trained facilitators for groups (Rzetelny and Mellor, 1981), and provided other types of assistance. In the Natural Supports System, for example, community agencies conducted a needs assessment, developed support group models in response to consumer demand and implemented programmes corresponding with the needs and demands of local populations (Buchsbaum and Sainer, 1981). The trend for such professionally led programmes has been towards task-oriented, time limited, short-term groups which later evolve into self-help groups (Hudis and Buchsbaum, 1981; Safford, 1980).

Support groups for care-givers depart from self-help groups for the elderly in that their focus tends to be on the entire family unit rather than individual group participants. The family orientation manifests itself in a number of ways. First, the issue of family relationships inevitably becomes a central theme in discussions of care-giving. As a result, support groups become conduits for emotional outpouring. Expression of anger towards family members who have relinquished their responsibilities of care, discomfort with inverted parent–child roles and guilt provoked by a desire to be released from care-giving burdens have been frequently observed in support group meetings (Barnes, Raskint, Scott *et al.*, 1981). Family communication patterns and accommodation of unresolved, lingering tensions between care-giver and the dependent older adult have been other recurrent themes. The expressive function of support groups with respect to family relationships appears to predominate on such a scale that researchers have noted the impossibility of conducting purely educational sessions (Streuer and Clark, 1982) due to the disruptive influence of family crises on group meetings (Priddy and Gallagher, 1984). Zarit (1983) has even proposed that, given the sensitive and volatile nature of family relationships, support group candidates should be screened through individual counselling and family meetings.

The family dimension of support groups also enlarges the range of their effects. Support groups have not only brought about favourable changes in the behaviour and attitudes of group participants, but have also contributed to improvements in the behaviour of elderly beneficiaries of care. Some groups emphasise training in techniques which eliminate or contain intolerable behaviours (Haley, 1983; Pinkston and Linsk, 1984). Evidence has indicated that care-giving stress can be predicted by the level of impairment of the aged recipient of care (Castro, 1982). However, evidence is inconsistent on this point. Zarit, Reever and Bach-Peterson (1980), for instance, discovered that behavioural impairment was not a predictor of care-giver burden. Hence diminishing the effects of impairment has been expected to reduce care-giving stress. While the impact of the support group on the elderly person is typically mediated through family members, some innovative groups feature dual sessions for care-givers and their elderly relatives (Aronson, Levin and Lipkowitz, 1984).

The family concerns around which support groups revolve influence their accessibility in a significant way. Paradoxically, the overwhelming family responsibilities which support groups seek to ease are often, by the same token, serious obstacles to group functioning. To accommodate participants with substantial family obligations and enable them to attend meetings, support groups have had to make provisions for respite care (Crossman, London and Barry, 1981). In light of the relative unavailability of respite care, this extra requirement places an undue strain on the viability of care-giver support groups. Moreover, the conflict between group participation and care-giving activities hinders the prospects for lay leadership.

Evaluation of care-giver support groups reflects their familial complexion. Appraisal of support groups has gone beyond their impact on care-giver knowledge of ageing (Johnson and Spence, 1982) and utilization of formal services (George and Gwyther, 1983) to include their effects on family responsibility (Hartford and Parsons, 1982), the quality of the family environment (Lazarus, Stafford, Cooper, *et al.*, 1981), care-giver's burden (Kahan, 1984) and the well-being of the elderly beneficiary (Paley, Axelroth, Bowers, *et al.*, 1982). Assessments of support groups suffer the same methodological flaws as those of self-help groups for the elderly, consisting primarily of case studies that are small-scale experimental designs or subjective accounts (Hausman, 1979). Clark and Rakowski (1983), in a review of literature on care-giving, confirm that the consensus as to the immediate benefits of support groups is derived from methodologically weak studies and point out that the lasting effects have yet to be demonstrated empirically. They conjecture that support groups may prove inadequate in developing the contingency planning and advocacy skills needed to accomplish more long-term goals.

In conclusion, support groups enable members to cope with care-giving via numerous strategies — through enlightened attitudes about ageing and care-giving, through mastery of stress management skills, through enhanced social support networks and through the control of unpleasant behaviours of the dependent older adult. However, their vitality lies primarily in their function as a channel for emotional release, a function which can also hamper group stability. Because of the very enormity of care-giving responsibilities, many care-givers cannot take advantage of the temporary escape that support groups give. Therefore, support groups may have to increasingly offer instrumental as well as expressive assistance to their members to ensure their perpetuity.

Peer Counselling

Peer counselling refers to a wide range of services given by older adults to their aged peers. Peer counsellors are often able to replace professionals in facilitating and leading support groups and educational programmes as well as in counselling on an individualised basis. Indigenous workers have also stimulated projects organised by older adults which were started and continued independently of direct professional or paraprofessional input. In effect, the purposes, approaches and merits of peer counselling are in many respects indistinguishable from those of the self-help groups, described in the preceding sections. Peer counselling has provided accessible and flexible services to meet the continuum of needs of the elderly, in successful cases making the psychotherapeutic and educational dimensions of services offered more palatable to the recipients than the traditional professional approach.

The majority of peer counsellors are trained by professionals before taking on their own clients and group responsibilities. Training is composed of both building a knowledge base on the ageing process, including topics of special interest, and learning pedagogical skills, group dynamics and counselling techniques (Kaye, Monk and Stuen, 1983). Peer counselling instruction is tailored to older students in the same way that educational self-help programmes are modified for older participants (Priddy and Knisely, 1982). The emphasis is on experiential rather than traditional training; in other words, it consists of demonstrating how personal experiences can be utilised to understand ageing tasks and problems and to assist others in coping with them. The anxiety of peer counsellors confronted with the prospect of acquiring new skills and applying them to help others has been decreased by introducing non-threatening session techniques. For example, counsellors are frequently not examined in any formal way at the end of the instructional period (Hoffman, 1983).

Peer counsellors are trained to be non-judgmental, active listeners and to avoid suggesting solutions prematurely. According to Strelow (1982), in a review of training literature, most counsellors are trained according to either the Carkhuff or Ivy model (Bolton and Dignum-Scott, 1979). The first stresses the use of open questioning, paraphrasing and summarising. The latter emphasises self-exploration and role-playing. Apart from counselling techniques and mastering information on specific topics, teaching future peer counsellors to identify problems beyond their capabilities is a major priority of training programmes. Peer counsellors have been instrumental in referring elderly clients for professional help when the need arises.

Peer counsellors are chosen more on the basis of personal than professional skills (Strelow, 1982). Older adults who are well-adjusted, stable and willing to commit themselves for the period of training are typically selected (Priddy and Knisely, 1982). In some cases, former participants of self-help (personal growth) programmes have become peer counsellors under professional supervision (Strelow, 1982). Personal qualities have been important criteria not only to guarantee competence but also to insure a suitable role model for elderly clients. Thus, peer counsellors fulfil another function by exemplifying that older persons can be active, capable, independent and needed by others.

The scope of the peer counsellor's expertise varies considerably. Peer counselling programmes have been founded to deal with specific issues such as nutrition (Shannon, Smiciklas-Wright, Davis, *et al.*. 1983), energy assistance (Luckey, 1982), widowhood (Romaniuk and Priddy, 1980; Silverman, 1970) and memory strengthening (Chenoweth *et al.*, 1980), as well as more general interpersonal problems such as the inability to sustain social contacts (Waters, Fink and White, 1976). The experience of the peer support system on the Turner Geriatric Clinic at the University of Michigan illustrates that peer support counselling concentrated in one area can be easily broadened to address a variety of concerns.

Campbell and Chenoweth (1981) observe that by involving peer counsellors in health-focused educational workshops in Michigan, a point of entry was created for more individualised support services. The original workshops led to requests for one-to-one counselling, spurred the emergence of small support groups and resulted in the compilation of pertinent literature and up-to-date referrals on a number of topics. In the same vein, Becker and Zarit (1978) have noted that peer counsellors at the Andrus Gerontology Center in Los Angeles have expanded their workload to include administration functions, group therapy and 'information and referral' services.

Peer counselling is only one of a number of programmes in which the elderly assist their aged peers. The elderly have been active in telephone reassurance, friendly visiting and retirement counselling programmes (Ward, 1978). Numerous papers have been devoted to outlining projects which have utilised elderly indigenous workers. Bokser (1982), for instance, describes a variation of the approach as applied to a crisis intervention project in New York City. Frail, impaired elderly residents of city housing were monitored using a 'buddy concept', with routine daily contact established through a floor captain. With linkage and back-up from community-based ageing services, the peer programme managed to prevent institutionalisation of housing authority residents.

Peer counselling and similar programmes have not been systematically evaluated. As is the case with self-help groups, the informal response of participants is enthusiastic. The benefits seem to accrue to both the recipients of assistance and to the peer counsellors, whose esteem is enhanced by the para-professional role.

To summarise, while peer counselling and other seniors-helping-seniors endeavours do not conform to the standard conceptualisation of self-help, they have been boosters to the self-help movement of the elderly. Indigenous workers have provided the manpower and leadership to organise self-care programmes, support groups and other mutual-help initiatives. Their techniques rely more on shared experiences between aged adults than on orthodox counselling treatment. Self-help groups, in turn, have been a source from which counsellors have been recruited. As peer counsellors have proved to be qualified substitutes for professionals, they have brought service delivery into the hands of the elderly themselves, with favourable results for both counsellor and client.

Informal Mutual Help Networks

Informal networks between elders are believed to be the most pervasive, influential and yet least visible forms of mutual help. Smithers (1981), in a qualitative investigation of a high-rise public housing retirement facility, discovered that supportive help between elderly residents was substantial but surrounded by secrecy. Networks, Smithers asserts, are defended against community intruders. Glimpses into these hidden networks have been afforded by but a few ethnographic accounts, most notably by Hochschild's (1973) report on the 'unexpected community'.

Informal networks, like other forms of self-help, represent alternatives to professional and bureaucratically administered services which are rejected or inaccessible to the elderly. Wang (1979), for instance, found that self-help was a significant mechanism used to deal with the uncertainties of later life among rural elderly who distrust and consequently underutilise formal services. Similarly, Rosel (1983), in her study of a neighbourhood support, concluded that routinised mutual assistance had arisen between individuals with a shared value of independence from formal assistance and without other sources of informal support.

One encounters the same problem in identifying informal mutual help networks among the elderly as in categorising self-help groups. The boundary between mutual help networks and friendships is a blurred one, yet it is important to distinguish network functioning independently of the affinal bonds between members. Exploration of the nature and extent of peer networks is further complicated by a tendency to focus on the overall social support system of the aged. The inconsistent evidence with respect to the relationship between social support and morale is most likely a result of the lack of differentiation between the various elements of the support network. When sources of support have been linked separately with dependent psychological variables, in some studies peer support has turned out to be a stronger influence on the morale and self-esteem of the elderly person than family interaction (Arling, 1976).

The full value of peer networks depends on how comprehensively they can fulfil the needs of elderly members. It has been a matter of dispute whether social networks are hierarchical and compensatory (Cantor, 1979) or task-specific (Dono, Falbe, Krail, *et al.*, 1979; Litwak and Szelenyi, 1969). In effect, it is unclear whether relatives, who are the first choice for source of assistance, can be substituted by peers when they are unavailable, or whether peers are appropriate for only certain tasks such as responding to emergencies or providing services based on territoriality (Ward, LaGory, Sherman, *et al.*, 1981). The potential utility of informal peer networks, as other forms of self-help, may therefore be circumscribed by culturally set limits on peer obligations in the helping domain.

The informal and spontaneous nature of mutual help networks puts them inside the purview of social engineering. While neighbourhoods are a likely source of mutual assistance, since the elderly are more homebound than other age groups, there is evidence that the elderly do not consistently choose aged neighbours for support and that aged neighbours who provide peer support do not contribute greatly to reported well-being (Ward *et al.*, 1981). Goodman's (1984) study of natural helping among older adults revealed that only one-third of her sample of elderly could be characterised as mutual helpers in relation to their neighbours. These individuals had enduring reciprocal relationships with their neighbours and were regarded as probable beneficiaries of self-help group membership. The remaining two-thirds of the sample were either isolated from their natural neighbourhood support or were 'high helpers' who volunteered to assist their neighbours but shunned assistance in return.

It can be surmised that informal mutual help networks, like other self-help modalities, are characterised by a self-selection process and cannot be propagated simply by age segregation of residential areas. Nevertheless, the existing informal networks have been exploited successfully in hybrid schemes integrating formal and informal resources. The Gofal project, neighbourhood care schemes and 'patch-working' in the United Kingdom have been cited by Grant and Wenger (1983) as three examples where lay care-givers collaborate with professionals to deliver individualised packages of services to elderly. (Informal care-giving in these projects is not confined to that provided by *aged peers* though it is defined as 'self-help'.) The professionals' role is redefined as an enabling and brokerage one through which the latent talents of the natural support network are tapped.

To summarise, informal networks have dependably performed extensive instrumental and expressive functions. Because of age homogeneity, these networks are particularly suited for dealing with the developmental tasks of ageing. Aged peers in informal networks can rehearse the transitions to be confronted in old age, can identify with each other's personal and social losses and exchange more tangible forms of assistance. The informal nature of networks has not precluded professional partnerships in which informal care-giving is interwoven with statutory and volunteer services (Darvill, 1983, pp. 245–6).

Conclusion

In a recent review of mutual self-help groups for the aged in the United States, Borkman (1982) sketches a picture strikingly different from the one delineated above. By pointing out the differences, the main issues covered here will be summarised and set in perspective. Borkman identifies only two mutual self-help groups for the elderly, one being the Grey Panthers, a political advocacy group, and the other bieng a second generation group for older alcoholics stemming from Alcoholics Anonymous. She stipulates that only these groups qualify as mutual self-help groups and must be distinguished from neighbouring self-help phenomena such as do-it-yourself initiatives that lack a mutual aid component, common-interest voluntary organisations and professionally controlled educational programmes with peer support. Further, she argues that the old do not view ageing as a problem and, consequently, the formation of self-help groups for the aged is not warranted. In contrast to these views, it is proposed here that a mutual self-help approach characterises a variety of groups, that the self-help, mutual aid and peer support aspects of groups overlap and can be combined in myriad ways and that professional and para-professional input is more likely to promote than impede the exchange of mutual assistance. Moreover, it is argued that the thesis of age homogeneity as a factor heightening group effectiveness is not tantamount to saying that the aged are all alike and problem-ridden. It suggests rather that ageing is a developmental process and that developmental tasks may be more successfully handled in the company of peers.

While formal evaluations of self-help groups are still lacking, the cumulative expertise in the self-help area has been widely disseminated with excellent results. Furthermore, objective, impartial assessment may not be altogether essential for the self-help strategy. By virtue of being defined and directed by their constituents, self-help groups may be most appropriately evaluated by the subjective accounts of consumers.

Self-help groups for the elderly and their families have flourished as collectivities for social action, personal change and mutual aid. Because they satisfy needs in the least restrictive setting possible and are cost-effective, they appeal to the elderly, their families and agencies/statutory bodies serving the aged. Given that community care has been shown not to be feasible without adequate social supports, self-help groups, as matrices of social support, are likely to remain an important element in alternatives to institutional care for the elderly.

References

Arling, G. (1976) 'The Elderly Widow and Her Family, Neighbors and Friends', *Journal of Marriage and the Family, 38* (4), pp. 757–68

Armstrong, D. and Warner, P.C. (1982) 'Elder Support Project: An Example of the Formal/Informal Coalition', Franklin/Hampshire Community Mental Health Center, *Journal of Human Services Abstracts, 7* (4) (Eric Document 223822)

Aronson, M.K., Levin, G. and Lipkowitz, R. (1984) 'A Community-based Family/Patient Group Program for Alzheimer's Disease', *The Gerontologist, 24* (4), pp. 339–42

Barnes, R.F., Raskind, M.A., Scott, M. *et al.* (1981) 'Problems of Families Caring for Alzheimer Patients: Use of a Support Group', *Journal of the American Geriatrics Society,*

29 (2), pp. 80–5

Becker, F. and Zarit, S.H. (1978) 'Training Older Adults as Peer Counselors', *Educational Gerontology, 3*, pp. 241–50

Bokser, K. (1982) 'Senior Resident Advisor Program: A First Step in a Continuum of Care', *Journal of Human Services Abstract, 7* (4) (Eric Document 223822)

Bolton, C. and Dignum-Scott, J. (1979) 'Peer Group Advocacy Counseling for the Elderly: A Conceptual Model', *Journal of Gerontological Social Work, 1* (4), pp. 321–31

Borkman, T. (1982) 'Where are Older Persons in Mutual Self-help Groups?' in A. Kolker and P.I. Ahmed (eds.), *Aging*, Elsevier Biomedical, New York, pp. 257–84

Bowles, E. (1976) 'Older Persons as Providers of Services: Three Federal Programs', *Social Policy, 7*, pp. 81–8

Brahce, I., Silverman, A.G. and Leon, J. (1981) 'Altering a Service Delivery System to Improve Family Care of the Elderly', *Journal of Human Services Abstracts, 7* (4) (Eric Document 223822)

Buchsbaum, M.D. and Sainer, J.S. (1981) 'The Natural Supports Program: A Service Model to Strengthen Families' Care for Their Older Relatives' in *Strengthening Informal Supports for the Aging*, The Community Service Society of New York, pp. 25–34

Butler, R.H., Gertman, J.S., Oberlander, D.L. *et al.* (1979) 'Self-care, Self-help and the Elderly', *International Journal of Aging and Human Development, 10* (1), pp. 95–117

Campbell, R. and Chenoweth, B. (1981) 'Health Education as a Basis of Social Support', *The Gerontologist, 21* (6), pp. 619–27

Cantor, M. (1979) 'Neighbors and Friends: An Overlooked Resource in the Informal Support System', *Research on Aging, 1*, pp. 434–63

——— (1983) 'Strain Among Caregivers: A Study of Experience in the United States', *The Gerontologist, 23* (6), pp. 597–604

Castro, C. (1984) 'Family Member Caregivers of Chronically Ill Elderly Persons: Their Stressors and Social Support', unpublished dissertation, Boston University

Chenoweth, B. *et al.* (1980) 'Didactic/Experiential Program for Memory Strengthening', Michigan University Hospital Paper presented at the 33rd Annual Meeting of the Gerontological Society of America, San Diego

Clark, N.M. and Rakowski, W. (1983) 'Family Caregivers of Older Adults — Improving Helping Skills', *The Gerontologist, 23* (6), pp. 637–42

Cohen, G.D. (1984) 'Psychotherapy of the Elderly', *Psychosomatics, 25* (6), 455–63

Cohen, P.M. (1983) 'A Group Approach for Working with Families of the Elderly', *The Gerontologist, 23* (3), pp. 248–50

Cooper, D.E. (1984) 'Group Psychotherapy with the Elderly Dealing with Loss and Death', *American Journal of Psychotherapy, 38* (2), pp. 203–14

Craven, R. (1984) 'Preventing Falls: An Educational Intervention Increasing Confidence and Safety Among Elderly Women', unpublished dissertation, Seattle University

Crossman, L., London, C. and Barry, C. (1981) 'Older Women Caring for Disabled Spouses: A Model for Supportive Services', *The Gerontologist, 21* (5), pp. 464–70

Darvill, G. (1983) 'Shuttle Diplomacy in the Personal Social Services: Interweaving Statutory and Informal Care in a Changing Britain' in D.L. Pancost *et al.* (eds.), *Rediscovering Self-Help*, Sage, Beverly Hills, pp. 239–60

Dono, J., Falbe, C., Krail, B. *et al.* (1979) 'Primary Groups in Old Age: Structure and Function', *Research on Aging, 1*, pp. 403–33

Dutro, J.W. II (1983) 'The Effects of Group Self-instructional Training on Positive Verbalizations in an Aged Population', unpublished dissertation, Oregon State University

Evans, R.L. and Jaureguy, B.M. (1982) 'Phone Therapy Outreach for Blind Elderly', *The Gerontologist, 22* (1), pp. 32–5

Feldman, R.N. (1982) 'Microcounselling Skill Training with the Elderly and its Effects on Self-concept and Self-esteem', unpublished dissertation, Syracuse University

Fuller, J., Ward, E., Evans, A. *et al.* (1979) 'Dementia: Supportive Groups for Relatives', *British Medical Journal, 1* (6179), pp. 1684–5

Galinsky, M. and Schopler, J. (1977) 'Warning: Groups May Be Dangerous', *Social Work, 22* (2), pp. 89–95

Gartner, A. and Riessman, F. (1977) *Self-help in the Human Services*, Jossey-Bass, San Francisco

George, L.K. and Gwyther, L.P. (1983) 'Family Caregivers of Alzheimer's Patients: Correlates of Burden and the Impact of Self-help Groups', paper presented at the 36th Annual Meeting of the Gerontological Society of America, San Francisco

Goodman, G.C. (1984) 'Natural Helping Among Older Adults', *The Gerontologist, 24* (2), pp. 138–43

Grant, G. and Wenger, C. (1983) 'Patterns of Partnership: Three Models of Care for the Elderly' in D.L. Pancost *et al.* (eds.), *Rediscovering Self-Help*, Sage, Beverly Hills, pp. 27–51

Gray, D. (1982) 'A Competency Oriented Small Group Intervention: Older Worker Job Clubs', paper presented at the annual convention of the American Psychological Association, Washington DC (Eric Document 229694)

Gwyther, L.P. (1982) 'Caregiver Self-help Groups: Roles for Professionals', *Generations, 37–8*, p. 53

Haber, D. (1983) 'Promoting Mutual Help Groups Among Older Persons', *The Gerontologist, 23* (3), pp. 251–3

Haley, W.E. (1983) 'A Family-behavioural Approach to the Treatment of the Cognitively Impaired Elderly', *The Gerontologist, 23* (1), pp. 18–20

Hammond, D.B. and Bonney, W.C. (1983) 'Counseling Families of the Elderly: A Group Experience', *Journal for Specialists in Group Work, 8* (4), pp. 198–204

Harper, D.C. (1980) 'The Effect of a Medication Self-care Program on Knowledge of Medication, Health, Locus of Control and Self-care Behavior Among Black Elderly Hypertensive Women', unpublished dissertation, University of Maryland

Hartford, M.E. and Parsons, R. (1982) 'Groups with Relatives of Dependent Older Adults', *The Gerontologist, 22* (3), pp. 394–8

Hausman, C.P. (1979) 'Short-term Counseling Groups for People with Elderly Parents', *The Gerontologist, 19* (1), pp. 102–7

Hawkins, B.L. (1983) 'Group Counseling as a Treatment Modality for the Elderly: A Group Snapshot', *Journal for Specialists in Group Work, 8* (4), pp. 186–93

Hess, B.B. (1976) 'Self-help Among the Aged', *Social Policy*, November–December, pp. 55–62

Hochschild, A. (1973) *The Unexpected Community*, Prentice Hall, New Jersey

Hoffman, S.B. (1983) 'Peer Counselor Training with the Elderly', *The Gerontologist, 23* (4), pp. 358–60

Hudis, I.E. and Buchsbaum, M.D. (1981) 'Components of Community-based Group Programs for Family Caregivers of the Aging', in *Strengthening Informal Supports for the Aging*, Commuinity Service Society of New York, New York, pp. 35–43

Jackson, R.N. (1980) 'Citizen Participation Workshops for the Elderly: Their Impact on Measures of Internal-external Locus of Control Among the Aged Population in the Piedmont Region of North Carolina', unpublished dissertation, North Carolina State University at Raleigh

Johnson, E.S. and Spence, D.L. (1982) 'Adult Children and Their Aging Parents: An Intervention Program', *Family Relations, 31* (1), pp. 115–22

Josephs, M.J. (1978) 'Adapting Institutions to the Adult Learner: Experiments in Progress', in *Current Issues in Higher Education*, American Association for Higher Education, Washington DC

Kahan, J.S. (1984) 'The Effects of a Group Support Program on Decreasing Feelings of Burden and Depression in Relatives of Patients with Alzheimer's Disease and Other Dementing Illnesses', unpublished dissertation, United States International University

Kamerman, S. (1981) 'Public Policy for the Elderly: The Dilemmas in a Family Policy Perspective' in *Strengthening Informal Supports for the Aging*, Community Service

Society of New York, New York, pp. 12–18

Kaye, L.W., Monk, A. and Stuen, S. (1983) 'The Efficacy of a Self-help Teacher Training Program for Older Adults', *Gerontology and Geriatrics Education, 4* (2), pp. 75–87

Klinger-Vartabedian, L.C. (1982) 'The Group Setting: A Viable Mental Health Alternative for the Elderly', paper presented at the 68th Annual Meeting of the Speech Communication Association, Louisville, KY (Eric Document 225195)

Kuypers, J.A. and Trute, B. (1978) 'The Older Family as the Locus of Crisis Intervention', *The Family Coordinator, 27* (4), pp. 405–11

Lakin, M., Bremer, J. and Oppenheimer, B. (1983) 'Group Processes in Helping Groups: Toward a Developmental Perspective', *International Journal of Aging and Human Development, 18* (1), pp. 13–24

Lazarus, L.W., Stafford, B., Cooper, K. *et al.* (1981) 'A Pilot Study of the Alzheimer Patients' Relatives Discussion Group', *The Gerontologist, 21* (4), pp. 353–8

Lidoff, L. and Abbott, S. (1983) 'Promoting Self-help Ventures in Food Production and Distribution. Program Innovations in Aging', *Journal of Human Services Abstract, 8* (4) (Eric Document 237765)

Lieberman, M.A., Yalom, I. and Miles, M. (1977) *Encounter Groups: First Facts*, Basic Books, New York

Lieberman, M.A. and Gourash, N. (1979) 'Evaluating the Effects of Change Groups on the Elderly', *International Journal of Group Psychotherapy, 29*, pp. 283–304

Litwak, E. and Szelenyi, I. (1969) 'Primary Group Structures and Their Functions: Kin, Neighbors and Friends', *American Sociological Review, 34*, pp. 465–81

Lopata, H. (1978) 'The Absence of Community Resources in Support Systems of Urban Widows', *The Family Coordinator, 27* (4), pp. 383–8

Luckey, I. (1982) 'Seniors Helping Seniors: Training Low Income Black Elderly to Cope with Cold Weather Energy and Housing-related Problems', unpublished dissertation, City University of New York

Lucks, H.C. (1981) 'Widow/widower Outreach Program (WWOP): The Social Work Role with Members of a Mutual-help Program and Their Families', Social Work Papers, School of Social Work, University of Southern California, Los Angeles, pp. 82–9

McCarthy, H. (1980) 'Coping with Stroke: Effects of Self-help Group Participation Among Disabled Seniors', paper presented at the 33rd Annual Meeting of the Gerontological Society of America, San Diego

Mellor, M.J., Rzetelny, H. and Hudis, I.E. (1981) 'Self-help Groups for Caregivers of the Aged' in *Strengthening Informal Supports for the Aging*, Community Service Society of New York, New York, pp. 52–9

Nahemow, L. (1981) 'People Care for People, Providing a Missing Link in the Chain of Natural Support Systems', NYU Medical Center, Office of Urban Health Affairs, *Journal of Human Services Abstracts, 7* (4) (Eric Document 223822)

Office for Senior Citizens and Handicapped (1981) 'Chicago Senior Citizen Self-help Project, Chicago', *Journal of Human Services Abstracts, 7* (4) (Eric Document 223822)

Orr, N.K. (1982) 'Support Groups for Caregivers of Senile Dementia Patients', paper presented at the 35th Annual Meeting of the Gerontological Society of America, Boston

Owen, G.R. (1981) 'Back to a Basic in Lifelong Learning: Personal and Small Group Problem Solving', paper presented at the meeting of the Speech Communication Association Conference in Communication and Gerontology, Edwardsville, IL (Eric Document 214221)

Paley, E.S., Axelroth, E., Bowers, M. *et al.* (1982) 'Multi-family Psychoeducational Support Group Therapy for Families with a Member Afflicted with Irreversible Brain Syndrome (Alzheimer's Disease): Report of a Pilot Study', School of Professional Psychology, University of Denver (Eric Document 237845)

Pancost, D.L., Parker, P. and Froland, C. (1983) (eds.), *Rediscovering Self-Help*, Sage, Beverly Hills

Parkes, C.M. and Weiss, R.S. (1983) *Recovery from Bereavement*, Basic Books, New York

Pearce, S.S. (1978) 'The Effect of Structured Group Counseling on Levels of Depression Among Retired Women in Institutional and Non-institutional Settings', unpublished dissertation, St Johns University

Petersen, C.H. (1979) 'The Effects of an Educational Intervention on the Elderly's Perception and Utilization of Problem-solving Skills', unpublished dissertation, University of Nebraska, Lincoln

Pilisuk, M. and Minkler, M. (1980) 'Supportive Networks: Life Ties for the Elderly', *Journal of Social Issues, 36* (2), pp. 95–116

Pinkston, E.M. and Linsk, N.L. (1984) 'Behavioral Family Intervention with the Impaired Elderly', *The Gerontologist, 24* (6), pp. 576–83

Priddy, J.M. and Gallagher, D. (1984) 'Clinical and Research Issues in the Study of Caregiver Support Groups', paper presented at the 37th Annual Meeting of the Gerontological Society of America, San Antonio

——— and Knisely, J.S. (1982) 'Older Adults as Peer Counselors: Considerations in Counselor Training with the Elderly', *Educational Gerontology, 8*, pp. 53–62

Rainey, J.S. (1980) 'Approaches to Successful Aging: A Field Study in Geriatric Preventive Community Mental Health', *Journal of Human Services Abstract, 8* (2) (Eric Document 231977)

Ray, R.W. (1983) 'Effects of Teaching Coping Skills to Widows in Groups', unpublished dissertation, the University of Arizona

Reifler, B. and Eisdorfer, C. (1980) 'A Clinic for Impaired Elderly and Their Families', *American Journal of Psychiatry, 137*, pp. 1399–403

Richardson, L.M. and Lowman, R.L. (1980) 'Group Intervention Strategy with the Aged', paper presented at the 33rd Annual Meeting of the Gerontological Society of America, San Diego (Eric Document 200885)

Richman, J. (1979) 'A Couples Therapy Group on a Geriatric Service', *Journal of Geriatric Psychiatry, 12* (2), pp. 203–12

Romaniuk, M. and Priddy, J.M. (1980) 'Widowhood Peer Counseling', *Counseling and Values, 24*, pp. 195–203

Rosel, N. (1983) 'The Hub of a Wheel: A Neighborhood Support Network', *International Journal of Aging and Human Development, 16* (3), pp. 193–200

Rzetelny, H. and Mellor, J. (1981) 'Support Groups for Caregivers of the Aged: A Training Manual for Facilitators', Community Service Society of New York, AOA, Washington DC, *Journal of Human Services Abstract, 8* (2) (Eric Document 231977)

Safford, F. (1980) 'A Program for Families of the Mentally Impaired Elderly', *The Gerontologist, 20* (6), pp. 656–60

Sanchez, D. (1984) 'Strengthening the Informal Support Systems of the Hispanic Elderly: Group Program for Caregivers and Potential Caregivers', unpublished dissertation, City University of New York

Schram, C.F. (1979) 'Citizen Participation in Community Planning for the Elderly', unpublished dissertation, State University of New York at Albany

Shannon, B.M., Smiciklas-Wright, H., Davis, B.W. *et al.* (1983) 'A Peer Educator Approach to Nutrition for the Elderly', *The Gerontologist, 23* (2), pp. 123–6

Silverman, P.R. (1980) *Mutual Help Groups*, Sage, Beverly Hills

Silverman, P.R. (1970) 'The Widow as a Caregiver in a Program of Preventive Intervention with Other Widows', *Mental Hygiene, 54*, pp. 540–7

Simons, R.L. (1984) 'Specificity and Substitution in the Social Networks of the Elderly', *International Journal of Aging and Human Development, 18* (2), pp. 121–39

Smithers, J. (1981) 'Determined Survivors: Coping Strategies Among the Urban Elderly', unpublished dissertation, University of California, Los Angeles

Strelow, A.C. (1982) 'Objectives and Teaching Methods Used in Older Adult Peer Counselor Training', University of Minnesota (Eric Document 223787)

Streuer, J.L. and E.O. Clark (1982) 'Family Support Systems Within a Research Project on Dementia', *Clinical Gerontologist, 1* (1), pp. 87–95

Strupp, H.H. and Hadley, S.W. (1977) 'A Tripartite Model of Mental Health and Therapeutic Outcomes', *American Psychologist, 32* (3), pp. 196–7

Szwabo, P. and Thale, T.T. (1983) 'Expressive Group Psychotherapy with the Older Adult', paper presented at the 36th Annual Meeting of the Gerontological Society of America, San Francisco

Troll, L. and Nowak, M. (1977) 'Age Bias in Counseling' in N. Schlossberg and A. Entine (eds.), *Counseling Adults*, Brooks/Cole, Monterey, CA

Wang, Y. (1979) 'Natural Support Systems and the Rural Elderly: A Missouri Case', unpublished dissertation, University of Missouri-Columbia

Ward, R.A. (1978) 'Limitations of the Family as a Supportive Institution in the Lives of the Aged', *The Family Coordinator, 27* (4), pp. 365–73

——— (1979) 'The Implications of Neighborhood Age Structure for Older People', *Sociological Symposium, 26*, 42–63

——— LaGory, M., Sherman, S. *et al*. (1981) 'Neighborhood Age Structure and Support Networks', paper presented at the joint annual meeting of the Scientitic Gerontological Society (34th) and the Scientific and Educational Canadian Association on Gerontology (10th), Toronto

Washington University, Seattle Center for Social Welfare Research (1982) 'Wallingford Wellness Project: An Innovative Health Promotion Project with Older Adults', AOA, Washington DC, *Journal of Human Services Abstract, 8* (4) (Eric Document 237765)

Waters, E., Fink, S. and White, B. (1976) 'Peer Group Counseling for Older People', *Educational Gerontology, 1*, pp. 157–70

Weiner, M.B. and Weinstock, C.S. (1979) 'Group Progress of Community Elderly as Measured by Tape Recordings, Group Tempo and Group Evaluation', *International Journal of Aging and Human Development, 10* (2), pp. 177–85

Wenger, G.C. (1982) 'Ageing and Rural Communities: Family Contacts and Community Integration', *Ageing and Society, 2*, pp. 211–29

West, H.L. and Ernst, M. (1981) 'The Life Enrichment Program for Older Adults: An Alternative Educational Model', *Educational Gerontology, 7*, pp. 257–74

Wollert, R. and Barron, N. (1983) 'Avenues of Collaboration' in D.L. Pancost *et al*. (eds.), *Rediscovering Self-Help*, Sage, Beverly Hills, pp. 105–23

Zarit, S.H. (1983) 'Interventions with Families of Impaired Elderly', paper presented at the 36th Annual Meeting of the Gerontological Society of America, San Francisco

Zarit, S.H., Reever, K.E. and Bach-Peterson, J. (1980) 'Relatives of the Impaired Elderly: Correlates of Feelings of Burden', *The Gerontologist, 20* (6), pp. 649–55

Zgliczynski, S.M. (1982) 'Multimodal Behavior Therapy with Groups of Aged', *Small Group Behavior, 13* (1), pp. 53–62

7 THE SYSTEMS APPROACH TO CHANGING PRACTICE IN RESIDENTIAL CARE

David P. Jeffery

The Problem of Implementing Successful Cost-effective Therapy

It has been argued that it is not cost-effective for therapists to see elderly clients for psychotherapy. The ageist position is: that the elderly either are not able or not willing to respond to therapy; that it takes so long that therapy would be virtually unending; or that because they do not have long to live, old people give a poor return on the investment. These arguments have been put forward from the time of Freud and are one aspect of the reluctance of psychotherapists to work with the elderly (Lewis and Johansen, 1982). Hildebrand (1982) and Yesavage and Karasu (1981) among others have convincingly refuted these arguments and the recent developments documented in this volume and elsewhere (for instance, Woods and Britton, 1985) demonstrate the healthy interest being taken in psychological therapy with the elderly. However, there are other reasons why therapists may not be cost-effective when employed in psychotherapy (Hawkes, 1981; Jeffery and Saxby, 1984).

According to Hawkes (1981), since the problems faced in clinical practice are complex, therapy has itself to reflect some of this complexity. Sophisticated therapy is time-consuming and it can be readily demonstrated that the proportion of cases that can be dealt with in this way is very small in relation to the total demand, let alone the untapped need. It follows that it is not cost-effective to do individual therapy and something else must be done to meet the demand. Hawkes (1981) proposes that therapists should not in the main do therapy and they should only see sufficient clients to 'achieve a certain credibility as therapists'. Their main work should be to 'give away' psychological therapy skills to other practitioners and to promote the primary prevention of psychological problems. That is, the psychologist should work indirectly, at one remove from the client population. The skills and knowledge necessary have been outlined in an earlier paper (Jeffery and Saxby, 1984).

Although as yet little attention has been paid to prevention, psychologists working with the elderly have been 'giving away' psychological therapy skills, as it has been recognised that psychological care and therapy with old people is, to an overwhelming extent, provided by people other than psychotherapists. Three groups can be identified: (1) volunteers and relatives who provide care for the dependent elderly; (2) direct care staff such as nurses, nursing aides and care assistants in residential and daycare settings and domiciliary care; (3) other professional staff such as community nurses, occupational therapists, social workers and general medical practitioners who use psychological techniques in their daily work.

None of these groups receive extensive training in the practice of psychological therapy and those who have the most contact with the elderly in need of therapy have the least training. The role of the psychologist has been to develop the psychological therapies to be implemented by staff, evaluate their effectiveness and train staff in their use. Reality orientation (RO) is the best example of this development/evaluation/training effort and other therapies such as reminiscence (for instance, Kaminsky, 1983), remotivation (Burton, 1980), increasing engagement in activities (Powell, Felce, Jenkin *et al.*, 1979) and behavioural interventions for problem behaviours (Hodge, 1984) have also received the same attention. As this work has progressed, a problem has become apparent which is not often documented in the literature on these techniques (Davies, 1982). The problem is this: however well developed the therapy, whatever its success and whatever training programme is established, it is remarkably difficult to ensure that the staff who are to implement the therapy do so; and if they do implement the therapy it is as difficult to ensure the therapy programme is maintained over time. This means that it may well be no more cost-effective to work indirectly through care staff and carers than it is to work directly with a few people.

Let us consider the example of RO to illustrate the problem. It has been stated (for instance, Drummond, Kirchoff and Scarbrough, 1978; Holden and Woods, 1982) that 24-hour RO is the main form and that classroom RO is a useful adjunct. Yet, as Hanley (1984) makes clear, there is no evidence of successful implementation of 24-hour RO. Hanley (1984) presents research results which show *no change* in staff behaviour towards patients after training in 24-hour RO, even though the staff reported that they had changed. Hanley concludes that 'changes in staff behaviour cannot be *assumed* to occur when RO is introduced, even when staff are favourable to the programme' (1984; p. 172). Several demonstration programmes in 24-hour RO analogues and approaches to increase engagement (for example, Burton, 1980; Hanley, 1981; Powell *et al.*,

1979; Woods, 1980) have shown changes in patient behaviour and, by implication, prior changes in staff behaviour.

Hanley (1984) suggests that successes have been due to extremely specific detailing of the exact procedures to be carried out by the staff. While this may be an important feature, even more important may have been the actions taken by the researchers to establish the conditions whereby the specific instructions given to the staff were followed. Unfortunately, this information, which is of crucial interest to therapists concerned with the pragmatics of setting up a successful programme, is almost invariably omitted from reports.

Davies (1982) has commented on this phenomenon. She thinks that the lack of published information on the social psychological aspects of programme design and implementation reflects the tendency of those interested in behavioural work with the elderly to adopt too narrow a perspective to their therapy. Davies (1982) identifies four social psychological factors she considers important: (1) how elderly patients and younger groups from different professions view each others' roles; (2) which behaviours are regarded as 'expected', 'reasonable' and 'desirable'; (3) which duties are regarded as routine aspects of the job and which are exceptional; and (4) how the role and status of the innovater is related to the success of the programme. Gubrium and his coworkers (Buckholdt and Gubrium, 1983; Gubrium, 1974) have demonstrated powerfully that the interaction of the first three of Davies' factors can lead direct care workers in a residential home to ignore management directives aimed at improving residential care and can render ineffective RO programmes which, on the face of it, are running successfully.

In order successfully to implement meaningful cost-effective therapy, it is necessary to pay attention to the factors of social organisation surrounding a therapeutic application and to consider the nature of the relationship between the therapist/innovator and the care staff who will implement the therapy. This chapter will examine the effect of the behaviour of care staff on residents and the relationship between care staff behaviour and organisational variables. Then, the human systems approach to change will be outlined briefly, and the systems approach to changing practice in residential care described. Following a review of other systems theory organisational interventions, an attempt is made to draw together principles for successful interventions in care systems.

The Effects of the Behaviour of Care Staff on Residents

It is well-established that older adults in residential care are more likely to suffer from psychological problems than those living independently. Mann, Graham and Ashby (1984), for example, found in their investigation of 438 residents in 12 Social Services Part II residential homes that one-third were suffering from severe senile dementia and another one-third from mild to moderate senile dementia. Of the two-thirds who showed mild or no dementia, 38 per cent were found to be clinically depressed. Recent observational studies of staff behaviour with such residents have demonstrated the importance of such practices for the well-being of residents. Lipman and colleagues (Lipman and Slater, 1977; Lipman, Slater and Harris, 1979) found that social and emotional support for residents was provided, in the homes that they studied, more by other residents than by staff. They suggested that a greater separation between residents and staff should be encouraged in order to enhance mutual helpfulness and self-maintenance skills, a suggestion which was taken up by those supporting the group living approach in the United Kingdom (Marston, 1979).

However, the increasing levels of dependency in residential homes necessitates closer staff contact with residents and several studies (Culbertson and Caporael, 1983; Evans, Hughes, Wilkin *et al.*, 1981; Willcocks, Peace and Kellaher, 1982) have found that a great proportion of interaction between residents and staff reflects high dependency in that it is largely instructional, that is, related to the carrying out of physical care tasks. In their study of the speech of care staff, Culbertson and Caporael (1983) found two registers of speech to the elderly in a nursing home: 'baby talk' which is simple in structure and content, conveys positive affect and is potentially infantilising; and 'non-baby talk' which was associated with the offering of help or an object. In line with the findings of Barton, Baltes and Orzech (1980), they found that verbal offers of help were related to dependence in the aged. What would happen was that 'where an aged person would have been capable of some small act . . . the task was assumed by the care-giver prior to or simultaneously with a verbal offer to help' (Culbertson and Caporael, 1983; p. 311). In a subsequent study, Baltes, Honn, Barton *et al.* (1983) revealed discrepant social contingencies by care staff for different resident behaviours. Following dependent self-care behaviour, staff responded in a way which was supportive of such dependency while no social contingencies were observed following independent self-care. Obstructively engaged and non-engaged behaviours were not followed by any social contingencies, but constructively engaged behaviour was followed by intermittently supportive contingencies. So, in the nursing home that they studied, Baltes *et al.* (1983) found that staff behaviour was actively reinforcing dependency in self-care and constructive activity. These studies demonstrate the importance of the behaviour of care staff and also that, in Culverston and Caporael's words, 'it may be that it is not beneficial for care receivers when caregivers comply with an institutional policy to please and take care of residents. For the institutionalized aged, the road to helplessness may be paved with good intentions' (1983; p. 311).

The Use of Training to Change Care Staff Behaviour

Why do direct care staff behave in this manner? It is often suggested that they do not know any better and that if they were taught to have a better understanding of the problem and what to do, such as how to practice 24-hour RO, their behaviour would change. While this may happen, Briers (1979) found little agreement among supervisory staff as to the type of training necessary for residential work with the elderly. However, there is very little evidence that training of *any* sort has an effect on the quality of life of residents (Davies, 1982). Kart and Maynard (1976), for example, found no evidence of a relationship between the proportion of trained professionals in a nursing home and either the quality of care or well-being of residents. In a survey carried out of the knowledge of administrative and care staff of the principles and appropriate behaviour for caring for 'confused' residents (Saxby and Jeffery, 1984), it was found that all grades of staff had levels of knowledge sufficient for good practice and yet they were not putting that knowledge into action and were requesting further training. It seems that training is one of the most popular attempted solutions to the problem of poor care practice — and it may be one of the least successful because in many cases *the root of the problem lies not in sufficient staff knowledge or inappropriate attitudes but in the organisation of care*. No training, however sophisticated, can help if the systems of care provision do not permit or do not facilitate good care.

Training is also a poor solution to the problems of changing care systems, as Georgiades and Phillimore (1975) show. They argue that attempts to introduce innovation and change in institutions by focusing upon changing individuals through training are based on a fallacy that, since work organisations are made up of individuals, the organisation can be changed by changing its individual members. Having presented evidence on the negligible effect of training courses on trainees' later behaviour in the care situation, they demolish the individual focused position in the following paragraph:

> This then is the myth of a hero-innovator: the idea that you can produce, by training, a knight in shining armour who, loins girded with new technology and beliefs, will assault his organizational fortress and institute changes both in himself and others at a stroke. Such a view is ingenious. The fact of the matter is that organizations such as schools and hospitals will, like dragons, eat hero-innovators for breakfast (Georgiades and Phillimore, 1975; p. 315).

The Relationship Between Care Staff Behaviour and Institutional Variables

If education and training is insufficient for producing behavioural change in care staff, what other approaches to improving the quality of care are there? As already indicated, what is required is a focus upon care staff behaviour in the context of the organisation of care. Common to much of the writing on staff behaviour is the truism that the behaviour of individual staff members is a function of the person *and* the working environment (Capele, 1979; Davies, 1982; Kets de Vires and Miller, 1984; Leatt and Schneck, 1985; Menzies, 1970; Tizard, 1975).

The relationships between features of the working environment, staff performance and the outcome for the population served have been documented in various studies. Tizard (1975), summarising his pioneering studies of residential care regimes, reported on the quality of residential care for retarded children and described two types of child management practice — institutionally oriented practice and child-oriented practice. Institutionally oriented practice accorded with Goffman's (1961) description of 'total institutions', while child-oriented practice was flexible, took account of children's individual differences, gave choice, initiative, personal possessions and privacy and there was reduced social distance between staff and residents. The occurrence of these two types of practice could not be accounted for by the size of the establishment, the size of the care units within the establishment, the children's handicaps, staff-child ratios, the facilities available or the personal qualities of the staff.

There were only two factors which accounted for the difference in management: there was a greater delegation of responsibility to the heads of the care units in child-oriented homes and the unit heads had a greater awareness of social and emotional needs. These findings led Tizard (1975) to conclude that the organisational structure of a residential establishment in large part determines staff roles and role performances.

Similar findings have emerged from studies of residential care for the elderly. Evans *et al.* (1981), for example, showed in their intensive study of six residential homes in Manchester, Great Britain, that resident-oriented care practice (as opposed to institution-oriented practice) was dependent not upon staff levels or size of institution, but upon high levels of communication and consensus between members of staff and upon the commitment and style of leadership of the supervisory staff. In their review of aspects of the residential social environment which positively affects residents' quality of life, Goldberg and Connelly (1982) identified nine dimensions:

1. Flexibility of management practice;
2. Individualisation and autonomy for residents;
3. Opportunities for privacy;
4. Opportunities for social stimulation;
5. Communication and interaction with the outside world;
6. Social interaction between staff and residents (in addition to instrumental communication);
7. Maximum delegation of decision-making to care staff and to residents;
8. Good communication channels between staff;
9. A minimum degree of specialisation of roles and tasks among staff.

Four of these dimensions are not concerned directly with residents or staff behaviour towards residents but with staff–staff interactions and staff management. One recent analysis of the effects of organisational processes on staff focused upon stress in hospital nursing units for the elderly (Leatt and Schneck, 1985). Five kinds of stress were identified: stress from traumatic personal experiences; psychogeriatric workload; scheduling of work; doctor–nurse relationships; and personality and role stress. They found that the first two types of stress were due to technological features of the work and would not be amenable to change in the management of the nursing unit, but scheduling of work, doctor–nurse relationships and personality and role stresses could be reduced by changes in management aimed at increasing the efficiency and scope of communication within and between work groups, decentralising decision-making and fostering communication and good leadership — all of which, as Leatt and Schneck (1985) say, are rather basic principles of good management to be found in any textbook (for instance, Dunnette, 1970; Staw, 1983).

It is clear, therefore, that organisational processes are a major influence on the behaviour of staff working in residential care settings and that to improve the quality of residential care, staff must not only know what to do and be prepared to do it, but they must also be helped in doing it by the organisation. Staff who do not practise 24-hour RO, even though they are interested and have been taught to do so, need not be obtuse, unco-operative or stupid. They may simply be responding to a work-system that leaves them little option but to act in their non-24-hour RO way. The psychotherapist who wants to 'give away' psychological therapy skills must determine if the conditions are such that they may be put into practice.

There are thus *two* issues — how to 'give away' therapy skills and then how to deal with the managerial and process consequences of that (Street, 1984). To do this, he or she must become a facilitator or manager of organisational change. The organisation must be treated as a client, just as the individual is a client for the therapist or educator. It is becoming recognised (Jeffery and Saxby, 1984; Sutton and MacPherson, 1981) that the potential change agent has two sources of ideas and methods for facilitating change to draw on: the literature on family therapy (for instance, Herr and Weakland, 1979; Watzlawick, Weakland and Fisch, 1974); and the work of organisation and industrial psychology (for instance, Abrahams, 1985; Pettigrew, 1975), and that there is a common ground between the two in their use of human system theories (Haley, 1981).

Human Systems Theory

In order to establish the terminology, some of the main features of human systems theory are outlined. Detailed treatment of human systems may be found in Bateson (1973) and Watzlawick *et al.* (1974). Systems theory is a new orientation to human dilemmas in that problems are located not within an individual but within the *pattern of relationships* that the individual who is the 'identified patient' has. It is these continuing patterns of interactions of communication that constitute the human system. A second feature of systems theory is the emphasis on the *interconnectedness* of human behaviour — any action on one part of a human system will, sooner or later, impinge on other parts of the system, sometimes in ways that are unexpected. Also important is the concept of *homeostasis* — systems maintain their form over time, and the patterns of communications that comprise human systems persist. This introduces a fourth feature, the concept of *boundary*. In order to maintain itself, any system will have a boundary between it and its environment. Systems can be defined as 'closed' or 'open' depending on whether the boundary is permeable (allows transfer across it) or not. Human systems are open systems and are homeostatic by maintaining a dynamic equilibrium of transfer in both directions across the boundary. Human systems differ in the degree of boundary permeability.

Within its boundaries, a human system generates an internal organisation series of *sub-systems*, which serve different functions within the system. These sub-systems are organised in a *hierarchy* whereby one will have executive functions and exert more or less control over other sub-systems, which may themselves be organised hierarchically. There may be more than one hierarchy ordering the same individuals or sub-systems at different times depending on the task being undertaken. When studying a human system it is important to: (1) take note of the boundary that the system maintains and (2) understand the hierarchies within the system. This is done by (3) discovering the flow of information and pattern of communication within the system. A system will itself be a sub-system of some larger (or meta-) system which may have to be considered when examining its functioning.

A residential care establishment will have two principal sub-systems, the staff sub-system and the resident or patient sub-system. Within the staff system there will be at least two sub-systems comprising the management and direct care staff, and these two or more sub-divisions will constitute a formal hierarchy. There will also be informal hierarchies within the staff group, such as length of time in the establishment, which will structure the system. The rigidity or permeability of boundaries between the various staff sub-systems will differ between establishments; cross-boundary alliances (for example, between one of the staff and an influential care worker) may form in some systems which, if they challenge the authority of the management, may lead to reduced effectiveness in functioning (Haley, 1981; Palazzoli, 1984). The work on organisational processes in residential care already discussed implies that hierarchy should be reduced or eliminated and boundaries made as permeable as possible in order that flexible practice, good communication between staff, minimum specialisation among staff and close communication with the outside world is facilitated. However, it is a principle of systems theory that any grouping of people will form hierarchies and it is being recognised in organisational psychology (for example, Abrahams, 1985) that some hierarchy is necessary and has to be worked with, but that extreme and rigid hierarchy is dysfunctional.

A Systems Based Project to Improve Residential Care Practice

The project described here is the systems based approach to improving care in a number of Social Services Residential Homes in Devon, Great Britain. The project is still in progress and has been published elsewhere in a different form (Crocker and Jeffery, 1986). In accordance with Garfinkel's (1967) description of how actors make sense out of the events and occurrences in their world, Crocker and Jeffery discovered the nature of the situation in the course of their career of actions. Earlier work (Jeffery, 1980; Jeffery and Saxby, 1984; Saxby and Jeffery, 1983) had highlighted the importance of the functioning of the organisation in the successful implementation of psychological therapies in residential care and identified the management sub-system as crucial. This focus upon the executive sub-system in dysfunctional systems is evident in family therapy (for instance, Minuchin, 1974), where the functioning of the parental sub-system is often the focus of intervention, and in organisational psychology's concern with the adequacy of industrial management (for instance, de Board, 1978).

Therapists rarely have direct access to residential care establishments as managers or staff and so it is important to have some vehicle for engaging with the home. The approach in this project (Crocker and Jeffery, 1986) was through the provision of training. Other common entries may be as a consultant to staff about resident management problems (for example, Street, 1981) as a researcher (for example, Davies, 1982) or as a change facilitator employed by the wider organisation (for example, Towell and Harris, 1979), although it is not unknown to be asked to directly facilitate staff functioning (Palazzoli, 1985). An intervention team was formed consisting of a social services training officer and a health service clinical psychologist. The aim in establishing this small team was to respond positively to demands from three sources: the area management of the social services department, which required that the training department provide (unspecified) training to the residential homes; the district health service psychiatric team for the elderly was concerned about the level of care provided for psychiatric patients in the homes and wanted to see it improved; the officers-in-charge of some of the homes were, in different ways and with different intensity, seeking training and advice for care staff in managing 'confused' and difficult residents. It would have been possible to meet these demands by setting up and running in each home a standard training package for care staff on handling 'confused' behaviour. However, the authors' emphasis upon the functioning of the organisation and previous survey work on the knowledge of residential care staff led them to design a systems intervention instead.

The Intervention Model

The systems intervention model followed in designing the programme was provided by Walton (1982) in his description of training as problem-focused consultancy practice. There are some important differences between this approach and the training approach in which the trainer simply accepts or assumes a training brief from the managers and then gets on with setting up and running the training. These approaches are contrasted in Table 7.1.

Table 7.1: Some Differences in Approaches to Training (Watton, 1982)

Five key factors	Traditional training approaches	Problem-focused training
1. Type of relationship	Servant–master Expert–novice	Collaborative; exploring; 'engaged'
2. Focus of the work	To provide a prescriptive training activity	To explore a 'live' issue — then see what that leads to
3. Way of working	Accepts training requests — then does it	Accepts opportunity to be involved — works with and for client manager
4. Style	Works for client	Works with client
5. Outcomes	Completed set task successfully: End	More 'open-ended' type of work contract; likely continuing contact

This systems intervention had a dual concern with (1) care practice, and (2) management and organisation practice. However, since the mode of engagement with the system was with the 'presenting problem' of care practice, this was the overt focus of interactions with the homes, while the unstated concern was with management practice and the organisation of care. Capele (1979), in describing organisational change, emphasises that the level of intervention (management) may often not be the same as the target of change (care practice). It is not necessary, and sometimes counterproductive, to make it clear to the system members what is being done; it is frequently emphasised in systemic family therapy that insight into the systemic cause of the problem is unnecessary and often not helpful (Haley, 1981; Herr and Weakland, 1979).

The key features of Crocker and Jeffery's (1986) programme were:

1. Training officer engages in an open-ended consulting relationship with the officer-in-charge as well as acting as a learning resource provider. This is the intervention model outlined by Walton (1982);

2. Management has to take responsibility for development and training. This was the major systems intervention strategy and served two principal functions. First, it reinforced the authority of management. This can be undermined if the trainer or specialist related directly to care staff about the organisation of training. By requiring management to be responsible for the organisation of training, the relationship between management and staff was normalised, and it also made it difficult for the training effort to be marginalised by either management or staff. Second, the intervention required management to consider the implications of training for operational practice and so gave the training team an envoy to work with management about organisational processes;

3. Access to specialist advice on the needs of and care of mentally infirm people was via the trainer. This respected the sub-system boundaries and avoided the possibility of cross-boundary alliances. The flow of communications about the project is shown in the systems map in Figure 7.1. The training officer and the psychologist had direct contact with care staff during teaching phases of the project, but this was always mediated by management;

4. Flexibility with the programme as to the content of learning material used, the amount of staff time set aside for training and the staff towards whom the training was aimed. This flexibility allowed the programme to meet the different needs of the different residential units in a flexible but organised way.

Outcomes

The programme has had very different results in the different homes. Common themes in management practice issues that arose during the programme were: (1) how the officers (management sub-system) work together, especially in how they organise communication, how they plan together for developments and how the officer-in-charge delegates tasks and authority to his or her juniors; (2) the supervisory relationship

Figure 7.1: Flow of Communication About Training Between Sub-systems

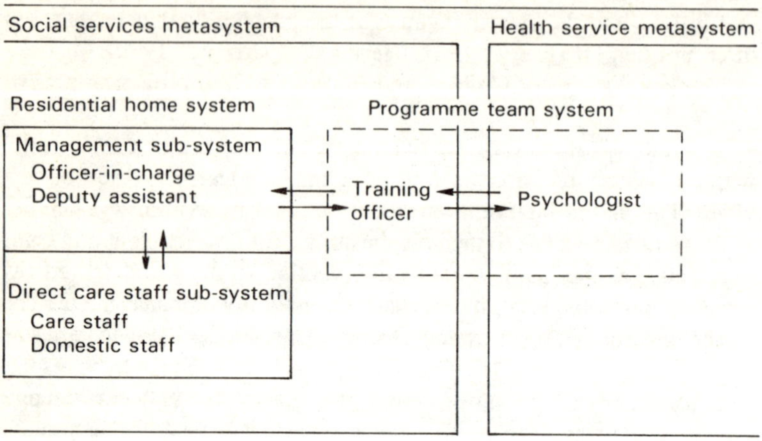

between management and direct care staff; and (3) communication between management and health service specialists. Quite how these issues were confronted or resolved varied between the homes.

Developments in resident care have differed between the homes as each has gone in its own direction. The following new care practices have been implemented in at least one home: 24-hour RO; identifying and developing current good care practice; planned management of disruptive residents; reminiscence therapy; extending the contribution to care made by volunteers; establishing a key worker system for allocation of individual residents to designated care staff members. None of these developments are particularly startling or revolutionary and many had been the object of discussion in the past, but it took the influence of the programme to mature them into practice. This unspectacular but solid development which builds securely on the already established practice in the home is the sort of thing that will be maintained when the influence of the project fades.

Structure of the Programme

The programme had a four-phase structure, as shown in Table 7.2. The preliminary phase was designed to alert the managers to how the programme aimed to support their development and training roles. During this phase, the phase I and II materials that would be used with the direct care staff and the guidance roles for managers were presented. In Crocker

Table 7.2: Content of the Programme

Preliminary
Officers from different homes and others involved in the programme meet for a day of training

Phase I. Stimulation
(1) Helping the elderly — video film and discussion notes after an interval of up to three weeks
(b) Responding to residents' needs — a group training session for officers and staff; covers causes of confused behaviour, examples from this home, ways of helping

Phase II. Problem-solving
Co-ordinator, homes officers and staff consult to:
(a) evaluate information on how work is done
(b) identify problems or issues
(c) decide what area of work to concentrate on
(d) decide what change to aim for
(e) decide what to do next

Phase III. Following through over an indefinite period
(a) People working in the homes do what they have decided to do
(b) Co-ordinator meets homes' officers at intervals to:
(i) help with planning and review
(ii) provide training resources for officers and staff

and Jeffery (1986) this phase is presented as being the beginning of the programme but there was much pre-programme work which had to be successfully negotiated in order to reach the stage of being able to put the programme into action. This vital work is now described here as an example of the careful way in which it is necessary to engage systems and negotiate communication across boundaries.

Two separate pre-programme steps were necessary to lead to the formation and engagement of the systems shown in Figure 7.1 and, given the pivotal role of the training officer, it was his work that was crucial. In the first step, the training officer had to establish a facilitative relationship with the officers-in-charge of the homes. This was done in the first instance at an interdepartmental level between the training department and the residential care department in the area social services office. From this small beginning, the management of the residential care units was introduced to the idea of training at a short workshop for all the officers-in-charge. During this stage, the styles of leadership of the officers were evaluated, their preparedness for involvement in further training assessed and the likely chance of such training being successful estimated. In the first instance, only those who were judged to be responsive were pursued in the initiative described here.

The second pre-programme step undertaken was the formation of the programme team. This also happened in two phases, with an intersystem preliminary approach from the training department to the National Health Service psychiatric team for the elderly for assistance with the technical aspects of the care of disturbed elderly people. From this approach, the psychologist met with the training officer and, over a series of meetings to plan the training, formed the team. One of the important factors in forming a successful team is the sharing of a common language, approach and aims, and it was fortunate that a background in family therapy was shared.

Phase I (Stimulation). The aim here was to stimulate awareness of issues in the care of disturbed elderly people among direct care staff and provide minimum background knowledge. The video film and playing equipment were left in the home for about ten days, and the group training session was run at least twice in each home to enable maximum numbers of staff to participate. This also allowed an evaluation of management style and communication, as the organisation of viewing the film and attending the training session were the responsibility of the officers. In some homes rigid timetables were drawn up for staff to attend the training events; in other homes a more relaxed schedule was sufficient to ensure that all staff participated; while in yet other homes some staff missed out on the training events due to poor organisation and/or communication.

In one home, it was concluded that the video film was useless and irrelevant, which indeed it was as they had somehow wound on to another part of the tape and seen a different programme, and had not searched the tape for the programme they had been told to expect. This lack of initiative led to the conclusion that they expected training to be useless and irrelevant to their needs. Both here and later, information-gathering communications between management and staff were encouraged. Management was asked to discuss the film with staff members and to ask the staff what their ideas were for developments within the home. This served three important functions: an opportunity for the manager to take on a trainer role and reinforce learning; providing a focus of attention on communication processes in the home; and setting up an assumption that change will happen.

Phase II (Problem-solving). Here, the steps leading towards deciding what to do next (see Table 7.2) are derived from problem-solving principles documented in the family therapy literature and in the management literature. Figure 7.2 shows a comparison between the brief therapy

Figure 7.2: A Comparison of Systems Problem-solving Models

Human system change model (Capelle)

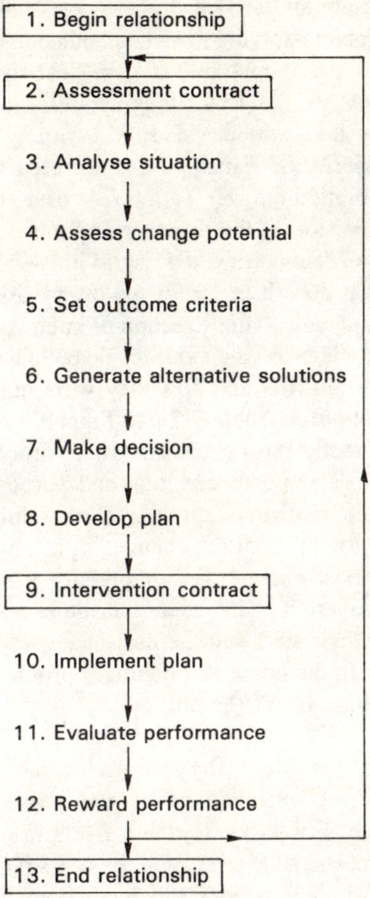

Brief therapy model (Herr and Weakland)

1. Approach family system and establish initial contact
2. Determining the problem
3. Determining attempted solutions to the problem
4. Determining minimal goals
5. Comprehending the family system
6. Review and strategic planning
7. Mobilising the family system through specific interventions and evaluation of their effects
8. Winding up, giving credit and terminating relationship

model presented by Herr and Weakland (1979) and the human systems change model of Capele (1979). Although they appear commonsensical and are also documented in other places (for example, behavioural psychotherapy literature), these steps can be extraordinarily elusive in practice.

A very useful aid to purposeful planning was found to be a set of notes produced in a booklet entitled *Deciding What To Do Next* and given to every officer-in-charge. The booklet had the following section headings: discussion with members of staff; recognising good work; identifying problems; deciding what you aim to achieve; deciding what to do next; where to get additional help and advice; training materials.

Some managers followed the problem-solving model embodied in the booklet and when they next met with the training officer were clear about what they wanted to do. Others went straight to the long list of training materials at the back and, treating it as a menu, selected a variety of interesting-looking items. The majority of managers had not used the booklet thoroughly (so much for bibliotherapy!). In the first case, the training officer could accept the decision of the manager and move on to the organisational process issue of 'How are you going to implement what you have decided to do? What does it mean for the organisation of you and your staff?' In the second case — the selection of interesting training items — the stages of the problem-solving model could be followed by asking which they wanted to do first and how they were going to decide. Of course, the model set out in Table 7.2 and Figure 7.2 is an ideal and is seldom followed exactly throughout the whole process — what is important is to maintain a sense of direction and purpose.

In phase II, the aim is to come to decisions at the level of training for improved care practice *and* at the level of the changes in management practice required to support those changes in care practice which should result from training. Moreover, it is intended that the *process* that management go through with their staff and the project team will improve communication processes in the home and highlight problems in management practice and organisation of the unit.

Phase III (Following Through). In this phase, the authors learned, as have others before them, to adjust expectations of the pace of developments to a longer time span. For example, the officers in one home decided they wanted the domestic staff to engage residents more in cleaning their bedrooms in order to help residents maintain daily living skills. They were also helped to decide that the means to achieving this end included the deputy officer-in-charge learning how to assume delegated authority, changes in the arrangements for communication between officers and all the officers adopting a different style of staff supervision. These system changes take some time to implement and become firmly established. Thus it is important to be sensitive to the pace of work and to have an awareness of the process of the establishment of an innovation. Flexibility of approach is crucial.

It was difficult to judge when the intervention was complete and the authors found that their involvement went in phases which depended on the stage of the work, the amount of advice and training needed, the readiness of managers and staff to engage in development work and unpredictable interruptions such as staff sickness and so on.

The aim was to make changes in the care systems of the homes with which there was contact, so that the intitiatives were maintained after the authors' departure, and to reduce the likelihood of problems being thrown up as a result of poor management or communication. It is worth reiterating the principles which the authors think made this possible:

1. Care in the approach to the homes so that the support of the appropriate senior management was gained and flexibility of response maintained;
2. Working only with homes that were judged to be responsive;
3. Working through the management in every home; supporting them in their position as the executive sub-system and, where possible, facilitating their development as innovators and trainers;
4. Taking steps to improve communication among managers and between management and staff; focusing on evaluating and improving the management functions of planning, decision-making, delegating and supervising in each home;
5. Being sensitive to the process of change and concerned to move change forward when that appeared possible and to take a back seat and mark time when it was not possible;
6. Forming a team which was supportive and helped maintain a sense of direction and purpose for the programme. Team meetings allowed exchange of information and enabled closer understandings of the particular problems of each system to be developed;
7. Adopting a systems problem-solving format which provided a useful tool with which to engage the homes in directed decision-making.

Other Systems Interventions

The principles followed in this work with social services residential homes for the elderly are also to be found in descriptions of interventions in other human service organisations. These reports can be characterised into two types — team-based institutional change programmes and interventions by family therapists into work systems.

Team-based Institutional Change Programmes

The best-known paper on team-based institutional change is that by Georgiades and Phillimore (1975), already referred to. Their alternative to the creation of 'hero-innovators' by training is to become an institutional change agent. They emphasise that the primary step in establishing permanent change is to 'cultivate the host culture' so that any changes that are later attempted are rooted in fertile ground. In order to do this, they outline two major strategic goals for the organisational change agent — to gain influence based in expertise and ability rather than attempting to use channels of authority which he or she may not control and, second, to maintain a cohesive organisational change team. In order to achieve these goals, Georgiades and Phillimore (1975) give six guidelines which they stress are intended more as a checklist or reminder than as a comprehensive treatise. These guidelines are given in Table 7.3, where they are compared with guidelines from the other institutional change programmes.

Towell and Dartington (1976) and Towell and Haris (1979) describe a long term programme to encourage innovation in inpatient care which was set up in Fulbourn Hospital, Cambridge, U.K. They established action research project teams which consisted of a 'social researcher' and care staff involved in care in various settings in the hospital. Since it was the direct care staff who were being required to change, they were given responsibility through the teams for establishing the methods and pace of change. Having keyed into a perceived need for change in the units, the social researchers and his unit-based project teams were facilitated in determining what change of necessary and how to make it through the use of an action research model, which is very similar to the systems problem-solving framework. Towell and Dartington (1976) emphasise that staff engaging in such innovation need leadership and support, and require protection from other hospital staff groups resistant to change. Their general principles for change can be found in Table 7.3. Towell and Dartington (1975) also suggest that unit innovations are further encouraged where the hospital organisation as a whole provides conditions facilitating innovation, although they give no clues as to how to foster this. They identify multidisciplinary participative working, decentralisation of the management of treatment services and an atmosphere valuing openness and experiment as key conditions. These are similar to the characteristics of 'open systems' given by Jones (1982) in his description of innovative therapeutic hospital communities.

Burden (1981) describes a project-based institutional change

Table 7.3: A Comparison of Guidelines From Project-based Institutional Change Programmes

Georgiades and Phillimore (1975) Guidelines for strategies of change (hospitals and community settings)	Towell and Dartington (1976) General principles for planning change efforts (hospitals)	Burden (1981) Keystone to success with the stages of the systems approach (school)
1. The manager of change effort should work with the forces in the organisation which are supportive of change rather than working against those which are defensive and resistant to change 2. Develop a 'critical mass' for change by: (i) producing a self-sustaining team of workers (ii) locating key people in the organisation to be an internal support system 3. Wherever possible the manager of change should work with the organisationally 'healthy' parts of the system which have the will and resources to improve 4. Try to work with individuals and groups who have as much freedom and discretion in managing their own operations and resources as possible 5. Obtain appropriate and realistic levels of involvement by key personnel. Obtain top management permission, and support and encouragement from those just below the top 6. Protect the members of the team from undue pressue and stress. Build strong personal support relationships among the unit members. Programme frequent meetings and external contacts	1. Employ multiple strategies for change. At each level adopt flexible tactics to allow advantage to be taken of opportunities 2. Activate those in local key positions to influence the adoption of new practices and to guide and advise small groups of concerned staff seeking to make changes 3. Disseminate teaching reports and documents (a 'top down' approach). Use a 'bottom up' approach which starts with direct care staff and helps them discover their capacities for bringing about change 4. Provide support for staff and opportunities in a protected forum to review, consider problems and find new solutions 5. For staff in key roles, provide access to both information on progressive practice *and* expertise in the social and psychological aspects of innovation 6. Senior managers are able to create the organisational conditions for innovation 7. Foster sharing of experience and support with staff in other hospitals who have the same experience 8. Efforts to produce change focused on hospital should keep in mind the relationship with the total system of patient care, so that improvements in one area are not gained at the expense of deterioration elsewhere	*Preparation* Spend time in the school to: 1. Get respect, trust and liking 2. Find out who has high status and ally with them 3. Work out the power structure 4. Sort out the school's educational priorities Work with good head teacher and make sure you are identified with him/her Find out and clarify the problem being offered Decide whether conditions are sufficient to continue *Planning and Implementing the Intervention* Establish a systems team with a leader secretary, systems engineers, statistician, expert in areas under investigation and consumer ('mole') Establish a contract with realistic goals for innovators and recipients Ensure school staff are informed of their role by head *Data collection* Decide on scope of systems analysis, looking at the ways individuals function in a sub-system *Pulling it all together* The leader must maintain a coherent view of the project Make a written report of the findings with the implications for the future organisation of the school Ensure wide distribution of report

programme initiated by educational psychologists in schools. This programme, based explicitly on an application of systems theory, falls short of the authors' requirements in its emphasis on systems analysis and not systems change, but contains some useful ideas. He describes four crucial stages of work: preparation; planning and implementing the innovation; data collection; and putting it all together. The 'keystones to success' with this approach are outlined in Table 7.3.

Family Therapists in Work Systems

Family therapists have only recently been documenting interventions in larger systems and their interventions tend to be on a smaller scale than the programmes outlined above. While institutional change approaches enjoy a variety of potential entries into the system (for example, research, problems with individual clients, a desire to improve efficiency, staff training) family therapists with their problem focus necessarily enter with a brief to help with or to solve a problem. Herr and Weakland (1979) and Pottle (1984), for example, describe the use of the brief therapy model of family therapy (see Figure 7.2) with older adults and their families. Often the 'family' that they work with is composed more of the statutory and voluntary workers who comprise the elderly person's social network than that of family members, and their interventions in hospital and residential settings necessarily involve the institution's staff. While these interventions often influence the behaviour of direct care staff, the work is focused on one resident problem and only has incidental effects on resident care in general.

A family therapist's interventions in children's homes staff systems through consultancy is described by Street (1981). He observes that the staff system in such homes often takes on the appearance of a family with 'parents', 'adolescents' and 'little children'. There may be problems if there are 'cross-generational' alliances within the staff group, or if the hierarchy is too rigid or steep, or if the authority of powerful figures is denied, particularly in the area of decision-making. Street (1981) says that the therapist must stay superordinate ('meta') to the system by moving freely in the organisation's hierarchies, by avoiding coalitions with staff members and by not becoming involved in the care of individual children. He employs a variety of family therapy interventions (see, for example, Minuchin and Fishman, 1981) with the principal aim of clarifying and normalising channels of communication and freeing decision-making.

Palazzoli (1984, 1985) has been developing the systemic approach to organisational change from the Milan school of family therapy (Palazzoli, Cecchin, Boscolo *et al.*, 1978). She recognises that human relations experts are often called in by the potential 'loser' in an organisation 'game' and that this consultation is the most recent move in the organisation's power struggle which is rendering it ineffective. It is therefore imperative to use every occasion of contact with the organisation, even the very first, to understand the game, the how and the why of the therapist's involvement.

A second concern of this approach is to ensure that the change agent does not lose power and manoeuverability within the organisation by getting into covert coalitions with one part of the system against another. Held (1982) also explored family therapy-based strategies for entering mental health systems, but her approach differs from that of Palazzoli as she treats the staff system as reactive to the arrival of the new member rather than proactive. She formulated four axioms for joining successfully with a system: proceed slowly; be respectful of the system you are joining; accept and respect criticism; and resist being drawn into coalitions.

Palazzoli (1984) recommends that covert coalitions can be avoided by: (1) strictly respecting the hierarchical order when defining a working relationship, by starting with the boss and working down; (2) promoting as comprehensively as possible the circulation of information in the organisation; and (3) actively and explicitly seeking open alliances *for* concrete objectives. If secret coalitions can be avoided, hidden conflicts spotted and an understanding of the system's attempted solutions achieved, the outside consultant who is concerned with systemic change is already halfway there. Guidelines for achieving these things with families are available in Palazzoli *et al.* (1978) and Herr and Weakland (1979), and many suggestions for achieving the same thing as a member of a work organisation are available in LaRouche and Ryan (1985).

In terms of the tactics and actions necessary to intervene in an organisational system, Palazzoli (1985) gives an example from her own practice of the importance of action rather than discussion. She is convinced that the family therapy guideline 'prescription (of action) works better than explanation (of the problem)' also applies to systemic interventions in small organisational units. Palazzoli (1985) goes on to describe how a therapeutic incident with one of the unit's most difficult clients was capitalised on to develop a prescription of action for the staff and thereby mobilise a stuck and ineffective staff system.

Common Themes in Systems Approaches to Changing Care Practice

There are several features common to systems approaches to

organisational change, although different reports highlight different aspects. The present author considers the following to be essential to success:

1. Large-scale permanent organisational change requires a time scale of years to achieve and the process is not an easy one;
2. Change agents must maintain their power within the system and, since they are unlikely to find themselves in positions of executive power, must ensure that those in positions of power are recruited to support and facilitate the change initiative. They must also ensure that they have access to sources of power other than executive;
3. The change agent must be careful in his or her engagement with the organisational system, making sure to maintain manoeuverability and avoiding covert alliances or making powerful enemies. This means maintaining a distance from the system while at the same time working within it. Assistance in doing this may be gained from establishing a change sub-system (a team) which is cohesive and mutually supportive;
4. It is very important to achieve a systematic understanding of the organisation. It is necessary to understand the rules of the 'game', acquire a knowledge of the political processes and map out the hierarchies and boundaries within the organisation;
5. Organisational change is a process and any process within a system is complex. Psychologists have come some way from Lewin's (1948) description of the change process as 'unfreezing, changing and refreezing' and have some idea of the process of planned change in the systems problem-solving and action research models. Psychologists still need to learn how organisations change spontaneously and how to capitalise on this in planned change endeavours;
6. A strategy and tactics for the implementation of change, based upon the systems analysis of the organisation, must be planned and followed in a flexible fashion. The literature on family therapy and organisational change contains many examples found helpful in the specific situations reported and which may be adapted for use in other settings;
7. There are particular skills of observation, analysis, interaction and persistence involved in being a successful change agent. Relationship skills of warmth, accurate empathy and geniuneness are not sufficient. Psychologists do not yet know enough to be specific about these skills but they may be similar to those required of a successful strategic family therapist (for example, Haley, 1976). This chapter has been concerned with the conditions necessary for the implementation of these skills.

Developments

The systems approach to improving care, which emphasises the efficient and effective use of already deployed resources, fits well in the financial climate of the late 1980s with stable or reducing expenditure on care systems and the increasing numbers and levels of dependency of older adults. As indicated above, future developments have to include gaining an understanding of spontaneous systems change, discovering the skills required to be a successful change agent and analysing the activities required for successful change.

Hall and Hord (1984) have made progress in this direction by developing a typology of organisational change interventions and a methodology for recording the sequence of interventions, ranging from policy level to the small incidents which are the building blocks of any change effort. As the method becomes established and documented, change agents must embark on the difficult task of evaluating their programmes.

References

Abrahams, B. (1985) 'On Form and Function in Organization Theory', *Organization Studies, 6*, pp. 39–53

Baltes, M., Honn, S., Barton, E. *et al.* (1983) 'On The Social Ecology of Dependence and Independence in Elderly Nursing Home Residents: A Replication and Extension', *Journal of Gerontology, 38*, pp. 556–64

Barton, E., Baltes, M. and Orzech, M. (1980) 'On the Etiology of Dependence in Older Nursing Home Residents During Morning Care: The Role of Staff Behaviour', *Journal of Personality and Social Psychology, 38*, pp. 423–31

Bateson, G. (1973) *Steps to an Ecology of Mind*, Granada, St Albans

Briers, J. (1979) *Residential Care for the Elderly in London*, DHSS Social Work Service, London

Buckholdt, D. and Gubrium, J. (1983) 'Therapeutic Pretense in Reality Orientation', *International Journal of Aging and Human Development, 16*, pp. 161–81

Burden, R. (1981) 'The Educational Psychologist as an Instigator and Agent of Change in Schools: Some Guidelines for Successful Practice' in I. McPherson and A. Sutton (eds.), *Reconstructing Psychological Practice*, Croom Helm, London, pp. 42–51

Burton, M. (1980) 'Evaluation and Change in a Psychogeriatric Ward Through Direct Observation and Feedback', *British Journal of Psychiatry, 137*, pp. 566–71

Capele, R. (1979) *Changing Human Systems*, International Human Systems Institute, Toronto

Crocker, A. and Jeffery, D. (1986) 'Developing Practice in Caring for Confused Elderly People', *Social Work Education* (in press)

Culbertson, G. and Caporael, L. (1983) 'Baby Talk Speech to the Elderly: Complexity and Content of Messages', *Personality and Social Psychology Bulletin, 9*, pp. 305–12

Davies, A. (1982) 'Research with Elderly People in Long-term Care: Some Social and Organisational Factors Affecting Psychological Interventions', *Ageing and Society, 2*, pp. 283–98 de Board, R. (1978) *The Psychoanalysis of Organisations*, Tavistock, London

Drummond, L., Kirchoff, L. and Scarbrough, D.R. (1978) 'A Practical Guide to Reality Orientation', *The Gerontologist, 18* (6), pp. 568–73

Dunnette, M. (1970) (ed.) *Handbook of Industrial and Organisational Psychology*, Rand McNally, Chicago

Evans, G., Hughes, B., Wilkin, D. *et al.* (1981) 'The Management of Mental and Physical Impairments in Non-specialist Homes for the Elderly', *Research Report No. 4*, Research Section, Psychogeriatric Unit, University Hospital of South Manchester

Garfinkel, H. (1967) *Studies in Ethnomethodology*, Prentice-Hall, Englewood Cliffs, New Jersey

Georgiades, N. and Phillimore, L. (1975) 'The Myth of the Hero-innovator and Alternative Strategies for Organisational Change' in C. Kiernan and P. Woodford (eds.), *Behaviour Modification with the Severely Retarded*, Associated Scientific Publishers, New York, pp. 313–19

Goffman, E. (1961) *Asylums*, Doubleday, New York

Gubrium, J. (1974) 'On Multiple Realities in a Nursing Home' in J. Gubrium (ed.), *Late Life: Communities and Environmental Policy*, Thomas, Springfield, Illinois, pp. 31–52

Haley, J. (1976) *Problem Solving Therapy: New Strategies for Effective Family Therapy*, Harper and Row, London

——— (1981) 'Reflections on Therapy and Other Essays' The Family Therapy Institute of Washington D.C., Chevy Chase, Maryland

Hall, G. and Hord, S. (1984) 'Analyzing What Change Facilitators Do: The Intervention Taxonomy', *Knowledge, 5*, pp. 275–307

Hanley, I. (1981) 'The Use of Signposts and Active Training to Modify Ward Disorientation in Elderly Patients', *Journal of Behaviour Therapy and Experimental Psychiatry, 12*, pp. 241–7

——— (1984) 'Theoretical and Practical Considerations in Reality Orientation Therapy with the Elderly' in I. Hanley and J. Hodge (eds.), *Psychological Approaches to the Care of the Elderly*, Croom Helm, London/Methuen, New York, pp. 164–91

Hawkes, D. (1981) 'The Dilemma of Clinical Practice — Surviving as a Clinical Psychologist' in I. MacPherson and A. Sutton (eds.), *Reconstructing Psychological Practice*, Croom Helm, London, pp. 11–20

Held, B. (1982) 'Entering a Mental Health System: A Strategic-systemic Approach', *Journal of Strategies and Systemic Therapies, 1*, pp. 40–50

Herr, J. and Weakland, J. (1979) *Counselling Elders and Their Families*, Springer, New York

Hildebrand, H. (1982) 'Psychotherapy with Older Patients', *British Journal of Medical Psychology, 55*, pp. 19–28

Hodge, J. (1984) 'Towards a Behavioural Analysis of Dementia' in I. Hanley and J. Hodge (eds.), *Psychological Approaches to the Care of the Elderly*, Croom Helm, London/Methuen, New York, pp. 61–87

Holden, U.P. and Woods, R.T. (1982) *Reality Orientation*, Churchill-Livingstone, Edinburgh

Jeffery, D. (1980) 'Involuntary Relocation and the Quality of Life of Chronic Psychogeriatric Hospital Patients', MSc thesis, University of Exeter

——— and Saxby, P. (1984) 'Effective Psychological Care for the Elderly' in I. Hanley and J. Hodge (eds.), *Psychological Approaches to the Care of the Elderly*, Croom Helm, London, pp. 255–82

Jones, M. (1982) *The Process of Change*, Routledge and Kegan Paul, London

Kaminsky, M. (1984) (ed.) 'The Uses of Reminiscence: New Ways of Working With Older Adults', *Journal of Geriatological Social Work, 7* (1–2)

Kart, C. and Maynard, B. (1976) 'Quality of Care in Old-age Institutions', *Gerontologist, 16*, pp. 250–6

Kets de Vries, M. and Miller, D. (1984) 'Group Fantasies and Organisational Functioning',

Human Relations, 37, pp. 111–34
LaRouche, J. and Ryan, R. (1985) *Strategies for Women at Work*, Unwin, London
Leatt, P. and Schneck, R. (1985) 'Sources and Management of Organisational Stress in Nursing Sub-units in Canada', *Organisation Studies, 6*, pp. 55–79
Lewin, K. (1948) *Resolving Social Conflict*, Harper and Row, New York
Lewis, J. and Johansen, K. (1982) 'Resistances to Psychotherapy with the Elderly', *American Journal of Psychotherapy, 36*, pp. 497–504
Lipman, A. and Slater, R. (1977) 'Homes for Old People: Towards a Positive Environment', *Gerontologist, 17*, pp. 146–56
——— Slater, R. and Harris, H. (1979) 'The Quality of Verbal Interaction in Homes for Old People', *Gerontology, 25*, pp. 275–84
Mann, A., Graham, N. and Ashby, D. (1984) 'Psychiatric Illness in Residential Homes for the Elderly: A Survey in One London Borough', *Age and Ageing, 13*, pp. 257–65
Marston, N. (1979) 'Can We De-institutionalise an Institution? Part 1', *Concord, 13*, pp. 27–45
Menzies, I. (1970) *The Functioning of Social Systems as a Defence Against Anxiety*, Tavistock Institute of Human Relations, London
Minuchin, S. (1974) *Families and Family Therapy*, Harvard University Press, Cambridge, Massachussetts
——— and Fishman, C. (1981) *Family Therapy Techniques*, Harvard University Press, Cambridge, Massachussettes
Palazzoli, M. (1984) 'Behind the Scenes of the Organisation: Some Guidelines for the Expert in Human Relations', *Journal of Family Therapy, 6*, pp. 299–307'
——— (1985) 'The Emergence of a Comprehensive Systems Approach. Supervisor and Team Problems in a District Psychiatric Centre', *Journal of Family Therapy, 7*, pp. 135–46
——— Cecchin, G., Boscolo, C. *et al.* (1978) *Paradox and Counterparadox*, Aranson, New York
Pettigrew, A. (1975) 'Towards a Political Theory of Organisational Intevention', *Human Relations, 28*, pp. 191–208
Pottle, S. (1984) 'Developing a Network-oriented Service for Elderly People and their Carers' in A. Treacher and J. Carpenter (eds.), *Using Family Therapy*, Blackwell, Oxford, pp. 149–65
Powell, L., Felce, O., Jenkin, J. *et al.* (1979) 'Increasing Engagement in a Home for the Elderly by Providing an Indoor Gardening Activity', *Behaviour Research and Therapy, 17*, pp. 127–35
Saxby, P. and Jeffery, D. (1984) 'In a Strange Land', *Social Work Today, 15*
Staw, B. (1983) (ed.), *Psychological Foundations of Organisational Behaviour*, 2nd edn, Scott Foresman, London
Street, E. (1981) 'The Family Therapist and Staff Group Consultancy', *Journal of Family Therapy, 3*, pp. 187–99
——— (1984) 'Family Therapy in Residential Homes for Children' in A. Treacher and J. Carpenter (eds.), *Using Family Therapy*, Blackwell, Oxford, pp. 47–68
Sutton, A. and McPherson, I. (1981) 'Psychological Practice in a Social Context' in I. McPherson and A. Sutton (eds.), *Reconstructing Psychological Practice*, Croom Helm, London, pp. 165–72
Tizard, J. (1975) 'Quality of Residential Care for Retarded Children' in J. Tizard, I. Sinclair and R. Clarke (eds.), *Varieties of Residential Experiences*, Routledge and Kegan Paul, London
Towell, D. and Dartington, I. (1976) 'Encouraging Innovation in Hospital Care', *Journal of Advanced Nursing, 1*, pp. 391–8
——— and Harries, C. (eds.), *Innovation in Patient Care*, Croom Helm, London
Walton, M. (1982) 'Training as Consultancy Practice', *Training and Development*, September

Watzlawick, P., Weakland, J. and Fisch, R. (1974) *Change Principles of Problem Formulation and Problem Resolution*, Norton, London

Willcocks, D., Peace, S. and Kellaher, L. (1982) 'The Residential Life of Old People: A Study in 100 Local Authority Homes', Polytechnic of North London Department of Applied Social Studies, *Survey Research Unit Reports Nos. 12 and 13*

Woods, R. (1980) cited by Hanley, I. (1984) 'Theoretical and Practical Considerations in RO Therapy' in I. Hanley and J. Hodge (eds.), *Psychological Approaches in the Care of the Elderly*, Croom Helm, London/Methuen, New York

——— and Britton, P. (1985) *Clinical Psychology with the Elderly*, Croom Helm, London/Aspen, Rockville, MD

Yesavage, J. and Karasu, T. (1982) 'Psychotherapy with Elderly Patients', *American Journal of Psychotherapy, 36*, pp. 41–55

8 'OVER THE HILL AND FAR AWAY': THE PRODUCTION OF A VIDEO-ASSISTED TRAINING PACKAGE

Gerry Murphy

Over the Hill and Far Away is a five-day video-assisted course offering a comprehensive introduction to work with elderly mentally infirm people and designed to be used with direct care workers such as home helps, care assistants in homes for elderly people and sheltered housing wardens (East Sussex Consultancy and Training Agency, 1984). The material has been attractively produced as a package comprising trainer's handbook, workbooks (for course participants), video-tape, script of video-tape and posters, all of which is packed in a neat plastic briefcase.

The package is pitched at fairly elementary level but does provide virtually everything that one would need to know for effective work with this client group, with particular emphasis on the learning and using of appropriate skills. Therefore, it is primarily a practice-based course which aims to engender in participants a positive, proactive attitude to the work and towards the clients.

The material, with full accompanying trainer's notes, has been written in such a way that people of even limited training experience should be able to tutor the course. This widens considerably its potential use, since its operation need not depend on the availability of skilled trainers.

This chapter will attempt to describe the complex process of producing the video-assisted course, from initial conceptualisation to completed project. The context of the operational and developmental training needs which led to the generation of the package in a local authority social services department will also be described. The package itself will be described in detail and the principles which underpin its characteristics will be outlined.

Local Operational Context

East Sussex, on the south coast of England, has a very high proportion of elderly people in its population. The 1981 census showed that there are 90,000 in the 65- to 75-year-old bracket, representing 14 per cent of the total population, and 70,000 in the 75-plus bracket, representing 11% of the total population. These local figures linked to the general estimated incidence of confusion in elderly people over the age of 80 years at 20 per cent (1 in 5) suggested a problem of some magnitude for those responsible for the delivery of welfare services for the old in the county.

Certainly, the social services training and development section was receiving many requests for help, primarily in training manual staff to deal with the more problematical behaviours of elderly mentally infirm people. The two most common messages received were that staff knew nothing about confusion and did not know how to react to behaviour such as wandering or aggression. Manual staff, of whom there are about 2,400, provide domiciliary services and work in the department's residential homes. As a staff group, they spend more time on a regular basis with their clients than any other.

Clearly, a piecemeal training response would not be sufficient or appropriate given the scale of the problem and the number of people in need of training. At this stage consideration was given to packaging some material which could be made available throughout the department and written in such a way that it would be accessible to and usable by line managers to train their own staff. Packaging means bringing together complete training material and supplementing it with full training notes in a pack which can be taken off the shelf and used with minimal preparation. In this case, it was thought that the addition of video material would greatly enhance the learning potential for users. Such a package could facilitate a concerted and immediate response to the training demand by line managers rather than training and development officers, insufficient in number and spread too thinly to make an impact on such a large group of manual staff.

In thinking about such a package, the resource options available to the planners were quite extensive. A fully equipped media team in the social services department would provide a complete range of professional services from scripting to video-tape editing. Design and printing would be available from the planning department of the county council. The possibilities could range from a modest pamphlet to a full-blown package including video. Whatever was chosen it would be well-produced and available for sale outside the department as well as for use within it.

The planners decided to produce a video-assisted learning package. Two factors influenced their decision. First, it was clear from publications like *The Rising Tide* (Health Advisory Service, 1982) that most areas in the country would be facing the same sort of problems being experienced in East Sussex, caused by the increasing numbers of elderly mentally infirm people. Second, the training personnel in the planning group suspected that very little training material existed for work with this client group, so there was almost certainly a gap in the market. The latter was confirmed later that year (1983) when all existing material was formally reviewed. Only one course was found which offered a comprehensive training programme. (This review has been published by the Local Government Training Board as *Training Resources Available for Those Working with Elderly and Mentally Infirm People*.)

General Description of the Package

The course has six modules, all of which are inter-related and part of the whole package. They have, however, been designed to stand alone and can be used independently. The modules are:

Part One: Understanding the problem
- Module 1: Attitudes
- Module 2: Definitions
- Module 3: Explanations of behaviour

Part Two: Solving the problem
- Module 4: Management of behaviour
- Module 5: Communication
- Module 6: Methods of work

The contents of these are described fully below.

The learning approach built into the package is broadly an experiential/participative one. Thus there are plenty of exercises, some of which are experiential, and plenty of room for discussion so that participants can share their experiences. The participative nature of the material is emphasised at the beginning of the course in the workbook: 'The trainer will guide you through the material but the success of the course will largely depend on your active participation through sharing experiences. The responsibility for learning lies with the group as a whole and not just with the trainer.'

There is sufficient material for a five-day block course, arranged to give maximum flexibility and choice to the intending trainer. It is therefore possible to use a one-day-a-week-for-five-weeks format, or half-a-day-a-week-for-ten-weeks, and so on.

In considering how to use the package, the trainer is given maximum assistance in the form of very full training notes in the trainer's handbook. The layout in the handbook gives the entire contents of the course participant's workbook on the right-hand pages, with the relevant trainer's notes on facing left-hand pages. So, page 22 (right-hand) in 'Explanations of Behaviour' has an exercise 'Understanding Extreme Behaviour' as follows:

> What aspects of work do you find most difficult to manage? Which leaves you most anxious or worried? Mark the activities from the list below and add any others.
> Incontinence
> Wandering
> Aggression
> Suspicion
> Not eating
> Memory loss
> Destructive/Dangerous behaviour
> Repetitive actions
> Overt sexual behaviour
> Spitting
> Swearing
> Eating things
> Any other
> Share your responses with the group. Taking each activity in turn, discuss the reasons for your feelings.

On the left-hand side (page T22) are the trainer's notes for the exercise:

> Ask the group to mark the things they find most difficult. Note the ones marked by the majority. Discuss why it is difficult. Answers may include: physically repugnant (cleaning up faeces); disgusting (anti-social, masturbating, etc); think people do it on purpose; risk (may come to harm); simply don't know what to do (frustrating); irritating/repeating questions; upset — different person to former self; angry/hurt (personal abuse); ungrateful (the feelings of rejection).
> Stress the importance of the carer's *response* to the behaviour itself. Each individual will respond in a different way from another. Emphasise the differences within the group to the same problem and emphasise the need for consistency between carers. Stress that you must not take things personally. Rejection, suspicion, lack of recognition, etc.

The written material and the video-tape material are integrated and closely related to each other. The course participants are intended to work their way through the workbooks under the guidance of a course trainer and to look at a portion of video-tape when directed in the workbook. Thus, the video-tape material is used to reinforce, to 'bring alive' or to check understanding of what has been worked through in the written word. For instance, in the communication module there is an information input about communication as a creative, learnable process. Course participants look at verbal and non-verbal communication, verbal approaches in conversation and barriers to communication, doing exercises and participating in discussion at appropriate times. The two sequences on the video-tape are viewed critically. One shows a good example of communication, one a not so good example. These sequences are looked at in terms of verbal communication, non-verbal communication and simply on the level of 'what would it feel like to be talked to and treated in these ways?' The module, which lasts for two-and-a-half hours, ends with a good communications summary containing the most important points from the preceding material.

Description of the Modules

In the first half of the course, entitled 'Understanding the Problem', is the module on attitudes. This seeks to encourage participants to think about society's attitudes towards old people and their own and then to consider how attitudes can affect the way people behave at work, both positively and negatively. Negative stereotypes are examined and different cultural attitudes which illustrate the varying status of old people in certain societies considered.

Module 2 is called 'Definitions'. This is the technical part of the course, in which the four major conditions that cause confusion in elderly people are examined and contrasted. Participants are asked to chart the signs and causes of different confusions on a grid in their workbooks. This shows very clearly that similarities in behaviour can cloud or muddle assessment and diagnosis. It underlines the importance of decision-making with this group and how the observations of a care assistant, for instance, can fit into the assessment or diagnosis process. The piece of video in this module shows an elderly man who suddenly becomes confused. The participants are asked to look for clues and say what is wrong. Finally, they are asked to consider the client in the context of the professionals that can help and the services that ideally are available. This encourages them to think of themselves as part of a network of help.

The third module is called 'Explanations of Behaviour'. The aim here is to encourage course participants to look beyond or behind behaviour for explanations of that behaviour. The rationale is that if you can explain behaviour, you are more likely to be able to work out strategies for dealing with it. The participants start with a couple of exercises, one of which is experiential — ear plugs, foam on feet and so on. They are then asked to consider how they feel about some forms of extreme behaviour. They are given a model to use in looking for explanation which takes into account medical factors, personal factors (life history) and environmental factors. The participants then watch a video sequence and look for the clues. It is about an elderly man being aggressive in a home. The medical clue is his deafness, the personal clue is his having been a senior manager in his work and the environmental clue is to do with his recent admission to institutional care.

The second half of the course, entitled 'Solving the Problem', begins with module 4, 'Management of Behaviour'. This is about responding in a positive and thoughtful way to behaviour which is problematical. The responses of collusion, diversion and removal are introduced and brought alive through a series of video sequences which look at aggression, repetitive questioning, risk-taking, wandering behaviour and incontinence. There is a substantial written section on legal aspects, based on the 1983 Mental Health Act and Section 47 of the National Assistance Act, 1948.

Module 5 is about communication. It is in the package because good communication is a necessary prerequisite for good work of any kind with elderly, mentally infirm, people. It introduces the notion of communication as a learnable skill, and participants carry out a series of exercises which illuminate the written material. The video sequence shows two examples of communication — one good, one bad. The participants look critically at the sequences, and make suggestions about how communication could have been improved.

The sixth and final module is called 'Methods of Work'. This looks at some of the methods of intervention used in work with elderly infirm people, including teamwork (including key workers and care programmes), reality orientation, group activities, daily living skills, and carers' support groups.

The course ends with a review of gains from it. Each participant is asked to identify three things learned from each module and then think about transferring the learning to his/her workplace in a very concrete way, formulating plans for something they will do when they return there.

The Video-tape

The video-tape, which lasts 75 minutes, is composed of a number of sections, each of which is related to a part of the written text in the workbook and trainer's handbook. Some of the sections are scenarios which are performed by actors, some are tape/slide sequences transferred to video-tape with voice-over and some are of 'real' people and clients in everyday situations.

A role that runs through most of the tape is that of 'Pat'. She is seen working both in residential and in domiciliary settings. This merged role is intended to reflect the development on an experimental basis in East Sussex of the care worker role. The care worker, instead of being located in one base, relates to a small number of clients in an ongoing way, working with the client in whatever the service-delivery setting happens to be. Over a period of time with one client, a care worker may need to function in a domiciliary setting, in a day-care setting, in a residential setting or whatever.

Using actors wherever possible, although expensive, does produce the best possible realisation of the authors' intentions for the training material. In addition, ethical problems connected with filming elderly mentally infirm people are considerably reduced.

Design Process

The decision to produce the package was made in February 1983, with publication planned for May 1984, to coincide with an international seminar in London 'Group Care Practice'. The major activities during this period are listed in Table 8.1.

It is more a model of what happened, rather than a literal account of reality. The whole process was in fact too messy, too bitty and at times too painful for memory to be possible or accurate. There was a recognisable sequence though, which is useful to think about and record for future work on packages.

In conceptual terms, getting clear on aims, objectives and principles were among the most difficult work. The producers knew the target group and roughly what they wanted to include in the package. They also had a fairly clear idea of the type of training approach which would be embodied in the material. What was needed was a framework which would give coherence to a mass of material and also be a means of transmitting certain principles which would underpin the course contents. At the same

Table 8.1: Producing the Package

Date	Activities	People involved
February 1983	Clarification of aims and objectives; research	Media producer; training and development officers (2)
September 1983	Production planning; writing; research; consultation (with experts)	project manager; media producer; training and development officers; script writer; designer; production assistant
December 1983	Writing; pilots; rewriting; video shoot	Training and development officers (2); media unit; script writer
March 1984	Video edit; print deadline; proof reading	Media unit training and development officers
May 1984	Publication	ESCATA (East Sussex Training and Consultancy Agency)

time, marketing considerations would have to be borne in mind — the material would have to be presented in such a way that it would be relevant to any work setting, without diluting the effect it might have on workers from a particular situation.

Achieving clarity about these issues was the first and most demanding task the planning group faced. During this part of the process, most of its meetings were lengthy, difficult and stormy. A growing realisation of the enormity of the task intensified the pressures for the group members, many of whom were embarking on such an exercise for the first time. That clarity at this stage was achieved considerably assisted the later progress of the work. The importance of overcoming this early obstacle cannot be overemphasised. The production of such a package is so lengthy and so complex, involving many different skills, timescales and activities, that completion would not be possible within a planned timescale without initial consensus.

Research and writing of both the course material and the video script was an ongoing concern for the two training and development officers and the script writer between February and December 1983. These activities moved from the general and random to the particular and relevant as time progressed. As sense was made of a mass of information, the written course material and the video script began to emerge as related parts of the package. Drafts were produced and checked for accuracy by experts in the field recruited from both inside and outside the social services department. Other people, not elderly mentally infirm experts, were asked to comment on the style, lay-out and general intelligibility of subsequent drafts. Such comments were useful to the writers who were so close to their work, and they benefited from fresh eyes being cast over it.

This was particularly so in terms of the level of writing. The production team aimed at a level roughly equivalent to that which can be found in a popular tabloid-type newspaper, so that the course material would be accessible to the target groups. This was not an easy task for people accustomed and attached to the beloved jargon of their profession, and they were not able to keep the package completely free of it in the end, mainly because time ran out for further editing. Also, there were some unavoidably technical parts, especially in the module dealing with definitions and causes of mental infirmity in elderly people.

By the end of 1983, the written material was more or less finished and the video-shoot was 'in the can' but yet to be edited. After the rough edit stage in February 1984, the package was tried out as a whole in two pilots with staff in the department. These went well, most probably because some parts of the material (but not the video) had already been extensively tested. Comparatively few amendments were needed before the print deadline was reached and the final editing of the video-tape finished. *Over the Hill and Far Away* was published on schedule in May 1984.

Underlying Principles

There are a number of principles which underpin the whole package, which to a greater or lesser extent are explicit in various parts of the material. However, they are present as threads which run through the entire course, informing every part. This is a very effective way of transmitting messages through training which are fundamental to good practice. The principles are stated below, with examples of their place in the text.

Respect for the Individual

The course encourages the participants to think of their clients as individuals with life histories, feelings and needs which are singular to them. Examples of this can be found in the attitudes module, which aims to undermine the negative stereotyping of elderly people in most western societies and their consequent treatment as 'batches', especially in residential settings. The module on explanation of behaviour suggests that problematical behaviour can only be understood and dealt with if detailed explanation is sought for that behaviour. A simple model which includes medical factors (other than those specifically related to the disease of senile dementia), personal factors (history, circumstances and feelings) and environmental factors lays stress on the client as an individual, for whom an individual assessment and care programme needs to be formulated.

Self-determination

This is important in work with mentally infirm elderly people because of the ease with which negative assumptions about general levels of competency can be expressed in bad work practice. At the very outset, one of the course objectives warns about under-estimating what even very mentally frail clients can do. The participant is encouraged to maximise the remaining faculties of the client. This general exhortation is made concrete in the risk-taking section of the management of behaviour section. Also, in the actual running of the course, there is usually much discussion generated by this point, especially in groups which include domiciliary workers.

'Critical' Working

This means being thoughtful, imaginative and observant all the time; in short, adopting a proactive approach of the work. This is made explicit in many places in the material, for instance, in the definitions module which stresses the similarities in appearance between the four major conditions that cause confusion in elderly people (acute confusional states, depression, paraphrenia and dementia) and the importance, therefore, of adequate assessment based on observation. The role of the direct care worker in contributing to assessment is emphasised, as that worker may have more information of a behavioural nature over time than any other.

Team Working

The importance of everyone working with the client having the same goals and a similar approach is emphasised in the teamwork section of the methods module. This theme is developed in the material on keyworkers in the same section. As in 'critical' working above, responsibility for playing a part in the team, which may be as small as a group of people based in a residential establishment, or as large as the range of disciplines serving a whole neighbourhood, is underlined. Team working also appears, for instance, in the management of behaviour summary:

'Ensure there is consistency of approach in handling behaviour by sharing information about clients with colleagues and by ageeing with them a uniform way of responding.'

Minimum Standards

Actually, this principle is nowhere explicit but everywhere implicit in the material and, as such, represents an important aim of the package designers, as it must be a main aim for almost any form of training. Even courses which claim not to be prescriptive, as this one does, cannot avoid transmitting information about minimum standards.

Thus, each module presents information about a range of standards: the attitudes module says that negative attitudes can result in bad practice and that, therefore, a degree of self-knowledge and knowledge of negative stereotyping is required of the worker to prevent this; the definitions module says that knowledge of the four main causes of confusion is needed for understanding both the client and the worker's role *vis à vis* other professions and agencies; the explanations of behaviour module says that understanding of behaviour can only be obtained by looking behind it for explanations in the individual client's history and situation; the module on management of behaviour says that effective management needs to be proactive rather than reactive — this requires a thoughtful and imaginative approach rather than simply going through the motions of the job; the communication module presents its subject as a necessary prerequisite for work of any kind with elderly mentally infirm people and, moreover, presents it as a learnable skill; finally, the methods of work module lists a range of approaches which in itself advocates positive attitudes to the work, as well as offering specific methods from which to choose planned interventions.

Conclusion

Over the Hill and Far Away has been used extensively in the author's department as part of a training programme which has offered courses to over 1,300 direct care staff during the last 18 months. It has been well received both by course participants and line managers. In strategic terms, the package will have raised standards across the board in a consistent and powerful way, which should result in an overall improvement in services for elderly mentally infirm people in the whole of East Sussex.

In addition, well over 100 packages have been sold to other local authorities and statutorily-based agencies like health authorities. It is also likely in the near future that the package will be issued under franchise in the United States and Japan, suitably altered to meet local needs in both cases.

This paper has looked back on a complex process of design and production, which to some extent has been clarified by hindsight. The actual experience for the designers of the package was an exciting albeit at times painful one, especially as immoveable deadlines loomed large. Knowledge of the process is probably only fully attainable through experience but it is hoped that this account will be of some use to others thinking of a similar project.

References

East Sussex Consultancy and Training Agency (1984) *Over the Hill and Far Away*

Health Advisory Service (1982) *The Rising Tide: Developing Services for Mental Illness in Old Age*, National Health Service, London

Local Government Training Board (1984) *Training Resources Available for Those Working with Elderly Mentally Infirm People*, LGTB, London

9 GROUP CARE AND NATURAL LIVING IN A RESIDENTIAL HOME FOR THE ELDERLY

Edith McCallum and Ian Hanley

This chapter is an account of life in an old people's home in the north of Scotland. It was presented by the senior author (McCallum, 1985) at a local conference on the theme of improving the quality of life of elderly people in institutional care. The contents are reproduced here verbatim. This is quite intentional as it was felt that changing the style would alter the message . . .

I require to start off by directing an apology to you Ian, and I must make it a public apology. When you spoke to me on the 'phone I said yes, no problem, I will bring the video that the residents and staff at the home made. Wrong; I hadn't discussed it with the rest of the staff or the residents and they decided later that it was too personal to be shown with such a group. I must respect that and I do apologise; it's my own fault. So that tells you something about how the home is run!

The home dates back to 1845. It is detailed in the statistical account of Scotland. It was built as a poor house. There were four houses, each with its own matron, where elderly people could be looked after and couples could stay together. Now that was revolutionary. That made me feel that this was a hard act to follow from 1845. Nine years ago that particular building was demolished and we now have a nine-year-old purpose-built home for 36 elderly residents with accommodation for couples. Our residents are of very mixed abilities, with an age range from 65 to 98. Some of our older residents are our fitter residents, both mentally and physically; some of the younger ones less so. Many have had a diagnosis of dementia. The way that we 'care' is the way that we would like to be cared for ourselves. We feel that through group care and what we call natural living, and I'll explain what all these mean to us, that we can allow all of us to 'live' together as a team. When I talk of the team I am talking of residents and the staff, all of us. We are the team that makes the home what it is. Not the staff, not me as the officer-in-charge, not the residents individually, but all of us. It also includes the outside people who come in from other services — hospitals, community care, community psychiatric care, chiropodists, hairdressers.

Every aspect that you yourselves embrace in your own daily life comes into the daily life of the home.

Group care is a method of care within an institution and we are an institution. Let's admit that from the start. Thirty-six residents plus staff cannot 'live' together in a group and say they are not an institution. We *are* an institution. We can make it as little like a total institution as we can, but this is a method of care within an institution which, by giving special responsibility to a specific group of staff for a specific group of residents, promotes trust and a family atmosphere. Staff and residents are involved together in the decision-making that effects the nature of life in their home. It is not our home, it is not my home, it is not the local authority's home, it is *their* home. It is their front door, their rooms are their houses. We are the interlopers, we as the staff are interlopers, and the sooner we realise that the sooner we reach a more amicable relationship.

Natural living is a philosophy whereby residents in care are encouraged to live lives as they have always done, regardless of any routine imposed by the establishment: in other words, resident-orientated care. Now, by that I mean that if, for example, you have never risen from your bed for your breakfast in the morning and you go into care, and you are told that breakfast is at 8.30 am and you are expected to be there, I don't suppose you'd be very happy about it. You know when you go to stay in a hotel that if you can't get your breakfast at the time you would normally have it, it's irritating. Again, this is the resident's home, they are the residents. They must be allowed, they have a right to be allowed, no, they have a right to live their lives as they wish.

Group living, if I can make the contrast between group care and group living, is a method of care where people live totally in small groups, cared for by the same group of staff, that make all decisions concerning aspects of living of that group. We do not have group living at our home for a variety of reasons. We have a group care system. The proposal when we opened was to try to combine the philosophy of natural living with the methodology of group care, thus creating a home with a small 'h', rather than a home with a big 'H'. We set out to develop the literal meaning of the word 'home', and improve the quality of life of the residents in our care. The aims of group care are to promote an air of confidence which will enable the residents to act as independently as their physical and mental state will allow. Independence is a word we bandy about quite a lot; independence, choice. Independence in being able to take decisions for yourself, being able to instruct someone else to do something for you, that you are unable to do yourself. To promote an atmosphere of relaxation and homeliness, thus making it less like an institution. To afford the residents the security of a family-type home and the personal attention of constant members of staff. This requires some explanation. The staff are divided into groups of roughly four. The staff are the care staff, the domestic staff, the cooks, the night staff. The staff are all experts in their own field, in their own right, and they all have responsibility within the home, to the residents and with the residents. To allow the staff to get to know a few members of the resident group we divide the residents into groups of around seven or eight who constantly have the personal attention for the more intimate side of life of these particular members of staff within the home. Instead of knowing all of them, instead of all the staff knowing all the residents only slightly, they know a few residents very intimately and the other residents less well. This gives the resident someone they can identify with both before and after admission and throughout their stay at the home.

Before a resident comes to stay with us they know the situation pretty well. They are visited at home by us before they make the decision even to come into care, if that is possible.

They know something about the place before they come for their first visit. They come to see the home again, if possible, before they make the decision to come into care. You wouldn't choose a hotel without seeing a brochure. Why should they make a decision to come into care without seeing it first? We also endeavour to give the relatives of each resident someone other than the officer-in-charge to identify with in relation to their relatives care. Unfortunately, I feel society still holds officers of old folks homes somewhere 'up there', which is a load of nonsense. We are very ordinary people and we should not make it difficult for them to come to an officer-in-charge if they feel they wish to make a complaint, or are concerned that it will be seen as a complaint, as opposed to discussion. This is not so, but to try and ease the strain for them, the relatives also have a chance to get to know the members of staff well before their relative goes into care. This gives them a more intimate relationship with the home.

To enable the staff to continually assess the needs of residents in their groups and work with the officer-in-charge, we have group care meetings, what we term continuity of care. We have records on each resident which the resident helps us to devise and these records contain the little simple things that make daily life more human. Does the resident like to bath or shower? How hot do they like the water? Which bits do they prefer to wash themselves? Do they prefer you to disappear for ten minutes?

Can you make them safe enough to do this? All these little things that if a member of staff was off sick and there was a relief person there, then that person does not continually have to ask. They have a knowledge of each resident when they go to work with them . . . of what they basically like. Now if the resident wishes to change this from time to time that's fine, that's their choice, but at least there is a basis to work on without someone strange having to go and say, 'What was it you like, Mrs So-and-so? I think I'll just give you a bath', when the person does not like to say, 'Well, actually, I don't like a bath; I like a shower'. It takes a lot of courage in these circumstances, when someone else has the initiative, the clothes are off, and it is a very intimate situation. It takes a lot of courage, as anyone who has ever been in hospital as a patient will know. It is very difficult to say, 'I don't like you doing that. I would prefer to do that myself'.

To assess the needs of residents we have care meetings, as I said, where the resident is invited if they wish. Some do, some don't. We discuss any points about their care and we would hope that the resident will take part in the decision-making within that meeting. It is a very informal thing, and as a resident gains confidence you find that they are more willing to challenge you and to say what they want, and how they see you filling their needs.

We encourage inter-group activity by injecting some competition into the lives of residents and staff. I don't mean that one group is caring for their residents better than the other. I don't mean that at all; I mean inter-group darts matches, snooker, cards, scrabble, whatever, the residents want. The residents can organise these themselves. They are not formally organised unless the residents wish them to be so and then we take part in the organisation of them. The aim is to motivate staff to work together as a team in order to improve the service to our clients the elderly. To improve their quality of life. That is the aim that we have in everything that we do. That is our way of life.

The aims of natural living are to give continuity of living, the basic premise being to give as much continuity as possible to the already established lifestyle of the resident when they enter care. I've mentioned about breakfast and rising time. The same goes for every aspect of someone's life. When someone comes into care there is a transition period. I don't like the term admission to care — there is a transition which is when someone steps over your threshold to make place for their home. There is a transition period where there is a settling in for all concerned and this is often a long period. During that period everyone is getting to know everyone else and developing a feeling of trust. Only from that trust is the knowledge gained and the resident begins to settle in their home and begins to continue their natural life. The process begins when the officer-in-charge or a member of staff visits the resident's home and the resident is then encouraged to visit us as often as is possible prior to admission. It is often possible to bring someone to day care. We have day care as well and it is often a good idea, if someone is uncertain, that they come and join us for day care. We should remember that for the age group we are talking about there were no old folks' homes as we know them or as we are supposed to know them. There were poor houses where poor and destitute people lived and that myth still lives. It is up to all of us as professionals to dispel that myth whenever we can.

What of the responsibilities of the residents and staff who are living together in one home? Each has areas of responsibility. There is no strong reason why the responsibility should not be interchangeable. For example, the setting of the dining room and the serving of meals can equally well be done by a resident, by a member of staff, by an officer-in-charge, a member of care staff or by a member of domestic staff. Manning the telephone, answering the door bell — it's their door, don't ever forget that, it's their front door and they have a right to answer it. I have said a right and I mean a right. When we have a staff meeting at the home, one of our residents mans the telephone and sits with her pad and takes messages. She can get very stroppy with anyone who won't believe that Mrs McCallum isn't available and will only be available at such and such a time. She can be quite shirty with people and that's fine. It is natural living. Washing dishes, making beds, tidying rooms jointly in one's own home can be shared jointly in an establishment and that makes sure the officer-in-charge's function is not just to sit behind a desk and stay there for the duration of a shift. In other words, we are all part of the same team.

Resident-orientated living. Setting a timetable for living to suit 36 residents, to me, is an impossible task, utterly impossible. In an environment promoting natural living, meal times, bath times, bed-making, bed time, should be tailored where possible to the desires of the residents rather than the convenience of the staff. In other words, everything is negotiable. What the residents must understand as well as the staff is that we do not jump when someone snaps their fingers. If we are busy with another resident and you as a resident wish to go to bed immediately . . . I am sorry, but we need to discuss it because I am busy right now with someone else and will ten minutes do? There are responsibilities on both sides and to know each other's responsibilities is important.

A resident's programme for their day should give them the chance to express all aspects of life as they see it.

Residents should be encouraged to do any work they wish to do and are capable of doing both within the home and in any other capacity that is possible. You care for your own homes, why shouldn't the resident be allowed to care for their own room if they wish? If they wish to make their bed and it is not perfect, are you really going to tell me that you would straighten it up, not for their own comfort, but so that it looks better? Too often I've heard, 'But it's wrinkled'. Tough, so it's wrinkled, the resident has achieved something. Are you going to take that away from them? I don't think you've got the right to do that. You can take the resident with you and say, 'Would you like me to straighten the bottom sheet before you get back into your bed?' That's different, but to go behind their back and do again work that they have done because it isn't up to your standard equates with going into a friend's home and doing her housework because it doesn't come up to your standard.

Education? There is no reason why residents shouldn't be involved in further education of either a purely educational or leisure variety. Classes either run outwith the home or classes run by the home. That comes back to a point I made earlier of the worth of residents and their abilities and, again, we'll talk a bit more about that later on. Decision-making? Responsibilities and decisions are taken by residents themselves. Group decisions would be taken by the group at group meetings and implemented by whoever the group designates. The points of identity, self-identification, recognition and esteem are encouraged in various ways: staff address the residents by the name that they have intimated they wish to be known by. That goes on two counts. It goes for the resident and it goes for the member of staff. It is a two-way thing like everything that happens in the home. Like keeping the continuity of the past through your favourite belongings, pictures, ornaments. Everything, even if it means that the residents bring tons of belongings with them and keep them in boxes in their rooms or somewhere that they know they are — if there isn't room to have all the ornaments and china out at once. What's wrong with changing them over every so often? As long as they have got them with them, that's the main thing. One lady we discovered had prized possessions which her family had given her when she moved to her pensioner's house. We now have a beautiful rose garden because we dug out all her roses and they came too, along with the budgie and the goldfish and three ducks. Now, the dog and ducks didn't get on too well, so that was a problem!

Orientation? The name of the home is prominently placed and identifies where we all are. Clocks and calendars are prominently placed and are large enough to be seen from a distance to identify time and date. There is also identification of toilets, kitchens, lounges and so on. Menus identify meal times as well as what is for the meal and they also have the day and the month on them and the year. Expectation? An air of expectation can be achieved by the use of a noticeboard to intimate coming events and any news items from within the staff or residents' groups. For example, the birth of a grandchild, a wedding, an anniversary . . . of a member of staff or a resident. They can all be intimated and it means that everyone can take part in that celebration.

Community involvement? The place of a home in the community has to be developed to make the home an accepted part of the community. Local pensioners' clubs, fund-raising, residents taking part in community activities where its possible, church activities where the resident has been in the habit of being involved, are appropriate. Remembering that it's if the individual wishes to be involved. It is not 'thou shalt'. Our community involvement has been far-reaching. It has reached as far as Poland.

In many cases the residents have been able to give, and a lot of people in care are not able to do that. They are not often allowed to do that. For example we have contact with the Girl Guides. Some of the residents are examiners for the Guide badges and sometimes the residents are invited to go down to the Guide meetings.

One of the local theatres has a musical group and one of them 'phoned me and said they'd like to do a show on World War Two. What they meant was an ongoing show with poetry, songs and words describing events in 1945 and they came along and did this show for the residents. We didn't say to them, 'Don't you think the residents could help you with this?' However, they are helping out with one on World War One and hopefully they'll be presenting that soon.

Self-care? Caring for each other in a physical sense is most important to build relationships within the home. Why seek the help of a volunteer? I have nothing against volunteers before someone jumps down my throat — but why seek the help of a volunteer when someone within the resident's group can help each other? We can all help each other; it would do us the world of good if we did help each other. It gives residents a sense of purpose, a sense of worth, and a knowledge that they are needed and wanted and they have the ability.

Illness? Residents who are ill are left at home unless they need to go to hospital, in which case the resident is transferred. The ill person is not otherwise moved away from their home at this time as he or she needs the people and surroundings he knows most.

For all this to be accomplished, it is vital that officers-in-charge show a leadership example in their contact with residents and staff. How can you expect staff to sit and talk to residents if you won't? Those of you at management level and senior nurses must know that. Residents and staff should be interchangeable in their roles, too, as carers and domestic staff, administrators and managers. They must be able to fill all of these functions and officers-in-charge, more importantly, must be willing to exchange their roles.

Risk-taking? Under the philosophy of natural living, it is important to give some thought to risk-taking and how far we as staff are willing to watch residents taking risks in going about their daily life. We as staff must discuss this and decide what constitutes a risk in the first place for each particular resident. We cannot have a list of risks because each individual is different. They are different individuals in their own right and its going to be different for each individual. Do you stop a resident making tea for themselves in case they burn themselves, or stop a frail person walking in case they fall? Do you deny the resident the privacy of bathing on their own in case they drown? If we deny people the right to take risks, we deny them the right to live. Do you have the right? I don't. Privacy and self-respect go together and if you don't afford the residents the privacy in all aspects of their lives you will ruin their self-respect and you cannot expect privacy from them. This means that you must knock on doors, shut doors, keep confidences. Respect the resident's wishes. Remember it could be you in that shower. You must not talk over residents at any time.

One of the best things that has ever happened to me was about a year ago. I was taken with a group of other social workers, for want of a better description, to a university residential building and I spent the day as a resident in an old folk's home. My disabilities were poor sight, my eyes were bandaged. I was very badly arthritic, my hands were bandaged. My knees were buckled and bandaged, I walked with a Zimmer frame and I spent a day like that along with 12 others with other disabilities. Some were acting roles as confused people. Other people who had previously been on the course were playing roles of the way a multitude of staff act. Some very well, some pretty awful, some absolutely disastrous. On one occasion we had gone for a meal and another girl and myself had had our meal, which can be very traumatic as you can imagine, trying to eat this way, and even go to the loo you needed help. You were physically taken to the loo by a stranger, people who were strangers to us. It's no different in an old folk's home. I got up after lunch to come out of the dining room and she went first and as we were making for the door, a voice boomed, 'Why are you leaving the table?'

'Because I want to,' I said, and went. I got back to the sitting room and thought, 'Who the hell did she think she was?' This female who was playing the officer-in-charge came across to me and said, 'Do you know that you have no right whatsoever to leave that table without permission?' I just about collapsed. Apparently this kind of behaviour does happen. Please, please don't let it happen in your home. If you are ever in any doubt of how it feels to be treated by a member of staff then go through one of these exercises. To be desperate for the loo and someone saying, 'Oh, be quiet, not just now, not just now.' To want to eat, but not being able to see and to be too disabled to cut up your food and not have the courage to ask. To be worried about something and not have the trust or the courage to say, 'Could someone help me?' because everyone is flying past you, or saying, 'Not just now; wait; go away'. You should try it some time, it is worthwhile. It's frightening, but it's worthwhile.

What I'd like to do now is tell you a little bit about the actual philosophy that we work under. This is the basis for everything we do. It is used as a means to combat both staff and resident dependency. First of all, you must ask yourself some questions — what is old age, when are we elderly people, how do you know when you are old? I did a study recently with some elderly people, looking for someone who felt old — me. I'm the only one that felt old. I'm only 40 but I felt old. No one felt old. It's a good thought. You'd better believe that the majority of elderly people can cope with life. They can learn new skills, they can solve the problems, retain and use knowledge and skills, verbalise their thoughts and have a variety of intellectual standards and have faulty or good memories, as with any other group. Remember, that if an elderly person mixes up a telephone message then they're labelled confused. If a teenager does it, they're scatterbrained. What's the difference? Remember that according to Erikson (1968), elderly people have a desire to leave something behind them when they die, a need to function in the elderly community, a need for attachments to familiar objects, places and people. They need a sense of time, and a sense of fulfilment in life. The philosophy of reminiscence sees each individual as a whole. The man as a whole, the man as part of his environment. Man is proactive rather than reactive. Man is capable of being aware of his own sensations, thoughts, emotions and perceptions. Man possesses the wherewith-all and resources to live effectively and to restore to himself his own assets. Man can experience himself only through the present. The past and the future can be experienced only in the now, through remembering and anticipating.

To use this philosophy, you will require the following skills. The ability to both hear and see what a person is saying; patience and stamina to wait until the time is right for a person to discuss their personal life with you. The ability to hear and recognise triggers when you are sitting talking to someone; to begin to recognise when they are trying to tell you something that they can't quite manage because it might just be something very important. The ability to create the correct atmosphere where it is permissible to display or feel emotion and not to be frightened of your own emotions. The intuition to feel when you are being invited to enter painful areas in that person's life and the self-awareness to know your own no-go areas and know that they, too, can be breached. The willingness to cope with your own pain with your clients when your own areas are breached. The ability to recognise and admit to your own inability to cope must be there.

If you do recognise that you cannot cope with someone's pain, please don't leave it, find someone who can. Personal pain and emotion go hand-in-hand with this philosophy. The outcome is a chance to reach self-actualisation for both you as members of staff and your clients as the residents in their home.

References

Erikson, E. (1968) *Identity, Youth and Crisis*, W.W. Norton and Co. Ltd, New York

McCallum, E. 'Motivation and Group Care in Homes for the Elderly', paper presented at British Society of Gerontology Annual Conference, Liverpool, 1983

——— 'Group Care and Natural Living', paper presented at Carer's Conference 'Adding Life to Years', Dumfries and Galloway Health Board, September, 1985

10 ETHICAL AND LEGAL ISSUES IN THERAPY WITH THE ELDERLY

Mary L.M. Gilhooly

The aim of this chapter is to provide an overview of the main ethical and legal issues in psychological therapies for the elderly. The issues to be considered are: (1) diagnosis as an ethical problem; (2) consent to therapy and research participation; (3) confidentiality; and (4) the role of the psychologist as clinician, scientist and bureaucrat. The chapter ends with a description of ways in which good ethical practice can be promoted through the informed decision process, ethical review committees and training in ethics. The chapter is aimed primarily at psychologists, but other health professionals who are involved in therapy with the elderly may also be interested.

Why include a chapter on ethics in a book on psychological therapies with the elderly? There are two reasons: (1) the elderly, like children or the mentally handicapped, are vulnerable to ethical abuses; and (2) little in the way of ethics is taught during the training of psychologists. Few clinical psychology courses in Britain have a lecture series or seminars on ethics, and it is extremely rare for psychology textbooks to have a chapter on ethics. Of course, there is a widespread view that ethics cannot be taught; that the only way it can be assured that psychologists behave ethically is to select ethical people and train them as psychologists. This view is analogous to the view held by many doctors about the skills involved in the doctor–patient relationship. There are, however, at least two arguments against this view. First, this view confuses the study of ethics with morals. Ethics has to do with the way in which one thinks about and discusses choices and moral problems (Michels, 1981). Thus, a 'good' person might not understand ethics and a 'bad' person might be able to reason at a sophisticated ethical level. Second, ethical behaviour may have its origins in character, but at the same time can be refined or developed through education.

The coverage of the ethical issues in treatments of the elderly cannot, of course, be comprehensive in a single chapter. However, there are now several books on psychiatric and medical ethics, and readers wanting a more comprehensive coverage on the issues discussed here should see some of the books referenced in the chapter.

Before moving on to a consideration of some of the issues in therapy with the elderly, it might be worthwhile looking at why there has been so much interest in ethics lately.

Reasons for the Interest in Ethics

In the past 15 to 20 years, interest among practitioners in health care in the ethical foundations of their work has blossomed. There are now journals, many textbooks and an increasing amount of time at professional conferences has been devoted to ethical concerns. The outcome of many of these conferences has been the adoption of ethical guidelines (for instance, the Declaration of Hawaii). Psychiatry has recognised that its problems are unique and deserve special attention: hence, the emergence of 'psychiatric ethics' (Bloch and Chodoff, 1981). The interest in psychiatric ethics has spilled over into psychology, especially the practice of clinical psychology.

There are four reasons for contemporary interest in the ethics of mental health care. First, there is the 'medical consumer movement', which can be seen as part of a broader scepticism of authority in general. The doctor no longer compels blind reverence. There has been a growing demand that the view of patients, and family members, be respected and acknowledged. Patients' associations and community health councils, plus the proliferation of self-help groups reflect the demand that patients be given more responsibility and say in treatment. Recipients of health care have recently come to constitute a powerful and coherent social force (Bloch and Chodoff, 1981; Faulder, 1985).

Second, the interest in mental health ethics has been associated with attacks on psychiatry and psychology by the 'civil liberties approach' to mental illness (Bloch and Chodoff, 1981). This movement has been generated largely by psychiatrists, for example, Laing and Szasz, but mental health lawyers have also been influential. Faced with criticism by colleagues and the legal profession, mental health professionals have been provoked into considering the ethics of their practice.

Third, there has been a questioning of the efficacy of psychology and psychiatric treatments. This has contributed to the rise of health care consumer movement and criticisms from within the mental health professions.

Finally, there has been greater contact with moral philosophers and others which has been influential. Moral philosophers have become more sensitive to the needs and interests of health professionals.

Diagnosis

Psychiatry's ability to cancel a person's freedom through its power to commit people to institutions has been the subject of most of the criticism of ethical abuses in the mental health field. But, as noted by Reich (1981), underpinning the power to commit is diagnosis. It is the privilege or right to diagnose that enables commitment to an institution. Thus, assessment and diagnosis should be the subject of serious and careful ethical consideration. The ethical dilemma of diagnosis is discussed here because other professionals, especially clinical psychologists, often participate in assessment and diagnosis and are, therefore, frequently collaborators in curtailing patients' freedom.

The ethical problem of diagnosis has to do with its capacity for misuse, that is, the actual or potential misapplication of diagnostic categories to persons who do not deserve or require them (Reich, 1981). The harmful effects of a misapplication of a diagnosis include loss of personal freedom, and confinement to a less than pleasant and potentially harmful environment, subjection to treatments and the possibility of life-long stigmatising labelling.

As noted by Reich (1981), misdiagnoses can originate in two ways: (1) purposeful and (2) non-purposeful. Purposeful misdiagnosis can be of two types; (a) a diagnosis given to someone, which is incorrect or inappropriate, in order to achieve an end, for instance, pressure from a family to institutionalise a troublesome relative; and (b) the client may request a particular diagnosis as protection from something else, for example, a diagnosis as protection from a prison sentence, avoidance of work or military service, to be eligible for an abortion and so on. Harm may result to the person when there is a misdiagnosis; harm to the integrity of the profession nearly always results.

Although purposeful misdiagnosis is a serious ethical concern, as noted by Reich (1981) non-purposeful misdiagnosis deserves as much, perhaps more, attention. Non-purposeful misdiagnoses include non-medical needs, pressures and compromises that affect the diagnostic process. These are not things of which the psychiatrist, psychologist or other professional is always fully aware. Reich (1981) outlines three sources of misdiagnosis: (1) the inherent limitations of the diagnostic process; (2) the power of diagnostic theory to shape professional judgement; and (3) the attraction of diagnosis as a solution to human problems. These three sources of misdiagnosis will be considered briefly.

Limitations of the Diagnostic Process

The vulnerability of the diagnostic process to error is the simplest and probably most understood and recognised source of misdiagnosis. Diagnosis has low reliability, is biased, relies on subjective criteria and tends to result in a diagnosis of health rather than illness (Mehlman, 1952; Plutchik, Conte and Landau, 1972; Temerlin, 1970). These problems with diagnosis raise ethical concerns only when they are ignored. As noted by Reich (1981), it is the responsibility of the diagnostician to remember the limitations of diagnosis and to be prepared to review decisions and admit fallibility.

The Power of Diagnostic Theory to Shape Judgement

The way that the psychologist or psychiatrist assesses a person's behaviour and mental state can be influenced heavily by the assumptions underlying the diagnostic system he or she is using. In countries where the diagnostic system in use is not officially sanctioned, a rigid vision of psychological reality is not imposed. But there are systems, such as that in the Soviet Union, where the official diagnostic system imposes a vision of reality that strictly moulds psychiatrists' and psychologists' perceptions of the nature, meaning and limits of psychopathology. It should be emphasised, however, that one is not talking about deliberately misdiagnosing patients here; Soviet psychiatrists really believe, for example, that schizophrenic pathology includes mild forms or symptoms that in the West would not be regarded as evidence of psychosis. However, the Soviet diagnostic system should not be seen as so unique that it has no relevance to diagnosis in the West. Psychologists need to be sensitive to the capacity of the systems in use here to shape the way that they perceive attitudes and behaviour, and understand and categorise clients.

Diagnosis as a Solution to Human Problems

According to Reich (1981), this category of sources of misdiagnosis is probably the most significant. Diagnosis is attractive as a means of solving (or avoiding) complex problems for the following reasons:

Diagnosis Offers an Explanation, Mitigation and Exculpation. Although odd or objectionable behaviour may be a consequence of mental disorder, the capacity of diagnosis to explain away troublesome behaviour makes its use a temptation even in cases in which a disorder does not truly exist.

The Power of Reassurance. Here the diagnosis shifts the frame of behaviour from a threatening personal or social arena to a safer medical one. Thus, acts that might be interpreted as vulnerabilities in society's institutions, communal beliefs or vulnerabilities in humans are reinterpreted as acts resulting from a medical problem. The health care professional should be aware of the ease with which he or she might turn to diagnosing a mental disorder if such a diagnosis would allay multiple concerns, a diagnosis which might not be made in cases which do not raise such concerns.

Diagnosis as a Humane Transformation of Social Deviance into Medical Illness. The goal here is humanitarian. People are viewed as essentially good and behaviour which is detrimental to society must, therefore, be due to an illness. Society benefits because its authorities do not have to exact harsh punishments, and the deviant benefits because he or she can be 'cured' rather than punished. The danger of this type of misdiagnosis is that such reclassifications may not, in the end, prove to be humanitarian. For example, treating a rapist as psychologically disordered and then subjecting him to pharmacological or behavioural treatments may not be humane. Telling juvenile offenders that they will not be punished if they submit to psychological treatment raises ethical issues. Such people might be worse off labelled as psychologically disturbed rather than having a criminal record.

Diagnosis as Exclusion and Dehumanisation. The three categories above can be said to reflect the human desire to be or do good. But diagnosis can be used to enable us to do things that we would not normally regard as good. For example, with the help of a diagnosis we can commit someone to an institution; not only can we use the diagnosis to deprive someone of freedom, but we can say to ourselves that the person requires exclusion from society — he not only has a need to be put away, he deserves to be put away. This is referred to as 'diagnostic dehumanisation'. It has many advantages to health care professionals; they do not have to see themselves as violators of human dignity. In fact, as pointed out by Reich (1981), the professional can see himself as helping and can, thus, in good conscience 'allow himself to do unto the patient that which he would not have others do unto himself' (1981, p. 79).

Diagnosis as a Self-confirming Hypothesis. Because there are no objective criteria for a diagnosis of mental disorder, psychological diagnoses have a remarkable ability to be self-confirming. If the client or patient claims that he or she is not ill or crazy, the disclaimer is taken as evidence that he or she is indeed disordered. Everything done after assessment and diagnosis can be seen as evidence that the diagnosis is correct. Thus, the psychologist or psychiatrist is rarely ever proved to be wrong. Hasty and inaccurate diagnoses go undetected, further encouraging a cavalier issuance of diagnoses.

Diagnosis as Discreditation and Punishment. Here diagnosis is used as a weapon. The person's views and politics are said to be the result of a sick mind. Most readers will be aware of how political dissidents have been found mentally ill and committed to hospitals for the criminally insane (Bloch and Chodoff, 1981). Political leaders are often said to be mentally deranged and hence discredited.

Although some might wish to argue that using a diagnosis to help someone is unethical, the danger is that its use will get out of hand, that its use will extend, increasingly, to other uses which would not be considered good for society. All abuses of diagnosis become an abuse of the health professions. Professionals need to be aware of the attractions of diagnosis in order to keep from yielding unknowingly.

Consent

The issue of consent to treatment or research participation is one of the most contentious issues in health care. It is generally accepted that, with few exceptions, treatments and research cannot proceed without consent. Nevertheless, what counts as 'valid' consent is uncertain. The legal doctrine of consent is explained by reference to the law of trespass to the person and battery. Thus, health care professionals and researchers are exempted from the civil and criminal wrongs of intentionally and injuriously touching a person by the consent of that person (Kirby, 1983).

For consent to be valid, three elements must be considered: (1) whether or not the consent was 'informed'; (2) whether or not the patient or research participant was competent to understand or did understand the consequences and nature of the therapy or research project; and (3) whether or not the patient or potential research participant's consent was voluntary and not the result of coercion (Smith, 1979). Each of the elements of consent will be considered, as well as the exceptions to the general rule of informed consent.

Informed Consent

In law 'informed consent' stems from the law of negligence. The law of negligence holds researchers and therapists responsible for inadequate disclosures that might lead to injury (Beauchamp and Childress, 1983; Kirby, 1983; Mason and McCall Smith, 1983). The ethical principle underlying informed consent is the right of self-determination, a right stemming from the principle of autonomy. This general notion is said to be based on inherent natural rights, or a political notion of the importance of the individual (Kirby, 1983). Accepting the doctrine of informed consent leaves us with the question of exactly what the health professional must tell the patient or potential research subject; that is, how much information must or should be given to the patient. Although it is not easy to decide exactly how much information should be disclosed to meet the criteria of a truly informed consent, it is necesary to attempt to develop guidelines or criteria for disclosure.

Current opinion holds that to comprehend the significance of a treatment, the patient-client does not need to know 'everything' about the treatment (Faulder, 1985; Mason and McCall Smith, 1983). What is needed is specific information directly related to the type of a treatment being contemplated. Here the concept of the 'reasonable person' is relevant (Kirby, 1983). Reasonable people have, of course, reason in common; what they do not have in common are the same reasons for adopting a particular course of action. This variability in reasoning means that the objective standards by which a reasonable person would expect to give consent, must be judged by the people from whom consent is sought, rather than those seeking consent, that is, the doctor or therapist (Faulder, 1985). Thus, it is up to the patient to decide how much information is necessary and adequate.

Competency and Understanding

Meeting adequate information must be adequate understanding. It has, of course, been argued that patients can never be truly informed, that is, they will never (or certainly rarely) achieve the understanding of the doctors, psychologist and so on (Ingelfinger, 1972). However, as noted by Faulder (1985), though patients may never understand the intricacies of some treatments, they can quite adequately understand the significance of a treatment for themselves if it is 'properly' explained.

Adequate understanding requires skilled communication. The communicator must avoid technical jargon and be aware of class differences that hinder communication. Communicators must also constantly remind themselves that patients are in a vulnerable emotional state, may find it hard to absorb information, may be intimidated by therapists and are very likely to be afraid to ask for more information or voice worries.

Voluntary Consent

The therapist must also be thoroughly convinced that the consent process was not coercive. The possibility of coercion of an indirect nature must be very carefully considered when the patient is in an institutional setting. Even when asked to participate in research or to take part in group or individual therapy, when informed and consenting, elderly people in institutional settings (ranging from day centres to hospitals), may feel that they have to take part in research or treatment programmes. The higher status of the doctor, psychologist or researcher, the patient's needs to please nurses and so on are the basis of covert coercion.

Because institutional settings contain coercive elements, it is sometimes argued that people in institutions should never be asked to participate in research, especially non-therapeutic research. Counter-arguments can, of course, be offered to this view and some will now be considered along with other exceptions to consent.

Exceptions to Informed Consent

Most treatments administered by doctors are intended to cure or to alleviate pain. Psychological therapies with the elderly are also to cure (as in depression), to prevent excess decline (as in reality orientation) and to alleviate mental distress, and to aid coping (as in counselling).

Circumstances in which a doctor may proceed with treatment without consent include: (1) when the patient's mind is disturbed; (2) when the patient is unconscious; and (3) when the patient is a minor (British Medical Association, 1984). Because therapy with the elderly does not embrace points (2) and (3), the main exception to the principle of consent to consider here is the administration of therapy to clients who, by virtue of a mental disturbance, are unable to give consent.

Here it is worthwhile looking at what the law says about treating people with mental illness. To do so we must first distinguish between the involuntary patient and the 'informal' or voluntary patient. Anyone treated as an outpatient would have to consent to treatment; the law cannot compel treatment as an outpatient. In the same way, informal or voluntary hospital patients cannot be compelled to take part in therapy. However, it is possible to treat a person without consent if he or she has been detained in hospital under Part IV of the Mental Health Act 1983. However, there are certain treatments which cannot be administered even when a patient is detained under Part IV; psychosurgery and hormone implants are two examples. What is of interest is that people detained under Part IV can be treated when they are competent and refuse consent as well as when they are incompetent and refuse to consent. For this to happen, a doctor must state in writing that the patient has not consented and/or is incapable of understanding the nature of the treatment, but that treatment should be given to prevent deterioration or to alleviate a condition. Furthermore, before giving a certificate, the independent doctor (appointed by the Mental Health Act Commission) must consult two other people who have been professionally concerned with the patient's treatment, one a nurse and the other neither a nurse nor a doctor (Gostin, 1983; Whitehead, 1983).

Thus, Section 58 of Part IV represents a fundamental departure from traditional common law assumptions in that it specifies circumstances in which therapy can be imposed upon a mentally ill patient who is regarded as competent but refuses consent. Nevertheless, good ethical practice demands that consent should be sought. There certainly should be substantial justification relating to the patient's health if treatment is to be imposed (Gostin, 1981, 1982).

There are two other, more controversial, exceptions to consent: (1) when disclosure of information would so seriously upset the client that she or he would be unable to weigh dispassionately the potential risks and benefits that would attend participation in therapy or research (Bernstein and Nelson, 1975); and (2) when there is no danger in the procedure, that is, no risk to life. However, if one maintains that the purpose of informed consent is to protect autonomy, and not just to protect the patient, then there is an obligation to obtain informed consent even in situations or procedures involving no risk. Although this may seem clear, much of the work done by clinical psychologists is with people who are not competent to give informed consent and, second, the therapy or results of the research study would be invalidated if the client were fully informed of the aims and procedures.

Misinformed Consent

Psychological research and even psychological therapies with the elderly often necessitate limiting the type and amount of information given to participants. In many research studies — therapeutic and non-therapeutic — full information would invalidate the data obtained. This type of requirement — keeping patients or research participants uninformed — presents many ethical dilemmas. Most investigators get round this by debriefing participants upon completion of the research, that is, telling the participants the aim and goals of the study after the procedures are completed. But, many elderly, dementing or mentally disturbed people may not be able to comprehend the debriefing procedure or information, and the debriefing session may confuse them further.

Unfortunately, what one is to do in situations like this is not ethically straightforward.

Although safeguards protecting potential research subjects and patients are important, it is also important that both therapeutic and non-therapeutic research take place. Ethical and legal doctrine dictate that the elderly be protected from unscrupulous researchers. However, research with, for example, the dementing elderly, may be important enough to justify violations of autonomy on utilitarian grounds.

Confidentiality

Once a client has been diagnosed and informed of a diagnosis, indeed, even before the patient is given a diagnosis, ethical considerations arise concerning who is to have access to the diagnosis and the information given by the client in the process of bringing about a diagnosis. The principles of privacy, confidentiality and privileged communications are important here.

Privacy refers to the right of individuals to have control over personal information and to be free of intrusions into their lives. Confidentiality, an outgrowth of privacy, refers to the ethical obligation not to reveal to others anything said by the client or to acknowledge the existence of a relationship. The concept of confidentiality is an ancient one. The ethics of confidential communications were codified in the fourth century in the Hippocratic Oath which states, 'All that may come to my knowledge in the exercise of my profession or in the daily commerce with men, which ought not to be spread abroad, I will keep secret and will never reveal'. Although a confidential contractual association is often assumed, in the United Kingdom no formal or specific law of privacy exists (Mason and McCall Smith, 1983). However, there is considerable respect for medical confidentiality in British courts (Beigler, 1981, in Bloch and Chodoff).

Privileged communication refers to the legal protection provided patients and clients by statute or the courts in legal matters relating to the client. In the United Kingdom no privilege attaches to communications between patient and physician or between patient and psychologist in legal matters relating to the client. In the United States, theoretically, the physician, psychologist and so on is legally obliged to retain the confidences of the client in legal proceedings, unless the client has waived his or her right to the privilege or, as part of a lawsuit, has entered medical records or emotional condition as an important element in the litigation

(Noll and Rosen, 1982). In some European countries, the obligation to maintain confidentiality also extends to the courtroom (Mason and McCall Smith, 1983).

Unless a person has been declared legally incompetent, privacy and confidentiality should prevent the professional from disclosing information to others — unless the patient wants that information to be disclosed. Nevertheless, because of the numerous exceptions to the ethical rule of confidentiality, one is led to question the status of this principle (Phillips and Dawson, 1985).

The Exceptions to the Rule of Professional Secrecy

Five exceptions to the rule of professional secrecy are listed by most professional organisations (for instance, the British Medical Association, 1984; the British Psychological Society, 1985). They can be considered as allowable breaches of the principle of confidentiality; that is, they can be justified by other ethical principles such as beneficience and utilitarianism.

Consent to Disclosure. A patient may authorise disclosure of information given to a professional. Without that consent the information remains, technically, the property of the patient. This consent is only considered to be valid if the patient has understood the nature and consequences of disclosure.

It is generally assumed that when a patient seeks help from a psychologist or medical practitioner that he or she is seeking help from the 'team' and that confidentiality extends to the other members of the team (Wing, 1981). However, it is unlikely that many patients realise that their case may be discussed at team meetings, or the extent of the range and numbers of people to whom this extended confidentiality applies. The patient is also unlikely to be aware that some of these people, for instance, psychologists, may be members of professional bodies that do not have sanctions for breaches of confidence; that is, such professionals cannot be disqualified if found guilty of a breach of confidence. It is also unlikely for a patient to say 'no' when asked if other members of the team may have access to information because of the power and status of the professional and the vulnerable position of the patient. Even so, much treatment, for example, hospital treatment and treatment by general practitioners could not take place if information had to be restricted to one person. Nevertheless, professionals should explain to clients exactly what confidentiality means today; they should explain the practice of extended confidentiality and obtain consent for disclosure of information to team members before embarking upon treatment.

Exceptional Circumstances and Patient Interests. Most codes of ethical conduct for professionals allow for breaches of confidentiality under exceptional circumstances and if it is in the patient's interests. Examples given for breaches of confidentiality in medicine include 'Circumstances . . . which render it undesirable for a patient to be told the full implications of his condition' (British Medical Association, 1984), and when the doctor decides relatives with particular regard to the circumstances should be informed. Although the ethical principle of beneficience is used to justify breaches of confidentiality in such cases, the professional should always keep in mind that such practice involves a strong element of paternalism and a certain lack of respect for the principle of autonomy. Only the patient can decide or know what is in his or her best interests.

Duty to Society. Because 'duty to society' can be defined in so many different ways and by different groups with different values, this is perhaps the most controversial of the exceptions to confidentiality. Examples which would cause most psychologists difficulty include a revelation by a patient that he has committed one or several rapes, that he or she had been considering murder, that he or she was repeatedly battering a dementing parent and so on. Few patients would reveal such information if they thought that, for example, it would be disclosed to the police or if potential victims were warned. Without the trust of a confidential relationship, the person would not seek help and thus would remain a danger to others.

There is no general agreement as to how the psychologist ought to proceed in such circumstances, although most codes of practice indicate that where there is evidence which would raise serious concern about the safety of others, the professional may inform appropriate third parties without prior consent. However, it is recommended that an experienced and disinterested colleague should be consulted unless a delay would involve a significant risk to life or health (British Psychological Society, 1984).

The Law. Information required by law falls into two categories; that required by statutory instrument and non-statutory information, that is, information required by a court of law for individual cases. Information required by statute of medical practitioners includes the reporting of infectious diseases and industrial poisoning (Mason and McCall Smith, 1983). This type of information is not normally dealt with by psychologists and hence is rarely problematic for the practice of clinical psychology. However, courts of law can compel the disclosure of information through the production of documents or during evidence and cross-examination. Refusal to answer questions in court would expose a psychologist to a charge of contempt of court in Britain.

Storage and Access to Clinical Information for Research Purposes. It is generally accepted that information in medical, psychiatric, psychological and other types of records may be used for research purposes without the consent of the patient or client provided that certain practices are followed such as rendering the information anonymous, and safeguarding the security of records (British Psychological Society, 1984; Wing, 1981).

Breach of Confidence and the Law

Given that the principle of confidentiality is not absolute in the United Kingdom, what can the patient do when confidentiality is breached?

To prevent anticipated breaches of confidence, a patient can obtain an injunction. However, this does little for past breaches of confidentiality. Previous cases have resulted in the award of damages for disclosure of information, but in these cases the information has had commercial value. There is still considerable uncertainty as to whether or not the relevation of purely personal information, especially if it is true, will result in the award of damages (Mason and McCall Smith, 1983). However, the Law Commission has recommended the introduction of a new sort of breach of confidence which would allow for the awarding of damages where the plaintiff has suffered an insult to his feelings as a result of the improper disclosure of confidential information. This would, of course, have important implications for the practice of clinical psychology.

Maintaining Confidentiality After Death

The legal duty to maintain confidentiality ends with the death of the patient (Mason and McCall Smith, 1983). However, current opinion holds that the death of a patient does not erase the obligation to maintain secrecy. From a practical point of view, of course, the practice of clinical psychology, psychiatry or medicine would be impossible without the confidence that the patient has in the therapist and the trust that the therapist will not reveal all upon his or her death. The elderly, in particular, may be reluctant to confide in a psychologist if they knew that confidences would be revealed upon death.

The Role of the Psychologist as Clinician, Scientist and Bureaucrat

The practice of clinical psychology, like psychiatry and medicine, involves many competing roles. Three roles which frequently require different social and ethical positions are the roles of clinician, scientist and bureaucrat (Freidson, 1970; Mechanic, 1981). Although the activities involved in these three roles overlap, it is useful to separate them in order to examine the ethical dilemmas posed when operating as a clinician, scientist and bureaucrat. Because nearly all therapists dealing with the elderly think of themselves primarily as clinicians, the role of clinician will be contrasted with the roles of scientist and bureaucrat.

The roles of clinician and scientist require quite different stances. The main objective of the scientist is knowledge (Freidson, 1970). The pursuit of knowledge, on the other hand, requires detachment and sceptism, attitudes likely to discourage the patient and erode the suggestive powers of the therapeutic encounter (Mechanic, 1981). Clinicians, however, must believe in what they are doing; it would be dysfunctional for both clinicians and patients if clinicians lacked faith in their own ability to help patients.

The differences in the objectives of the clinician and scientist require different ways of acting out the two roles. For example, the therapist-scientist requires precise and reliable diagnoses. Without clear distinctions, knowledge about effective therapies cannot be acquired (Mechanic, 1978). But, efforts in making fine distinctions among clinical entities may yield no benefit for the patient. And, as noted by Mechanic (1981), such activities, plus the labelling of questionable conditions, may even divert the therapist-clinician from taking constructive therapeutic action and, furthermore, may cause harm by stigmatising the patient and inducing anxiety.

As a clinician, the psychologist works only partly on the basis of scientific knowledge. The role of clinician requires a dependence on subjective experience or trial and error in time of uncertainty; in other words, a pragmatic approach. The psychologist as clinician cannot be constrained by the state of established scientific knowledge. Were clinicians to be constrained by established knowledge, they would have to refuse help to many of those who suffer and seek help. However, this means that clinicians work, at least partly, on the basis of social judgement as to what is deviant and what is appropriate treatment. As problems become more uncertain, and in situations where there is little established knowledge as to what course of action should be taken, the clinician's values and social biography have a greater influence on decision-making.

This is what is meant by the political and social aspects of therapeutic work, and is something the psychologist as clinician should always keep in mind.

Psychologists as scientists may claim that the results of their research may benefit patients or others with similar problems. However, scientists are unlikely to claim or believe that they are acting solely in the interests of patients. On the other hand, when psychologists are acting as clinicians it is assumed that they are acting for the sake of patients alone. Clinicians' values and views may lead to behaviour which is not, in fact, in the interest of patients, but at least they are operating under the belief that all action is for the benefit of patients. Nevertheless, unless clinicians are practising privately, that is, being paid by patients, and are treating patients solely (for instance, not conducting family therapy), they cannot be absolutely certain that they represent only the interests of patients. Whenever a professional is employed by an organisation other than the patient, there is, by definition, a split loyalty.

Because conflict of loyalty is not a major issue in routine practice, few therapists are even aware of the ethical dilemmas in ways that eventually harm the interests of the patient and acting on behalf of parties other than the patient. For example, a dementing person seeks help and is assessed and diagnosed. The diagnosis and prognosis are then used by family members to obtain institutional care. The dementing elder's interests are harmed by institutionalisation; the elderly dementing person sought 'help' and gave information which was expected to lead to help, not harm.

The Promotion of Ethical Practice

In this section, ways in which good ethical practice can be promoted will be discussed. Professionals offering therapy or doing research can ensure that the process for gaining consent is not coercive. They can also ensure ethical practice by encouraging the formation and work of ethical review committees and by submitting their research plans or non-standard therapies, even when not required, to ethical committees. Patients can also be encouraged to take an active interest in consent procedures, and to know their rights. Finally, ethical practice can be promoted through the teaching of ethics during the training of psychologists and other mental health care professionals. These four aspects of the promotion of ethical practice will now be considered.

The Process of Informing for Decision

Until recently, little attention was paid to the 'process' of informed consent. It is frequently assumed that if a person presents for therapy, he or she 'consents'. Written 'informed consent' forms are rarely used in Britain for treatments other than surgery. The closest psychologists get to written consent forms are written agreements, or 'contracts', between therapist and patient for certain types of treatments and problems. For example, a therapist working with a person with an alcohol problem might devise a plan of therapy and then write it up as a contract for discussion and agreement with the patient. This is done not so much to protect the therapist against liability or to protect the autonomy of the patient (although it does all these), but because such a contract has been found to be useful in getting therapy off the ground and in keeping the patient in therapy.

There are arguments both for and against the use of written consent forms for psychological therapies. Consent forms force the therapist or researcher to think about the meaning of informed consent, the principle of personal autonomy and rights of self-determination. This should be of benefit to the patient.

The arguments against the use of written consent forms are at two levels. First, informed consent forms may be used to absolve the researcher or therapist of liability for harm or wrong-doing, rather than act as an instrument to protect autonomy. As noted by Goldstein (1978), so much attention is now devoted to the state of mind of the patient or potential research participant and his or her ability to comprehend the information given in order to give 'informed' consent, that attention is being directed away from the conduct of the therapist or researcher. Goldstein argues that less attention should be paid to the 'informed' part of informed consent and more to 'freedom to decide'. What we should be thinking about is informed decision-making, perhaps even informed refusal, and not informed consent. The whole process of getting people to sign informed consent forms is directed to getting consent.

The other reason for not having written consent forms actually relates to refusal rates. Many people are happy to consent to therapy or participation in research projects, especially research not involving risks of physical harm, but do not like the idea of signing consent forms. The need for written consent often makes people suspicious of the motives of the researchers or therapists. The elderly in particular may be suspicious of signing forms.

Perhaps written consent forms should be used in the spirit in which they are intended; that is, as a written contract between therapist and patient, a contract indicating that the therapist and patient have decided together to pursue a particular form of treatment. Since consent forms for research are usually perceived by potential participants as a method of limiting liability for the researcher, rather than as a way of promoting autonomy, perhaps they should not be used for psychological research. Not signing a consent form to participate in research may also make it easier for people to change their minds about participation.

Another method of ensuring that consent is valid, that is, informed and free from coercion, is to have the consent process witnessed. Although it would be more difficult for a therapist or researcher to coerce a person in front of a colleague or independent witness, there are problems of maintaining confidentiality when therapy contracts are witnessed. However, there are strong grounds for witnessed consent for non-therapeutic research.

Ethical Committees

In 1966 the United States Public Health Service mandated Institutional Review Committees (IRCs) to monitor the ethical aspects of research proposals for Public Health Service funding. The requirements have now been extended to all institutions in the United States which apply for health, education and welfare research support (Makarushka and McDonald, 1979). In Britain the Medical Research Council requires that all MRC-supported research be vetted by an ethical committee.

The primary functions of ethical committees are: (1) to protect the rights of the subjects and associated staff in terms of confidentiality and privacy by emphasising the voluntary aspects of participation via appropriate informed consent mechanisms; and (2) to evaluate the scientific merit of the research proposal and the qualifications of the investigators in order to assess the appropriateness of the risk–benefit relationship for subjects. Additional functions of ethical review committees which are not generally acknowledged are: (1) the effective utilisation of the finite resources of the institution *vis-à-vis* the particular research proposal; and (2) the development of consensus within the institution on the ethical treatment of research subjects (Makarushka and McDonald, 1979).

Ethical committees are usually composed of researchers, administrators and representatives of interested groups (legal staff, clergy, patients and nurses), plus a member of the lay public. Thus, ethical committees represent a new relationship between the scientific research community and the larger society.

In a broader sense, ethical committees reflect society's concern with real and potential abuses of research subjects. However, what must not be allowed to happen is to have ethical committees end up as primarily legitimising the conduct of research and the activities of researchers.

Ethical committees generally function to vet research proposals. However, ethical committees should also concern themselves with the conduct of therapy, and therapists would be wise to submit proposed therapeutic plans to ethical committees if they are non-standard therapies. It is not suggested, of course, that members of ethical committees are in a better position to judge the merits of a particular form of therapy (though some therapists do delude themselves as to the efficacy of their therapies), but the committee could ensure that consent to treatment is valid and informed and that coercion is not used to obtain consent. Standard therapies, that is, those with proven efficacy, would not of course need to be submitted to ethical committees. But many therapies have an almost 'experimental' or research quality to them when they are first utilised. Thus, independent opinion on new therapies would be desirable.

Another area which might be tackled by ethical committees is the special problems raised by computerised medical information systems. The scrutiny of an ethical committee would help the professional to focus his or her attention on the issues involved. There is, of course, no consensus on how committees would operate with regard to medical information systems. However, Wing (1981) suggests that those who supply information to registers should be represented and a member of the committee should understand the problems of computer security.

Patients' Bill of Rights

The trend in recent years has been towards viewing informal consent, confidentiality and so on, as more than a concession or a courtesy, but instead as a inalienable human right; rights protecting personal integrity and autonomy. In line with these views has been the drawing up of patients' bills of rights.

The American Hospital Association produced the first Patients' Bill of Rights (see Appendix A). This particular document has no legal standing but has been used as a model for a number of government bodies in the United States which have adopted legally binding bills of rights.

The European Parliament tabled a resolution in 1984 inviting the submission of proposals for a European Charter on the Rights of Patients (Appendix B). Among the 15 rights are the right to information concerning diagnosis, therapy and prognosis, rights of access to patients' own medical data, patients' right to refuse the treatment proposed and the right to complaint based on damage to the interests of the patient

(Faulder, 1985).

Even if not legally binding, such bills are important because they define certain human rights based on moral principles which must be recognised and honoured; thus, they are for the protection of the patient and not drawn up by a professional body to protect that group's interests.

Patients' bills of rights make the relationship between professional and patient more of a contractual one. Such bills make it more likely that the relationship is a 'partnership' mutually entered into, but underwritten by certain accepted obligations on both sides.

Training in Ethics

Most of the psychologists reading this book will have received little in the way of training in ethics. This, of course, is not to say that psychologists are more evil than other mental health professionals. However, the issue is not solely one of moral practice; instead, discussion needs to be conducted in an 'ethical', rather than merely a 'moral' framework.

How, then, are ethical sensitivities to develop? One prevalent view of the teaching of ethics is that the only appropriate way to teach ethics is through modelling. Two arguments against this approach are that: (1) to improve ethical practice, one then has to teach the teachers; and (2) one can only show the final product, that is, the decision through modelling and not most of the ethical 'reasoning' that went into the final decision (Michels, 1981).

Teaching can proceed in other ways. One approach is to teach by the case method; case conferences and supervision of specific therapies form the course work, and the ethical aspects of the psychologist's work are then studied alongside and in the same way as studying, for example, pharmacological aspects of treatment. Although this method of teaching has obvious appeal to students, there is a tendency to focus on unusual cases and issues related to specific patients, rather than problems that recognise the universality of ethics as a framework for understanding professional functioning and the relationship between the professional and society (Michels, 1981).

Another approach to the teaching of ethics is to provide a core curriculum with a fundamental body of knowledge taught through lectures and seminars, with applications of specific problems being considered during supervision of clinical practice. This model appears attractive, but in reality is rarely employed, even in medical or psychiatric training. However, professionals should aim towards this approach.

What should be taught depends, of course, on the goals and objectives of a teaching programme in ethics. A major goal should be an understanding of major systems of ethical reasoning. Another goal should be sensitising students to the ethical aspects of issues that might otherwise be seen as technical or scientific in nature (Michels, 1981). Thus, one would wish to include in an ethics course a basic introduction including the philosophical basis of moral discourse (meta-ethics), discussions of the normative rules, standards and codes of the profession, plus the teaching of specific issues in the field. At the end of the course, one would hope to have advanced the student's skill in recognising ethical problems, his ability to reason about them in a coherent, systematic and useful way, his understanding of the reasoning of others and his participation in ethical discourse.

Concluding Comments

Many of the ethical and legal issues considered in this chapter are relevant to groups other than the elderly. However, the elderly are a group particularly vulnerable to ethical abuses. A high proportion of the elderly, compared to younger age groups, suffer from dementia, and the dementing elderly are subject to considerable legal, administrative and professional involvement in their lives (Gilhooly, 1986). The elderly, because of both physical and mental infirmities, are at higher risk of institutionalisation. There are real problems of consent for therapy and research in institutional settings containing many indirect coercive elements. Finally, the elderly are vulnerable to ethical abuses because of the negative stereotypes that exist in Western society about old people. For example, it is frequently assumed that all old people are 'senile' and hence no longer need to be treated as competent to understand the details of a therapy or research programme. Such assumptions are used to excuse violations of the informed consent rule and hence the principle of autonomy.

It is hoped that this chapter will encourage psychologists and other mental health professionals to think more carefully about the ethical bases of their practices, both in therapy and in research.

Appendix A: American Hospital Association — A Patient's Bill of Rights

The American Hospital Association represents a Patient's Bill of Rights with the expectation that observance of these rights will contribute to more effective patient care and greater satisfaction for the patient, his physician, and the hospital organisation. Further, the Association presents these rights in the expectation that they will be supported by the hospital on behalf of its patients, as an integral part of the healing process. It is recognised that a personal relationship between the physician and the patient is essential for the provision of proper medical care. The traditional physician–patient relationship takes on a new dimension when care is rendered within an organisational structure. Legal precedent has established that the institution itself also has a responsibility to the patient. It is in recognition of these factors that these rights are affirmed:

1. The patient has the right to considerate and respectful care;

2. The patient has the right to obtain from his physician complete current information concerning his diagnosis, treatment and prognosis in terms the patient can be reasonably expected to understand. When it is not medically advisable to give such information to the patient, the information should be made available to an appropriate person on his behalf. He has the right to know, by name, the physician responsible for co-ordinating his care;

3. The patient has the right to receive from his physician information necessary to give informed consent prior to the start of any procedure and/or treatment. Except in emergencies, such information for informed consent should include but not necessarily be limited to the specific procedure and/or treatment, the medically significant risks involved and the probable duration of incapicitation. Where medically significant alternatives for care or treatment exist, or when the patient requires information concerning medical alternatives, the patient has the right to know the name of the person responsible for the procedures and/or treatment;

4. The patient has the right to refuse treatment to the extent permitted by law and to be informed of the medical consequences of his action;

5. The patient has the right to every consideration of his privacy concerning his own medical care programme. Case discussion, consultation, examination and treatment are confidential and should be conducted discreetly. Those not directly involved in his care must have the permission of the patient to be present;

6. The patient has the right to expect that within its capacity a hospital must make reasonable response to the request of a patient for services. The hospital must provide evaluation, service and/or referral as indicated by the urgency of the case. When medically permissible, a patient may be transferred to another facility only after he has received complete

information and explanation concerning the needs for and alternatives to such a transfer. The institution to which the patient is to be transferred must first have accepted the patient for transfer;

8. The patient has the right to obtain information as to any relationship of his hospital to other health care and educational institutions insofar as his care is concerned. The patient has the right to obtain information as to the existence of any professional relationships among individuals, by name, who are treating him;

9. The patient has the right to be advised if the hospital proposes to engage in or perform human experimentation affecting his care or treatment. The patient has the right to refuse to participate in such research projects;

10. The patient has the right to expect reasonable continuity of care. He has the right to know in advance what appointment times and physicians are available and where. The patient has the right to expect that the hospital will provide a mechanism whereby he is informed by his physician or a delegate of the physician of the patient's continuing health care requirements following discharge;

11. The patient has the right to examine and receive an explanation of his bill regardless of source of payment;

12. The patient has the right to know what hospital rules and regulations apply to his conduct as a patient.

No catalogue of rights can guarantee for the patient the kind of treatment he has a right to expect. A hospital has many functions to perform, including the prevention and treatment of disease, the education of both health professionals and patients and the conduct of clinical research. All these activities must be conducted with an overriding concern for the patient and, above all, the recognition of his dignity as a human being. Success in achieving this recognition assures success in the defence of the rights of the patient.

(Approved by the American Hospital Association of Delegates, 6 February 1973.)

Appendix B: Resolution on a European Charter on the Rights of Patients

(a) the right to available treatment and care appropriate to the illness;

(b) the right to prompt treatment;

(c) the right to adequate social security cover to allow the rights set out in (a) to be exercised;

(d) the right to free choice of medical practitioner and health care establishment;

(e) the right of access to hospital service within a reasonable travelling distance;

(f) the right to information concerning diagnosis, therapy and prognosis, the patient's right of access to his own medical data and the patient's right to give his consent to or refuse the treatment proposed;

(g) the right to medical confidentiality, the only possible exceptions to which should be on a limited number of serious and well-defined grounds, having due regard for the integrity of the human person;

(h) the patient's right to lift the obligation of confidentiality completely or in part as regards his own medical records;

(i) the right to complaint based on 'damage to the interests of the patient';

(j) the right to an appeal procedure before the courts;

(k) the rights and duties of medical practitioners;

(l) the patient's right to be represented by independent associations and organisations;

(m) the definition of the legal status of the patient in a health care establishment;

(n) the right to respect for private life and for religious and philosophical convictions;

(o) the right to a dignified death.

4. Considers that it may be necessary, in certain well-defined circumstances, to limit the rights of patients where they would involve a danger to public health;

5. Is of the opinion that the specific problems pertaining to the rights of the mentally ill and of children should not be dealt with in this context but in a special charter.

(Extract from Resolution tabled by the European Parliament on 19 January 1984 and forwarded by the President to the Commission with the instruction to submit as soon as possible a European Charter on the Rights of Patients.)

References

Beauchamp, T.L. and Childress, J.E. (1983) *Principles of Biomedical Ethics*, Oxford University Press, Oxford

Beigler, J. (1981) 'Psychiatric Confidentiality and the American Legal System: An Ethical Conflict' in S. Bloch and P. Chodoff (eds.), *Psychiatric Ethics*, Oxford University Press, Oxford, pp. 220–34

Bernstein, J.E. and Nelson, F.K. (1975) 'Medical Experimentation in the Elderly', *Journal of the American Geriatric Society, 23*, pp. 327–9
Bloch, S. and Chodoff, P. (eds.) (1981) *Psychiatric Ethics*, Oxford University Press, Oxford
British Medical Association (1984) *The Handbook of Medical Ethics*, The British Medical Association, London
British Psychological Society (1985) 'A Code of Conduct for Psychologists', *Bulletin of the British Psychological Society, 38*, pp. 41–3
Faulder, C. (1985) *Whose Body Is It? The Troubling Issue of Informed Consent*, Virago Press, London
Freidson, E. (1970) *Profession of Medicine: A Study of the Social Structure of Applied Knowledge*, Dodd, Mead, New York
Gilhooly, M.L.M. (1986) 'Legal and Ethical Issues in the Management of the Dementing Elderly' in M.L.M. Gilhooly, S.H. Zarit and J.E. Birren (eds.), *The Dementias: Policy and Management*, Prentice Hall, Englewood Cliffs, New Jersey
Goldstein, J. (1978) 'On the Right of the "Institutionalized Mentally Infirm" to Consent To or Refuse to Participate as Subjects in Biomedical and Behavioural Research' in *National Commission for the Protection of Human Subjects of Biomedical and Behavioural Research. Research Involving those Institutionalized as Mentally Infirm: Research and Recommendations*, DHEW Publication No (OS) 78–006, Washington DC
Gostin, L.O. (1981) 'Observations on Consent to Treatment and Review of Clinical Judgment in Psychiatry: A Discussion Paper', *Journal of the Royal Society of Medicine, 74*, pp. 742–52
——— (1982) 'Compulsory Treatment in Psychiatry: Some Reflections on Self-determination, Patient Competency and Professional Expertise', *Poly Law Review*, pp. 86–93
——— (1983) *A Detailed Guide to Mental Health Law: The Mental Health Act 1983 and Related Legislation*, MIND, London
Ingelfinger, F.J. (1972) 'Informed (but Uneducated) Consent', *New England Journal of Medicine, 287*, pp. 465–6
Kirby, M.D. (1983) 'Informed Consent: What Does it Mean?', *Journal of Medical Ethics, 9*, pp. 69–75
Makarushka, J.L. and McDonald, R.D. (1979) 'Informed Consent, Research, and Geriatric Patients: The Responsibility of Institutional Review Committees', *The Gerontologist, 19*, pp. 61–6
Mason, J.K. and McCall Smith, R.A. (1983) *Law and Medical Ethics*, Butterworths, London
Mechanic, D. (1978) *Medical Sociology*, The Free Press, New York
——— (1981) 'The Social Dimension' in S. Bloch and P. Chodoff (eds.), *Psychiatric Ethics*, Oxford University Press, Oxford, pp. 46–60
Mehlman, P. (1952) 'The Reliability of Psychiatric Diagnoses', *Journal of Abnormal and Social Psychology, 47*, pp. 577–8
Michels, R. (1981) 'Training in Psychiatric Ethics' in S. Bloch and P. Chodoff (eds.), *Psychiatric Ethics*, Oxford University Press, Oxford, pp. 295–305
Noll, J.O. and Rosen, C.E. (1982) 'Privacy, Confidentiality and Informed Consent in Psychotherapy' in B.L. Bloom and S.J. Asher (eds.), *Psychiatric Patients' Rights and Patient Advovacy: Issues and Evidence*, Human Sciences Press, New York, pp. 171–95
Phillips, M. and Dawson, J. (1985) *Doctors' Dilemmas: Medical Ethics and Contemporary Science*, The Harvester Press, Brighton, Sussex
Plutchik, R., Conte, H. and Landau, H. (1972) 'A Comparison of Symptom Evaluations by Psychiatrists and Social Workers', *Hospital and Community Psychiatry, 23*, pp. 13–14
Reich, W. (1981) 'Psychiatric Diagnosis as an Ethical Problem' in S. Bloch and P. Chodoff (eds.), *Psychiatric Ethics*, Oxford University Press, Oxford, pp. 61–88
Smith, H.L. (1979) 'Ethical Considerations in Research Involving Human Subjects', *Ethics in Science and Medicine, 6*, pp. 167–75
Temerlin, M.K. (1970) 'Diagnostic Bias in Community Health', *Community Mental Health*

Journal, 6, pp. 110–17
Whitehead, T. (1983) *Mental Illness and the Law*, Basil Blackwell, Oxford
Wing, J. (1981) 'Ethics and Psychiatric Research' in S. Bloch and P. Chodoff (eds.), *Psychiatric Ethics*, Oxford University Press, Oxford, pp. 277–94

INDEX

activities of daily living 92
ageing
  abnormal 4
  adjustments to 28–9
  as a problem 118
  demographics 151–2
  loss of roles 59
  normal 2, 43
  stereotypes 1, 27, 103, 106, 124, 155
alcoholism 83
Alzheimer's disease 84
  see also dementia
aphasia 4–5
assessment 90

behaviour management 156
  see also therapy
bereavement 15, 31–2, 60, 102, 109

care-givers
  and day care 87, 94–6
  stress in 18, 95
  support 84
  support groups 110–13
  willingness to care 95
  see also counselling
Clifton Assessment Procedures for the Elderly 70, 75
communication 138, 141, 155–6
community care 18–19, 84, 118
confidentiality *see* ethical issues
confusion 134, 151–62
  see also dementia, depression
consent *see* ethical issues
cost-benefit analysis 87, 91–2
counselling 12, 14, 84, 115
  see also self-help groups

day care 80–100, 167
  costs 91–2
  day centres 82, 94
  day hospitals 81, 94
  effects on client 92–4
  effects on family 94–6
  evaluation of 88–91

death and dying 22, 27–8, 106
dementia 4–8, 62, 65–79 *passim*, 127
  and day care 84–7, 94
  assessment of 65
  care-givers' well-being 95
  ethical issues 181–2
  problems with 4, 6, 66, 86, 93, 152
  segregation 85–7
  stigma 86
demonstration projects 88
dependency 94
depression 11–13, 30, 101, 127
development
  life-span 22–5, 38, 108, 117–18
diagnosis 5, 155
drugs 12–15 *passim*

education 168
  see also training
elderly mentally infirm *see* confusion, dementia
engagement 67, 125, 127
environment 2–16 *passim*, 129
ethical and legal issues 18, 156–7, 173–97
  confidentiality 182–5; exceptions to 183; privacy 182; privileged communication 182
  consent 71, 178–82; competency 179–80; exceptions to 180–1; informed consent 178–9, 188–9; misinformed consent 181–2
  diagnosis 175–8
  ethical committees 189–90
  interest in 174
  patients' bill of rights 190–5
  role of psychologist 186–7
  training in ethics 191–2
experimental design 88

family *see* care-giver
foster homes 83
functional impairment 80

grief *see* bereavement

home helps 7

incontinence 75–7
institutional care 92, 95

Korsakoff's psychosis 7

legal issues *see* ethical and legal issues
life review 43, 107
 see also reminiscence
life-span development *see* development
long-term care *see* residential care

Medicaid 94
memory 62–3, 83
morale *see* well-being

National Health Service (UK) 81
nurses 12, 82, 106
nursing homes 81, 87, 91

old peoples' homes *see* residential care
organisation psychology 131
 human systems theory 131–3
 see also systems interventions, services

physical impairment 83, 95
policy 16, 102
prevention 80, 124

quality of life 68, 94, 102, 128, 130, 163

reality orientation 4, 61, 65–79, 156, 168
 and grief therapy 71, 74
 and single case study design 77
 arguments against 66
 case management 67
 classroom 67
 components 66
 memory aids 67, 71
 signposts 67, 76
 staff 78, 125
 24-hour 66, 125
rehabilitation 80, 82, 87–8, 101
religion 58
reminiscence 28, 41–64, 107
 and adjustment 49–55, 62
 and mental deterioration 61–2
 attitudes to 41–3, 47–55
 functions of 43–7; normative process 45; preservation of identity 46; transmitting culture 46
 therapy 56–62, 136
residential care 81, 163–72
 community involvement 169
 group care 127, 164
 natural living philosophy 164, 166, 170
 organisational structure 129–33; management 133
 rights of residents 167–8, 170
 systems approach to change 124–47; an intervention model 134–41
respite care 80, 84, 94, 112
retirement 13, 24, 109
risk-taking 160, 170
roles of psychologist 124, 186–7

self-help groups 101–23, 174
 care-givers 110–13
 evaluation 104, 109–10, 112, 115
 mutual help networks 115–17
 peer counselling 113–15
 professional involvement 105–7, 111, 117
 self-care 104–10, 169
services 7–19 *passim*, 163
 see also systems interventions
sex differences 25–6
sexuality 23, 26–7, 36–7, 39
social behaviour 93
social networks 102, 109, 115–17
social work 19, 56, 82
stigma 88
stimulation 94
stress 93, 94, 108, 112
 in staff 130
suicide 11, 101
systems interventions
 common themes 145–6
 family therapists in work systems 144–5
 team based institutional change 142–4
 see also residential care

teamwork 11, 141, 156, 160, 163, 166
therapy
 behavioural 7, 11, 107

cognitive 11
cost-effectiveness *see* cost-benefit analysis
family 13–16, 144–5
grief 71
individual 8–13
insight-orientated 107
marital 12
psychoanalytic 8, 22–4
psychodynamic 22–40; and phase specific problems 31; evaluation of 35; transference 30, 34–5, 39
reminiscence 28, 44, 56–7, 107

training
counsellors 113–14
domiciliary staff 151–3
educational techniques 108
elderly persons 103; *see also* self-help groups
family care-givers 84
failure of 128
institutional care staff 128–9, 151–3
professional involvement 105
reality orientation 125
video-assisted package 151–62; design process 157–9; general description 153–5; modules 155–6; principles 159–61

voluntary organisations 81, 82, 118
volunteers 87, 125, 169

well-being 16, 82, 84, 93, 96, 101
morale 109, 116
self-esteem 86, 104, 168